6000+
PULLOVER
POSSIBILITIES

Interchangeable Options
for Custom Knitted Sweaters

FRONTS • BACKS • SLEEVES • NECKLINES
ARMHOLES • COLLARS • POCKETS • EDGINGS

MELISSA LEAPMAN

sixth&spring books
NEW YORK

For Peter, cultivator of secret potatoes and connoisseur of all things gummi, who always has one less stamp than he will ultimately possess. You're my beautiful dragon.

sixth&spring ◼ books

161 Avenue of the
Americas, New York, NY
10013
sixthandspring.com

Designs and Schematics
MELISSA LEAPMAN

Editor
LISA SILVERMAN

Editorial Assistant
JACOB SEIFERT

Yarn Editor
MATTHEW SCHRANK

Supervising Patterns Editor
CARLA SCOTT

Technical Editor
DEBBIE RADTKE

Technical Illustrations
LORETTA DACHMAN

Book Design
MICHELLE HENNING

Photography
JACK DEUTSCH

Stylist
JOSEFINA GARCIA

Hair/Makeup
ELENA LYAKIR

_____

Vice President/
Editorial Director
TRISHA MALCOLM

Publisher
CAROLINE KILMER

Production Manager
DAVID JOINNIDES

President
ART JOINNIDES

Chairman
JAY STEIN

Copyright © 2017 by Melissa Leapman

Library of Congress Cataloging-in-Publication Data

Names: Leapman, Melissa, author.
Title: 6000+ pullover possibilities : interchangeable options for custom knitted sweaters / by Melissa Leapman.
Other titles: Six thousand plus pullover possibilities
Description: New York : Sixth&Spring Books, 2017. | Includes index.
Identifiers: LCCN 2016034098 | ISBN 9781936096947 (spiral bound)
Subjects: LCSH: Knitting—Patterns. | Sweaters. | BISAC: CRAFTS & HOBBIES / Needlework / Knitting. | CRAFTS & HOBBIES / Needlework / General. | CRAFTS & HOBBIES / Reference.
Classification: LCC TT825 .L384 2017 | DDC 746.43/20432—dc23

Manufactured in China
1 3 5 7 9 10 8 6 4 2

First Edition

Acknowledgments

I am grateful to have had the following expert knitters work with me on samples for this book: Kally Aronis, Cindy Grosch, Nancy Harrington, Susan Hope, Cheryl Keeley, Chris Krauss, Mary Lewis, Wendy Moses, Joan Murphy, Patty Olson, Kristi Ostling, Jen Owens, Sue Paules, Debbie Prout, Margarete Shaw, Heather Start, Norma Jean Sternschein, Angie Tzoumakas, Matt Waldrop, Renae Woolsey, and Gail Zimmerman.

Special thanks go to Cascade Yarns for such incredible generosity in providing furniture-size cartons of beautiful, colorful *Cascade 220* yarn used to knit the modular pieces photographed throughout the book. Thank you, Jean, Bob, Shannon, Rob, and Carly, for supporting this project.

I'm appreciative of the following yarn companies for sending the gorgeous yarn used in our fashion gallery and gauge gallery sweaters: Berroco, Brown Sheep Company, Cascade Yarns, Classic Elite Yarns, Lion Brand Yarn, and Westminster Fibers. One of the best parts of my job as an author/designer is having the ability to choose to work with only the nicest yarns—and people—in the industry. Thank you for making my work enjoyable!

With so many moving parts, this was clearly the biggest and most demanding project I've ever done.
Thank you, Patty Lyons, Brooke Nico, and Carol Sulkoski, for keeping the author together—at least somewhat!
<grin>—during the process.

Contents

Introduction

How many hours have you spent leafing through knitting books and magazines, searching for the perfect sweater? One pattern is great except for the neckline; another has the wrong sleeve length or yarn weight. What if you could custom knit *exactly* the sweater you want, to precisely your desired size and specs, with yarn you love? Well, now you can!

Written modularly, with instructions for many body silhouettes, sleeve shapes, neckline openings, and trims, in eight sizes (from X-Small to 4X) and nine yarn gauges, all designed to fit together, this book delivers more than 6,000 sweater possibilities. You can match the style and the yarn you love and create the perfect sweater for you!

How to Use This Book

Don't let the unusual format of these modular patterns scare you! A step-by-step guide for creating a sweater with designer details you love will look different from most knitting patterns—but isn't a customized creation what handknitting is all about?

The sweaters in this book are knitted in flat pieces rather than in the round, for two reasons: 1) Modular flat pieces allow for maximum flexibility in customization, and 2) I firmly believe that side seams add stability to garments. If you are uncomfortable sewing seams, register for a class at your local yarn shop or a knitting event, or refer to the information on pages 256–258. You might discover you actually enjoy the process of watching your pieces fit perfectly together!

Now let's get started creating your favorite sweater.

ON THE EDGE

The modular patterns in this book *do not* include selvedge stitches. Depending on the types of seams you'll use to assemble your garment, you may wish to add one extra stitch to each side edge of the fabric. Mattress stitch seams (pages 256–257), for example, incorporate edge stitches into the seams; for these, you'll definitely want to add two stitches to your initial cast-on: one selvedge stitch on each side edge.

Step One: Choose the Yarn

Whether you shop your stash or your local yarn store, enjoy the freedom of selecting the yarn you most want to knit with. Easy-to-use tables in this book will allow you to customize every pattern to suit nearly any yarn imaginable.

Standards & Guidelines for Crochet and Knitting
Standard Yarn Weight System

Categories of yarn, gauge ranges, and recommended needle and hook sizes

Yarn Weight Symbol & Category	0 Lace	1 Super Fine	2 Fine	3 Light	4 Medium	5 Bulky	6 Super Bulky	7 Jumbo
Type of Yarns in Category	Fingering 10-count crochet thread	Sock, Fingering, Baby	Sport, Baby	DK, Light Worsted	Worsted, Afghan, Aran	Chunky, Craft, Rug	Super Bulky, Roving	Jumbo, Roving
Knit Gauge Range* in Stockinette Stitch to 4 inches	33–40** sts	27–32 sts	23–26 sts	21–24 sts	16–20 sts	12–15 sts	7–11 sts	6 sts and fewer
Recommended Needle in Metric Size Range	1.5–2.25 mm	2.25–3.25 mm	3.25–3.75 mm	3.75–4.5 mm	4.5–5.5 mm	5.5–8 mm	8–12.75 mm	12.75 mm and larger
Recommended Needle U.S. Size Range	000–1	1 to 3	3 to 5	5 to 7	7 to 9	9 to 11	11 to 17	17 and larger
Crochet Gauge* Ranges in Single Crochet to 4 inch	32–42 double crochets**	21–32 sts	16–20 sts	12–17 sts	11–14 sts	8–11 sts	6–9 sts	5 sts and fewer
Recommended Hook in Metric Size Range	Steel*** 1.6–1.4 mm	2.25–3.5 mm	3.5–4.5 mm	4.5–5.5 mm	5.5–6.5 mm	6.5–9 mm	9–16 mm	16 mm and larger
Recommended Hook U.S. Size Range	Steel*** 6, 7, 8 Regular hook B-1	B-1 to E-4	E-4 to 7	7 to I-9	I-9 to K-10 1/2	K-10 1/2 to M-13	M-13 to Q	Q and larger

* GUIDELINES ONLY: The above reflect the most commonly used gauges and needle or hook sizes for specific yarn categories.

** Lace weight yarns are usually knitted or crocheted on larger needles and hooks to create lacy, openwork patterns. Accordingly, a gauge range is difficult to determine. Always follow the gauge stated in your pattern.

*** Steel crochet hooks are sized differently from regular hooks—the higher the number, the smaller the hook, which is the reverse of regular hook sizing

This Standards & Guidelines booklet and downloadable symbol artwork are available at: **YarnStandards.com**

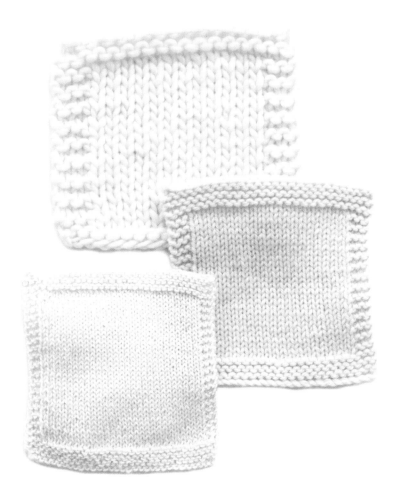

Step Two: Swatch, Swatch, Swatch!

All knitting projects—at least, most successful ones—begin with swatches. Once you select your yarn, take the time to do this important step! Swatching allows you to determine the number of stitches and rows per inch in your knitted fabric and will greatly reduce the chances of knitting yourself a sweater that will comfortably slipcover a sofa or would only fit your pet guppy.

Think of it this way: Casting on 100 stitches and knitting at 5 stitches to the inch will produce a piece of fabric that is 20"/51cm wide. Those same 100 stitches worked at a looser gauge of 4 stitches to the inch will be 25"/63.5cm wide. Combine a sweater front and back at that looser (or tighter) gauge, and your garment will be 10"/25.5cm larger (or smaller) than expected. That's a lot of weight to have to gain—or lose—in order to be able to wear a precious handknit! It's much wiser to have an accurate gauge measurement.

To begin, find the suggested gauge and needle size on the yarn label. Usually, this information is given over 4"/10cm in stockinette stitch. The patterns in this book are written for stockinette stitch, but if you plan to knit your garment in another stitch pattern, be sure to work your swatch in your desired texture instead.

Stitch Gauge

Row Gauge

Use the suggested knitting needle size, and cast on the number of stitches required to obtain 4"/10cm, plus 4 stitches. The extra stitches will serve as garter stitch selvedge stitches that will help keep your swatch flat and will frame the stockinette portion of the fabric. Begin by knitting 4 to 6 rows of garter stitch. Then, keeping the first and last 2 stitches in garter stitch with stockinette stitch in the middle, knit for the number of rows indicated on the yarn label for 4"/10 cm. Work 4 to 6 more rows of stockinette, and then bind off loosely.

Once you've bound off, you might choose to knit a second (or even third!) swatch, using a different needle size. If your original fabric seems tight and stiff, try another piece with larger knitting needles. If you'd prefer a firmer and more solid fabric, swatch again with smaller needles.

Be sure to tag each piece with the needle size you used, or tie that number of knots in the yarn tail of the swatch to remind you! (Been there, done that.)

Next, launder and block (page 256) your swatch(es), using the same method you'll use for your finished sweater. Don't skip this important step! Depending on the fiber content, this process can greatly affect the finished gauge of the fabric. Your beautiful sweater may match the desired specs perfectly—until it is worn and washed once. (Ask me how I know!)

Once the fabric is completely dry, choose the swatch with the drape, look, and feel you like the best, and pin it to a flat surface without stretching it.

Count the number of stitches and rows over 4"/10cm, avoiding the edges of the fabric and being careful not to distort the stitches by pressing down too hard. It's best to measure in several different spots and take the average.

When counting, do not ignore partial stitches and rows. The difference of only one-half of a stitch per inch seems inconsequential on a small piece of fabric but will become very important in a large one!

Divide those numbers by 4 to determine the stitch and row gauge over 1"/2.5cm. These numbers will determine which set of numbers in the pattern tables you will use to knit your sweater. In our illustration, there are 20 stitches over 4"/10cm, so the gauge is 5 stitches to the inch.

The patterns in this book are written for nine gauges, from 7 stitches to the inch to 3 stitches to the inch, with half-stitch increments in between. If your swatch yields a gauge that is not a whole or half stitch, change your needle size slightly to try to attain a gauge included in these patterns. For example, if your original swatch had a gauge of 5.75 stitches to the inch, try using knitting needles one size down to get a full 6 stitches to the inch. If the new fabric seems too stiff and tight, try going up a size in needles. This is your sweater! Knit the fabric that pleases you!

NEEDLE SIZES

In most cases, you will use two different sizes of knitting needles for a project: a main knitting needle size for the sweater fabric and smaller needles for the borders, depending on the edge treatment. Keep in mind, however, that certain silhouettes (such as A-Line or Empire Waist) look better with lower edges that do not draw in. If you prefer the lower edge of your garment not to draw in, simply use one needle size throughout the project.

Metric	U.S.	U.K
2mm	0	14
2.25mm	1	13
2.75mm	3	12
3mm	--	11
3.25mm	3	10
3.5mm	4	--
3.75mm	5	9
4mm	6	8
4.5mm	7	7
5mm	8	6
5.5mm	9	5
6mm	10	4
6.5mm	10½	3
7mm	--	2
7.5mm	--	1
8mm	11	0
9mm	13	00
10mm	15	000
12mm	17	--
16mm	19	--
19mm	35	--
25mm	50	--

ROW GAUGE

The patterns in this book are written for specific stitch and row gauges. Many factors affect the combination of stitch and row gauge, including the fiber content of the yarn and the material your knitting needles are composed of—even your mood while knitting! Check out the following table to see the stitch and matching row gauges used in this book. If your row gauge is off, try working with needles made of a different material. Or adapt the patterns to your new row gauge. The calculations are relatively easy! Just stay with me, and I'll show you how.

Shaping is usually done within a certain height of fabric (a V neckline, for instance, might be 6½"/16.5cm deep). If the pattern is written for 6 stitches and 8 rows to the inch, and if the neck opening is 7"/18cm wide, then 42 stitches will need to be decreased in total. Necklines tend to fit better if the upper 1"/2.5cm is straight, so all 42 stitches will need to be decreased within 6"/15cm or 48 rows (8 rows to the inch × 6" = 48 rows). If your row gauge is, say, 9 rows to the inch instead of 8 rows to the inch, you'll have 54 rows available to you to do the shaping. We'll be working 21 neck decrease rows (since we're decreasing half of the 42 stitches on each side of the opening), so 54 divided by 21 gives us 2.57. This means we would ideally decrease 1 stitch at each neck edge approximately every 2.57 rows. To make this knittable, we'd decrease 1 stitch each neck edge every other row 15 times, and then every 4 rows 6 times, using all 54 rows to get rid of the 42 neck stitches.

The modular patterns in this book are drafted using the following typical stitch and row gauge combinations. The symbols shown represent the standard yarn weight (based on the Craft Yarn Council's system) that will knit up to each gauge.

Typical Stitch and Row Gauges

Stitch Gauge	Row Gauge	Yarn Weights
7	9 rows	(1)
6½	8½ rows	(2)
6	8 rows	(3)
5½	7½ rows	(3)
5	7 rows	(4)
4½	6½ rows	(4)
4	6 rows	(4)
3½	5 rows	(5)
3	4 rows	(5)

IN THE THICK OF IT: GAUGE

Here are photos of the same sweater silhouette knitted at three different yarns and gauges.

Sweater #1
(shown in size small)

Yarn: Classic Elite
Vail **1** in color #6416
Gauge: 7 stitches and 9 rows = 1"
- Shaped silhouette
- Set-in construction
- Short set-in sleeves
- Round neck
- Turtleneck
- K1P1 rib edge treatment

Sweater #2
(shown in size small)

Yarn: Cascade Yarns
Cascade 220 **4** in color #8010
Gauge: 5 stitches and 7 rows = 1"
- Shaped silhouette
- Set-in construction
- Classic ¾-length set-in sleeves
- Scoop neck
- Garter stitch edge treatment

Sweater #3
(shown in size small)

Yarn: Brown Sheep Company
Lamb's Pride Bulky **5**
in color #M-10
Gauge: 3 stitches and 4 rows = 1"
- Shaped silhouette
- Set-in construction
- Classic long set-in sleeves
- V neck
- K1P1 rib edge treatment

Step Three: Choose a Sweater Silhouette

This book includes instructions for five unique sweater silhouettes (pages 19–118):

- Straight
- Shaped
- A-Line
- Tapered
- Empire Waist

The straight silhouette has no shaping in the torso and will have a casual, relaxed fit; the shaped silhouette gives an hourglass look; the A-line silhouette is wider at the lower edge, perfect for a less clingy fit; the tapered silhouette narrows slightly at the lower edge, accentuating the waist; the empire waist silhouette has a horizontal band just below the bust, and flares slightly toward the lower edge, making it an almost universally flattering shape.

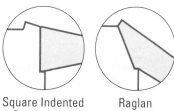

Square Indented
Construction

Raglan
Construction

Set-In
Construction

Saddle Shoulder
Construction

Step Four: Choose an Armhole Construction

Each silhouette includes instructions for four different armhole options (pages 18–194):

- Square Indented Construction
- Set-In Construction
- Raglan Construction
- Saddle Shoulder Construction

The armhole shape determines how the sleeve will fit into the armhole of the front and back of the garment. Square indented construction is the simplest and will yield a relaxed, casual fit; set-in construction is universally flattering, with a sleeve cap that fits vertically into a shaped armhole; raglan construction features diagonal seams that run from the armhole up to the neckline, as in an old-fashioned baseball shirt; sweaters with saddle shoulder construction have a strip of fabric along the shoulder line, often attracting attention upward, right where the wearer wants it.

Once you decide which armhole construction to use, be sure to knit your front, back, and sleeves with the same construction. Raglan sleeves will not fit neatly into a straight armhole, trust me, not even if you're knitting a garment for Quasimodo. Icons are provided with each pattern to make choosing matching modular pieces easy, as shown at left.

Step Five: Choose a Sleeve

Want short sleeves? Fine. Long sleeves? Done! Would you prefer a cute flared sleeve? You can have that, too. I've included several options for sleeve types and lengths for each armhole construction (pages 119–194) so you can customize every sweater.

Always be certain to choose a sleeve with the same armhole construction icon as your front and back. Quasimodo has enough sweaters.

Of course, sometimes you'll want to knit a sleeveless garment. Easy! Simply omit sleeves and add an edge treatment around the armholes. The set-in construction is perfect for this.

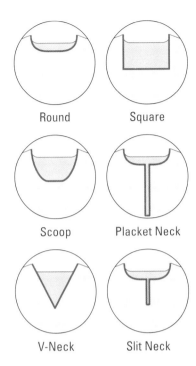

Round   Square

Scoop   Placket Neck

V-Neck   Slit Neck

Step Six: Choose Your Neckline

From a scoop neck to a placket neck to a round neck and more, customize your garment with the perfect neck opening (pages 195–212). Just select the shape you prefer! Included are the following six possibilities, each presented with icons:

- Round
- Scoop
- V-Neck
- Square
- Placket Neck
- Slit Neck

Each of the silhouettes and sleeves will work with any of the neck shapes. The back pieces for all of the garments have identical necklines—only the front necklines are different. Choose the one you like!

Step Seven: Choose a Neckline Treatment

Nearly every neckline treatment possibility is included (pages 195–212), from a basic crewneck to a comfy hood to an elegant square neck and more! Always be sure to choose one that is compatible with the neckline opening you selected. Once again, match the graphic icons, and you won't go wrong.

Step Eight: Choose an Edge Treatment

The sample modular pieces are all knitted with simple K1P1 ribbed edges, but don't limit yourself to this treatment. Choose the perfect edging for your garment, from a refined hem to a classic cable trim (pages 213–223).

Step Nine: Add Extra Details

Want to incorporate a cozy angled patch pocket or a refined knitted-in pocket? No problem! Refer to the Pockets section (pages 225–241) to make the sweater truly your own.

YARN AMOUNTS

One of the first things you'll notice about this book is that no yarn yardage requirements are included. That's because the yardage depends on all the choices you'll make while customizing your garment. Obviously, a tapered silhouette will use less yarn than a straight one; a classic long sleeve will require much more yarn than a short cap sleeve. You can rely on a knowledgeable yarn shop owner to help estimate how much yarn you'll need, but here's a reliable method for determining yarn requirements using schematic drawings of the sweater pieces and your gauge swatch. (See? Another good reason to knit a swatch!)

Refer to the schematic drawing for each sweater piece, and multiply the width of the back at its widest point by its length to determine its approximate surface area. Repeat for the front and sleeves. Obviously, most sleeves are far from square, but if you place the schematic for one sleeve upside down next to the first, you can "fill in" the empty space created from increases (or decreases), making it easier to calculate the surface area. It's always better to have too much yarn rather than not enough (just ask anyone!), so ignore cutouts such as neck openings and waist shaping.

Note: Imperial weights and measurements are shown here; however, the formulas also apply to the metric system.

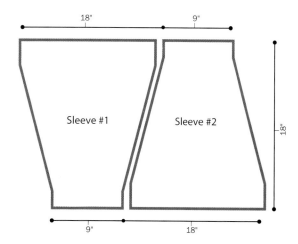

In the above illustration, if the width of the sleeve at the narrowest point is 9" and the width at the top is 18", with a finished length of 18", it's easy to estimate that the total surface area of two sleeves is approximately 486 square inches: (18 + 9) × 18 = 486.

Total up the surface area for all of the sweater pieces.

Next, determine the surface area of your swatch by multiplying its width by its height. Now, unravel your swatch and measure the length of yarn used.

Use the following formula to estimate the yarn requirements for your finished sweater. A is the yardage of yarn used to knit your gauge swatch, B is the total surface area of your entire finished project, C is the surface area of your gauge swatch, and X is the total yardage required for your entire project:

$$\frac{(A \times B)}{C} = X$$

Another way to say this is A times B divided by C = X, or the yardage used in the gauge swatch (A) times the estimated area of the finished sweater (B) divided by the surface area of the swatch (C), equals the approximate yardage needed (X).

For example, if your 4 x 4" swatch (i.e., 16 square inches) used 18 yards of yarn and the total surface area of your desired sweater is 1,366 square inches, then you can estimate the total required yardage like this:

$$\frac{(18 \times 1,366)}{16} = 1,536.75 \text{ yards required for project}$$

OR: 18 times 1,366 divided by 16 equals 1,536.75 yards.

Next, check out the label for the yarn you'd like to use to see how many yards are wound into each skein. Simply divide the number of yards required for your project by the number of yards per skein, and you'll know how many skeins of yarn you'll need to finish your project!

For example, if one skein of yarn contains 100 yards and you estimate that you will need 1,550 yards to complete your project, you will need 1,550 divided by 100, or 15½ skeins, so purchase 16.

If your project includes a big collar or hood, you'll want to purchase extra yarn, just so you don't run short. There's no such thing as too much yarn!

Step Ten: Choose a Size to Knit

Forget about your store-bought clothing size. You're going to knit this custom garment to fit you! Either measure the bust of your favorite sweater or else start from scratch and determine your actual body measurements.

Begin by taking an accurate bust measurement around the widest part of your bust. It's helpful to have a friend assist with this task in order to ensure the measuring tool doesn't dip down in the back. Also, since we tend to subconsciously round our body measurements up or down, I suggest that you take all measurements using a length of non-stretchy yarn or ribbon, and then measure it. Mercerized cotton or linen is ideal here; avoid silks and bouncy wools.

Once you know your bust measurement, you need to decide what type of fit you'd like your garment to have. Ease is the difference between your actual body measurement and the circumference of the finished garment. A close-fitting garment will have less ease than a loose-fitting one.

Use this grid, adapted from the Craft Yarn Council of America's standards, as a guide:

Fit	Amount of Ease
Very close-fitting	None, or even negative ease
Close-fitting	Add 1–2"/2.5–5cm total
Standard-fitting	Add 2–4"/5–10cm total
Loose-fitting	Add 4–6"/10–15cm total
Oversized	Add more than 6"/15cm total

The patterns in this book are written for 8 sizes, from X-Small to 4X, with the following *finished* bust measurements:

Finished Measurements

	XS	S	M	L	1X	2X	3X	4X
Bust	30"/76cm	34"/86.5cm	38"/96.5cm	42"/106.5cm	46"/117cm	50"/127cm	54"/137cm	58"/147.5cm

Just choose the one that's similar to your favorite sweater or matches your bust measurement plus (or minus) the desired ease!

Using the Tables

To make the patterns easy to use, you'll notice tables throughout this book. The 8 sizes are presented in columns, with X-Small at the left, 4X at the right, and the other sizes in between. The 9 gauges (number of stitches per inch) are shown in horizontal rows, with finer gauges toward the top, and successively bulkier ones below.

Sample Table (Blank)

	XS	S	M	L	1X	2X	3X	4X
7								
6½								
6								
5½								
5								
4½								
4								
3½								
3								

To use the table, just locate your project's gauge on the left, then look across to find the size you're knitting. You might find it convenient to circle all the numbers that pertain to the project before you start.

If only one number is mentioned, it is used for all gauges and sizes.

If a "--" appears, it signifies that those rows or stitches do not pertain to the size and gauge you are knitting; simply move your eye to the next set of instructions.

In the table below, for example, only sizes X-Small and 1X knitted at a gauge of 3½ stitches to the inch will have increases worked in the 20-row increment. All other sizes will ignore the grid completely, moving along to the next set of instructions.

Sample Table

Work fully fashioned increases each side every 20 rows ___ times. If no number is given, do not work these rows.

	XS	S	M	L	1X	2X	3X	4X
7	--	--	--	--	--	--	--	--
6½	--	--	--	--	--	--	--	--
6	--	--	--	--	--	--	--	--
5½	--	--	--	--	--	--	--	--
5	--	--	--	--	--	--	--	--
4½	--	--	--	--	--	--	--	--
4	--	--	--	--	--	--	--	--
3½	1	--	--	--	2	--	--	--
3	--	--	--	--	--	--	--	--

ADJUSTING LENGTH IN THE PATTERNS

These modular patterns are written to create sweaters of specific lengths, depending on the silhouette. If you are petite or especially tall, you may choose to adjust the length of the garment pieces. In order to ensure that the sleeves fit neatly into the armholes, I suggest that any such changes be made below the armholes on the front and back, and below the sleeve caps on the sleeves.

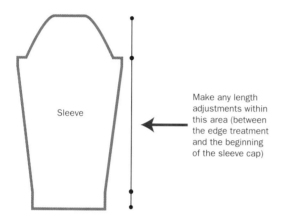

Sleeve

Make any length adjustments within this area (between the edge treatment and the beginning of the sleeve cap)

For pieces that are shaped, it will be necessary to change the rate of decreasing (or increasing). To do this, determine the difference in the number of stitches and the number of rows you have available to you. If you are lengthening your garment, you will work your shaping over more rows than what is listed in the pattern; if you are shortening your garment, you will work your shaping in fewer rows.

For example: If your sleeve requires 24 increases over 72 rows, it may call for increasing each side every 6 rows (24 divided by 2 each row = 12 increase rows total; 72 rows divided by 12 increase rows = 6).

If you decide to make the sleeve longer by 12 rows, to 84 rows, you will want to increase every 6 rows 6 times, and then every 8 rows 6 times. (84 rows divided by 12 increases = 7, but increasing every 7 rows would occasionally require shaping on wrong-side rows. Most knitters prefer doing shaping on right-side rows, and working half of the increases every 6 rows and the rest of them every 8 rows uses the same 84 rows total. Bingo!)

Using the Schematic Drawings

Schematic illustrations are provided for every sweater piece to show finished shape and dimensions. (The measurements on the schematics are given in inches; see the corresponding tables and instructions for metric measurements.) Refer to them frequently: prior to beginning your project to estimate yarn requirements, during the knitting process, and again during final blocking (page 256), to ensure that your sweater will fit as intended.

Final Checklist

Before you begin knitting your custom sweater, take a minute to write out your Fill-in-the-Blank Checklist on page 243. It'll help you keep all of the important details of your special project in one place.

Now you're ready to get started. Let's go!

BACKS

This section of the book includes modular patterns for the back pieces of your garment. Choose the silhouette (straight, shaped, A-line, tapered, or empire waist) and the armhole construction (square indented, set-in, raglan, or saddle shoulder) here.

Straight Silhouette

The straight silhouette falls straight from the armhole to the lower edge and gives a relaxed, comfortable fit.

Straight Silhouette with Square Indented Construction

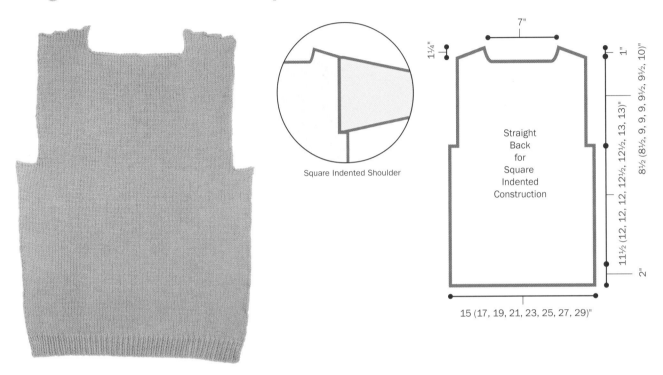

Square Indented Shoulder

Straight Back for Square Indented Construction

7"

1¼"

1"

8½ (8½, 9, 9, 9, 9½, 9½, 10)"

11½ (12, 12, 12, 12½, 12½, 13, 13)"

2"

15 (17, 19, 21, 23, 25, 27, 29)"

Finished Measurements

	XS	S	M	L	1X	2X	3X	4X
Bust	30"/76cm	34"/86.5cm	38"/96.5cm	42"/106.5cm	46"/117cm	50"/127cm	54"/137cm	58"/147.5cm
Waist	30"/76cm	34"/86.5cm	38"/96.5cm	42"/106.5cm	46"/117cm	50"/127cm	54"/137cm	58"/147.5cm
Hip	30"/76cm	34"/86.5cm	38"/96.5cm	42"/106.5cm	46"/117cm	50"/127cm	54"/137cm	58"/147.5cm
Length	23"/58.5cm	23½"/59.5cm	24"/61cm	24"/61cm	24½"/62cm	25"/63.5cm	25½"/65cm	26"/66cm

Notes

- This pattern is written for K1P1 ribbed edges. Refer to pages 213–223 for information on how to customize the edge treatment.
- For fully fashioned neck decreases: On right-side rows, first half, knit to 3 stitches before the neck edge, k2tog, k1; second half, k1, ssk, work to the end of the row. On wrong-side rows, first half, purl to 3 stitches before the neck edge, ssp (page 225), p1; second half, p1, p2tog, work to the end of the row.

Back

Cast on __ stitches.

	XS	S	M	L	1X	2X	3X	4X
7	106	120	134	148	162	176	190	204
6½	98	110	124	136	150	162	176	188
6	90	102	114	126	138	150	162	174
5½	84	94	104	116	126	138	148	160
5	76	86	94	106	116	126	136	144
4½	68	76	86	96	104	112	122	130
4	60	68	76	84	92	100	108	116
3½	52	60	66	74	80	88	94	102
3	46	52	58	64	70	76	82	88

Begin K1P1 rib (page 215), and work even until the piece measures approximately 2"/5cm from the beginning. Begin stockinette stitch, and work even until the piece measures approximately 13½ (14, 14, 14, 14½, 14½, 15, 15)"/34.5 (35.5, 35.5, 35.5, 37, 37, 38, 38)cm from the beginning, or 9½ (9½, 10, 10, 10, 10½, 10½, 11)"/24 (24, 25.5, 25.5, 25.5, 26.5, 26.5, 28)cm less than the desired finished length, ending after a wrong-side row.

Shape the Armholes

Bind off __ stitches at the beginning of the next 2 rows.

	XS	S	M	L	1X	2X	3X	4X
7	7	11	14	18	23	28	34	39
6½	7	9	13	16	21	26	31	35
6	6	9	12	15	19	24	28	33
5½	6	8	11	14	18	22	26	30
5	6	8	10	13	17	20	24	27
4½	5	6	9	12	15	18	22	24
4	4	6	8	10	13	16	19	22
3½	3	5	7	9	11	14	16	19
3	3	5	6	8	10	12	15	17

You will have __ stitches remaining.

	XS	S	M	L	1X	2X	3X	4X
7	92	98	106	112	116	120	122	126
6½	84	92	98	104	108	110	114	118
6	78	84	90	96	100	102	106	108
5½	72	78	82	88	90	94	96	100
5	64	70	74	80	82	86	88	90
4½	58	64	68	72	74	76	78	82
4	52	56	60	64	66	68	70	72
3½	46	50	52	56	58	60	62	64
3	40	42	46	48	50	52	52	54

Continue even until the piece measures approximately 21¾ (22¼, 22¾, 22¾, 23¼, 23¾, 24¼, 24¾)"/55 (56.5, 58, 58, 59, 60.5, 61.5, 63)cm from the beginning, or 1¼"/3cm less than the desired finished length, ending after a wrong-side row.

Shape the Neck

Place markers on both sides of the middle __ stitches.

	XS	S	M	L	1X	2X	3X	4X
7	46	46	46	46	46	46	46	46
6½	44	44	44	44	44	44	44	44
6	40	40	40	40	40	40	40	40
5½	36	36	36	36	36	36	36	36
5	32	32	32	32	32	32	32	32
4½	30	30	30	30	30	30	30	30
4	26	26	26	26	26	26	26	26
3½	22	22	22	22	22	22	22	22
3	20	20	20	20	20	20	20	20

Next Row (RS): Knit across to the first marker, join a second ball of yarn, and bind off the stitches between the markers, then knit across to end the row.

Work both sides at once with separate balls of yarn, and work fully fashioned neck decreases (see Notes) at each neck edge once.

You will have __ stitches remaining on each side.

	XS	S	M	L	1X	2X	3X	4X
7	22	25	29	32	34	36	37	39
6½	19	23	26	29	31	32	34	36
6	18	21	24	27	29	30	32	33
5½	17	20	22	25	26	28	29	31
5	15	18	20	23	24	26	27	28
4½	13	16	18	20	21	22	23	25
4	12	14	16	18	19	20	21	22
3½	11	13	14	16	17	18	19	20
3	9	10	12	13	14	15	15	16

Continue even, if necessary, until the piece measures approximately 22 (22½, 23, 23, 23½, 24, 24½, 25)"/56 (57, 58.5, 58.5, 59.5, 61, 62. 63.5)cm from the beginning, or 1"/2.5cm less than the desired finished length, ending after a wrong-side row.

Shape the Shoulders

Bind off __ stitches at the beginning of the next 2 rows.

	XS	S	M	L	1X	2X	3X	4X
7	6	6	7	8	9	9	9	10
6½	5	6	7	7	8	8	8	9
6	5	5	6	7	7	8	8	8
5½	4	5	6	6	7	7	7	8
5	4	5	5	6	6	6	7	7
4½	4	5	6	7	7	7	8	8
4	4	5	5	6	6	7	7	7
3½	4	4	5	5	6	6	6	7
3	5	5	6	7	7	8	8	8

Bind off __ stitches at the beginning of the next 2 rows.

	XS	S	M	L	1X	2X	3X	4X
7	6	6	7	8	9	9	9	10
6½	5	6	7	7	8	8	8	9
6	5	5	6	7	7	8	8	8
5½	4	5	6	6	7	7	7	8
5	4	5	5	6	6	6	7	7
4½	4	5	6	7	7	7	8	8
4	4	5	5	6	6	7	7	7
3½	4	4	5	5	6	6	6	7
3	4	5	6	6	7	7	7	8

Bind off __ stitches at the beginning of the next 2 rows. If no number is given, do not work these rows.

	XS	S	M	L	1X	2X	3X	4X
7	6	6	7	8	9	9	9	10
6½	5	6	7	7	8	8	8	9
6	5	5	6	7	7	8	8	8
5½	4	5	6	6	7	7	7	8
5	4	5	5	6	6	6	7	7
4½	5	6	6	6	7	8	7	9
4	4	4	6	6	7	6	7	8
3½	3	5	4	6	5	6	7	6
3	--	--	--	--	--	--	--	--

Bind off __ stitches at the beginning of the next 2 rows. If no number is given, do not work these rows.

	XS	S	M	L	1X	2X	3X	4X
7	4	7	8	8	7	9	10	9
6½	4	5	5	8	7	8	10	9
6	3	6	6	6	8	6	8	9
5½	5	5	4	7	5	7	8	7
5	3	3	5	5	6	8	6	7
4½	--	--	--	--	--	--	--	--
4	--	--	--	--	--	--	--	--
3½	--	--	--	--	--	--	--	--
3	--	--	--	--	--	--	--	--

Straight Silhouette with Set-In Construction

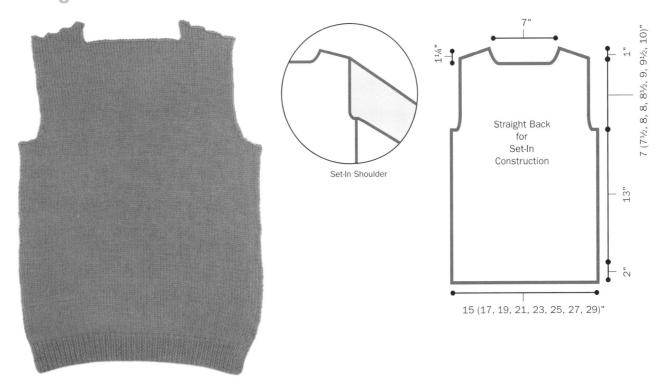

Set-In Shoulder

7"

1¼"

7 (7½, 8, 8, 8½, 9, 9½, 10)"

1"

Straight Back
for
Set-In
Construction

13"

2"

15 (17, 19, 21, 23, 25, 27, 29)"

Finished Measurements

	XS	S	M	L	1X	2X	3X	4X
Bust	30"/76cm	34"/86.5cm	38"/96.5cm	42"/106.5cm	46"/117cm	50"/127cm	54"/137cm	58"/147.5cm
Hip	30"/76cm	34"/86.5cm	38"/96.5cm	42"/106.5cm	46"/117cm	50"/127cm	54"/137cm	58"/147.5cm
Waist	30"/76cm	34"/86.5cm	38"/96.5cm	42"/106.5cm	46"/117cm	50"/127cm	54"/137cm	58"/147.5cm
Length	23"/58.5cm	23½"/59.5cm	24"/61cm	24"/61cm	24½"/62cm	25"/63.5cm	25½"/65cm	26"/66cm

Notes

- This pattern is written for K1P1 ribbed edges. Refer to pages 213–223 for information on how to customize the edge treatment.
- For fully fashioned decreases: On right-side rows, k1, ssk, knit to the last 3 stitches, k2tog, k1; on wrong-side rows, p1, p2tog, purl to the last 3 stitches, ssp (page 255), p1.
- For fully fashioned increases: On right-side rows, k1, M1R (page 253), knit to the last stitch, M1L (page 253), k1.
- For fully fashioned neck decreases: On the right-hand side of the neck, knit to 3 stitches before the neck edge, k2tog, k1; on the left-hand side of the neck, k1, ssk, work to the end of the row.

Back

Work same as for the straight silhouette with square indented construction (page 20) until the piece measures approximately 15"/38cm from the beginning, or 8 (8½, 9, 9, 9½, 10, 10½, 11)"/20.5 (21.5, 23, 23, 24, 25.5, 26.5, 28)cm less than the desired finished length, ending after a wrong-side row.

Shape the Armholes

Bind off __ stitches at the beginning of the next 2 rows.

	XS	S	M	L	1X	2X	3X	4X
7	3	4	4	5	5	6	9	10
6½	3	4	4	5	6	7	9	10
6	3	3	4	4	5	6	8	8
5½	2	3	3	4	4	5	7	7
5	2	3	3	4	4	5	6	6
4½	2	3	3	3	4	4	5	5
4	2	2	2	3	3	4	5	6
3½	2	2	2	3	3	4	5	5
3	2	2	2	3	3	4	4	5

Bind off __ stitches at the beginning of the next 2 rows. If no number is given, do not work these rows.

	XS	S	M	L	1X	2X	3X	4X
7	2	2	3	3	4	4	5	6
6½	2	2	3	3	4	4	5	6
6	2	2	2	2	3	3	4	5
5½	2	2	2	3	3	3	3	4
5	2	2	2	3	3	3	3	4
4½	2	2	2	2	2	3	3	3
4	--	--	2	2	2	3	3	3
3½	--	--	2	2	2	3	2	3
3	--	--	--	--	2	2	3	3

Work fully fashioned decreases each side every row __ times. If no number is given, do not work these rows.

	XS	S	M	L	1X	2X	3X	4X
7	--	--	--	6	12	18	18	22
6½	--	--	--	4	8	14	12	14
6	--	--	--	6	8	14	12	18
5½	--	--	2	4	10	14	14	18
5	--	--	--	2	8	10	14	16
4½	--	--	--	4	8	10	12	16
4	--	--	--	2	6	6	8	10
3½	--	--	--	2	6	6	8	10
3	--	2	2	4	5	6	8	9

Work fully fashioned decreases each side every other row __ time(s).
If no number is given, do not work these rows.

	XS	S	M	L	1X	2X	3X	4X
7	--	4	7	4	2	--	2	1
6½	--	1	6	4	3	1	5	5
6	--	3	6	3	3	1	4	2
5½	1	2	4	3	1	--	2	1
5	1	2	5	4	2	2	1	1
4½	--	--	3	3	1	1	2	--
4	1	4	4	3	2	3	3	3
3½	--	3	3	2	--	1	1	1
3	--	1	2	1	--	--	--	--

Work fully fashioned decreases each side every 4 rows __ time(s). If no number is given, do not work these rows.

	XS	S	M	L	1X	2X	3X	4X
7	1	1	--	--	--	--	--	--
6½	2	2	--	--	--	--	--	--
6	--	1	--	--	--	--	--	--
5½	1	1	--	--	--	--	--	--
5	1	1	--	--	--	--	--	--
4½	--	--	1	--	--	--	--	--
4	1	--	--	--	--	--	--	--
3½	1	--	--	--	--	--	--	--
3	1	--	--	--	--	--	--	--

Work fully fashioned decreases each side every 6 rows once, if indicated below.
If no number is given, do not work these rows.

	XS	S	M	L	1X	2X	3X	4X
7	1	--	--	--	--	--	--	--
6½	--	--	--	--	--	--	--	--
6	--	--	--	--	--	--	--	--
5½	--	--	--	--	--	--	--	--
5	--	--	--	--	--	--	--	--
4½	1	1	--	--	--	--	--	--
4	--	--	--	--	--	--	--	--
3½	--	--	--	--	--	--	--	--
3	--	--	--	--	--	--	--	--

Work fully fashioned decreases each side every 8 rows once, if indicated below.
If no number is given, do not work these rows.

	XS	S	M	L	1X	2X	3X	4X
7	--	--	--	--	--	--	--	--
6½	--	--	--	--	--	--	--	--
6	1	--	--	--	--	--	--	--
5½	--	--	--	--	--	--	--	--
5	--	--	--	--	--	--	--	--
4½	--	--	--	--	--	--	--	--
4	--	--	--	--	--	--	--	--
3½	--	--	--	--	--	--	--	--
3	--	--	--	--	--	--	--	--

You will have __ stitches remaining.

	XS	S	M	L	1X	2X	3X	4X
7	92	98	106	112	116	120	122	126
6½	84	92	98	104	108	110	114	118
6	78	84	90	96	100	102	106	108
5½	72	78	82	88	90	94	96	100
5	64	70	74	80	82	86	88	90
4½	58	64	68	72	74	76	78	82
4	52	56	60	64	66	68	70	72
3½	46	50	52	56	58	60	62	64
3	40	42	46	48	50	52	52	54

Continue even until the piece measures approximately 21¾ (22¼, 22¾, 22¾, 23¼, 23¾, 24¼, 24¾)"/55.5 (56.5, 58, 58, 59, 60.5, 62, 63)cm from the beginning, or 1¼"/3cm less than the desired finished length, ending after a wrong-side row.

Shape the Neck

Work same as for the straight silhouette with square indented construction (page 20).

You will have __ stitches remaining on each side.

	XS	S	M	L	1X	2X	3X	4X
7	22	25	29	32	34	36	37	39
6½	19	23	26	29	31	32	34	36
6	18	21	24	27	29	30	32	33
5½	17	20	22	25	26	28	29	31
5	15	18	20	23	24	26	27	28
4½	13	16	18	20	21	22	23	25
4	12	14	16	18	19	20	21	22
3½	11	13	14	16	17	18	19	20
3	9	10	12	13	14	15	15	16

Continue even, if necessary, until the piece measures approximately 22 (22½, 23, 23, 23½, 24, 24½, 25)"/56 (57, 58.5, 58.5, 59.5, 61, 62.5, 63.5)cm from the beginning, or 1"/2.5cm less than the desired finished length, ending after a wrong-side row.

Shape the Shoulders

Work same as for the straight silhouette with square indented construction (page 20).

Straight Silhouette with Raglan Construction

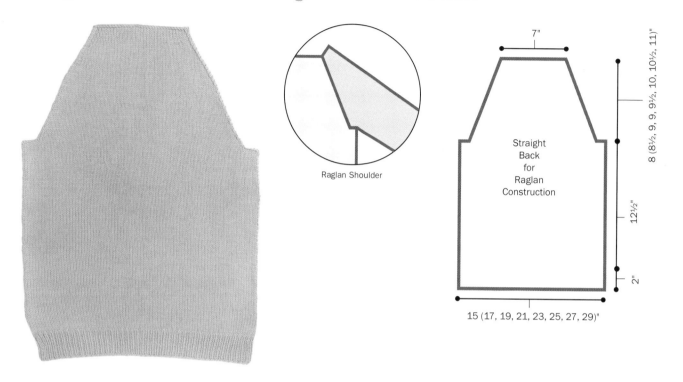

Raglan Shoulder

Straight
Back
for
Raglan
Construction

7"

8 (8½, 9, 9, 9½, 10, 10½, 11)"

12½"

2"

15 (17, 19, 21, 23, 25, 27, 29)"

Finished Measurements

	XS	S	M	L	1X	2X	3X	4X
Bust	30"/76cm	34"/86.5cm	38"/96.5cm	42"/106.5cm	46"/117cm	50"/127cm	54"/137cm	58"/147.5cm
Waist	30"/76cm	34"/86.5cm	38"/96.5cm	42"/106.5cm	46"/117cm	50"/127cm	54"/137cm	58"/147.5cm
Hip	30"/76cm	34"/86.5cm	38"/96.5cm	42"/106.5cm	46"/117cm	50"/127cm	54"/137cm	58"/147.5cm
Length	23¾"/60.5cm	24¼"/61.5cm	24¾"/63cm	24¾"/63cm	25¼"/64cm	25¾"/65.5cm	26¼"/66.5cm	26¾"/68cm

Notes

- The total finished length of this garment includes one-half of the width of the upper edge of the sleeves; the front and back pieces are 1¼"/3cm shorter than the total length of the garment.
- This pattern is written for K1P1 ribbed edges. Refer to pages 213–223 for information on how to customize the edge treatment.
- For fully fashioned decreases: On right-side rows, k1, ssk, knit to the last 3 stitches, k2tog, k1; on wrong-side rows, p1, p2tog, purl to the last 3 stitches, ssp (page 255), p1.

Back

Work same as for the straight silhouette with square indented construction (page 20) until the piece measures approximately 14½"/37cm from the beginning, or 9¼ (9¾, 10¼, 10¼, 10¾, 11¼, 11¾, 12¼)"/23.5 (24.5, 26, 26, 27, 28.5, 29.5, 31)cm less than the desired finished length, ending after a wrong-side row.

Shape the Armholes

Bind off __ stitches at the beginning of the next 2 rows.

	XS	S	M	L	1X	2X	3X	4X
7	7	7	7	7	11	11	11	11
6½	7	7	7	7	10	10	10	10
6	6	6	6	6	9	9	9	9
5½	6	6	6	6	8	8	8	8
5	5	5	5	5	8	8	8	8
4½	5	5	5	5	7	7	7	7
4	4	4	4	4	6	6	6	6
3½	4	4	4	4	6	6	6	6
3	3	3	3	3	5	5	5	5

Work fully fashioned decreases each side every 4 rows __ time(s). If no number is given, do not work these rows.

	XS	S	M	L	1X	2X	3X	4X
7	13	8	3	--	--	--	--	--
6½	14	10	5	--	--	--	--	--
6	13	9	5	--	--	--	--	--
5½	12	9	6	--	--	--	--	--
5	11	8	5	--	--	--	--	--
4½	12	9	6	1	1	--	--	--
4	11	8	6	2	1	--	--	--
3½	9	6	4	--	1	--	--	--
3	6	4	2	--	--	--	--	--

Work fully fashioned decreases each side every other row __ time(s).

	XS	S	M	L	1X	2X	3X	4X
7	9	21	33	36	38	35	33	30
6½	5	15	27	36	37	35	32	31
6	5	15	25	34	35	33	31	29
5½	5	13	21	33	33	31	30	28
5	5	13	20	29	32	30	29	28
4½	1	8	16	26	28	30	28	28
4	1	8	14	22	25	28	27	26
3½	1	8	13	21	21	22	21	19
3	3	8	13	16	17	16	15	14

Work fully fashioned decreases each side every row __ time(s). If no number is given, do not work these rows.

	XS	S	M	L	1X	2X	3X	4X
7	--	--	--	7	8	18	27	37
6½	--	--	--	2	5	13	23	30
6	--	--	--	2	4	12	20	28
5½	--	--	--	--	3	11	17	25
5	--	--	--	2	1	8	14	19
4½	--	--	--	--	--	3	10	14
4	--	--	--	--	--	2	7	12
3½	--	--	--	--	--	4	8	14
3	--	--	--	2	2	6	10	14

You will have __ stitches remaining.

	XS	S	M	L	1X	2X	3X	4X
7	48	48	48	48	48	48	48	48
6½	46	46	46	46	46	46	46	46
6	42	42	42	42	42	42	42	42
5½	38	38	38	38	38	38	38	38
5	34	34	34	34	34	34	34	34
4½	32	32	32	32	32	32	32	32
4	28	28	28	28	28	28	28	28
3½	24	24	24	24	24	24	24	24
3	22	22	22	22	22	22	22	22

Work 1 row even, if indicated below. If no number is given, do not work this row.

	XS	S	M	L	1X	2X	3X	4X
7	--	1	1	--	--	--	--	--
6½	--	--	1	1	--	--	--	--
6	--	--	--	--	--	--	--	--
5½	--	--	--	--	--	--	--	--
5	--	--	1	1	--	--	--	--
4½	--	1	1	1	--	--	--	--
4	--	1	--	--	1	--	--	--
3½	--	1	1	1	--	--	1	1
3	--	--	--	--	--	--	--	--

Bind off all stitches.

Straight Silhouette with Saddle Shoulder Construction

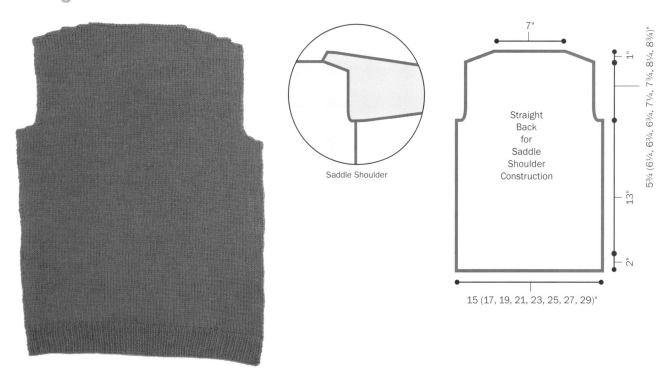

Saddle Shoulder

Straight
Back
for
Saddle
Shoulder
Construction

7"

1"

5¾ (6¼, 6¾, 6¾, 7¼, 7¾, 8¼, 8¾)"

13"

2"

15 (17, 19, 21, 23, 25, 27, 29)"

Finished Measurements

	XS	S	M	L	1X	2X	3X	4X
Bust	30"/76cm	34"/86.5cm	38"/96.5cm	42"/106.5cm	46"/117cm	50"/127cm	54"/137cm	58"/147.5cm
Waist	30"/76cm	34"/86.5cm	38"/96.5cm	42"/106.5cm	46"/117cm	50"/127cm	54"/137cm	58"/147.5cm
Hip	30"/76cm	34"/86.5cm	38"/96.5cm	42"/106.5cm	46"/117cm	50"/127cm	54"/137cm	58"/147.5cm
Length	23"/58.5cm	23½"/59.5cm	24"/61cm	24"/61cm	24½"/62cm	25"/63.5cm	25½"/64.5cm	26"/66cm

Notes

- The total finished length of this garment includes one-half of the width of the upper edge of the sleeves; the front and back pieces are 1¼"/3cm shorter than the total length of the garment.
- This pattern is written for K1P1 ribbed edges. Refer to pages 213–223 for information on how to customize the edge treatment.
- For fully fashioned decreases: On right-side rows, k1, ssk, knit to the last 3 stitches, k2tog, k1; on wrong-side rows, p1, p2tog, purl to the last 3 stitches, ssp (page 255), p1.

Back

Work same as for the straight silhouette with square indented construction (page 20) until the piece measures approximately 15"/38cm from the beginning, or 8 (8½, 9, 9, 9½, 10, 10½, 11)"/20.5 (21.5, 23, 23, 24, 25.5, 26.5, 28)cm less than the desired finished length, ending after a wrong-side row.

Shape the Armholes

Work same as for the straight silhouette with set-in construction (page 25).

You will have __ stitches remaining.

	XS	S	M	L	1X	2X	3X	4X
7	92	98	106	112	116	120	122	126
6½	84	92	98	104	108	110	114	118
6	78	84	90	96	100	102	106	108
5½	72	78	82	88	90	94	96	100
5	64	70	74	80	82	86	88	90
4½	58	64	68	72	74	76	78	82
4	52	56	60	64	66	68	70	72
3½	46	50	52	56	58	60	62	64
3	40	42	46	48	50	52	52	54

Continue even until the piece measures approximately 20¾ (21¼, 21¾, 21¾, 22¼, 22¾, 23¼, 23¾)"/53 (54, 55.5, 55.5, 56.5, 58, 59, 60.5)cm, or 2¼"/5.5cm less than the desired finished length, ending after a wrong-side row.

Shape the Shoulders

Work same as for the straight silhouette with square indented construction (page 20).

You will have __ stitches remaining.

	XS	S	M	L	1X	2X	3X	4X
7	48	48	48	48	48	48	48	48
6½	46	46	46	46	46	46	46	46
6	42	42	42	42	42	42	42	42
5½	38	38	38	38	38	38	38	38
5	34	34	34	34	34	34	34	34
4½	32	32	32	32	32	32	32	32
4	28	28	28	28	28	28	28	28
3½	24	24	24	24	24	24	24	24
3	22	22	22	22	22	22	22	22

Bind off all stitches.

Shaped Silhouette

This silhouette features waist shaping and flatters most figures.

Shaped Silhouette with Square Indented Construction

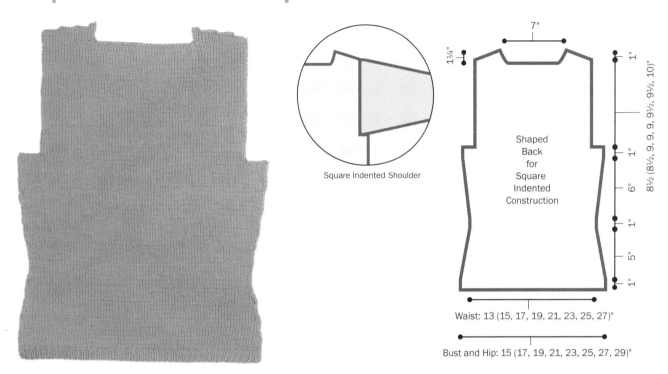

Square Indented Shoulder

7"

1¼"

1"

8½ (8½, 9, 9, 9, 9½, 9½, 10)"

1"

6"

1"

5"

1"

Shaped Back for Square Indented Construction

Waist: 13 (15, 17, 19, 21, 23, 25, 27)"

Bust and Hip: 15 (17, 19, 21, 23, 25, 27, 29)"

Finished Measurements

	XS	S	M	L	1X	2X	3X	4X
Bust	30"/76cm	34"/86.5cm	38"/96.5cm	42"/106.5cm	46"/117cm	50"/127cm	54"/137cm	58"/147.5cm
Waist	26"/66cm	30"/76cm	34"/86.5cm	38"/96.5cm	42"/106.5cm	46"/117cm	50"/127cm	54"/137cm
Hip	30"/76cm	34"/86.5cm	38"/96.5cm	42"/106.5cm	46"/117cm	50"/127cm	54"/137cm	58"/147.5cm
Length	23½"/59.5cm	23½"/59.5cm	24"/61cm	24"/61cm	24"/61cm	24½"/62cm	24½"/62cm	25"/63.5cm

Notes

- This pattern is written for K1P1 ribbed edges. Refer to pages 213–223 for information on how to customize the edge treatment.
- For fully fashioned decreases: On right-side rows, k1, ssk, knit to the last 3 stitches, k2tog, k1; on wrong-side rows, p1, p2tog, purl to the last 3 stitches, ssp (page 255), p1.
- For fully fashioned increases on right-side rows, k1, M1R (page 255), knit to the last stitch, M1L (page 253), k1.
- For fully fashioned neck decreases: On right-side rows, first half, knit to 3 stitches before the neck edge, k2tog, k1; second half, k1, ssk, work to the end of the row. On wrong-side rows, first half, purl to 3 stitches before the neck edge, ssp (page 255), p1; second half, p1, p2tog, work to the end of the row.

Back

Cast on ___ stitches.

	XS	S	M	L	1X	2X	3X	4X
7	106	120	134	148	162	176	190	204
6½	98	110	124	136	150	162	176	188
6	90	102	114	126	138	150	162	174
5½	84	94	104	116	126	138	148	160
5	76	86	94	106	116	126	136	144
4½	68	76	86	96	104	112	122	130
4	60	68	76	84	92	100	108	116
3½	52	60	66	74	80	88	94	102
3	46	52	58	64	70	76	82	88

Begin K1P1 rib (page 215), and work even until the piece measures approximately 1"/2.5cm from the beginning.

Decrease for the Waist

Begin stockinette stitch, and work fully fashioned decreases (see Notes) each side every 8 rows ___ time(s). If no number is given, do not work these rows.

	XS	S	M	L	1X	2X	3X	4X
7	1	1	1	1	1	1	1	1
6½	--	--	--	--	--	--	--	--
6	2	2	2	2	2	2	2	2
5½	1	1	1	1	1	1	1	1
5	2	2	2	2	2	2	2	2
4½	1	1	1	1	1	1	1	1
4	3	3	3	3	3	3	3	3
3½	--	--	--	--	--	--	--	--
3	1	1	1	1	1	1	1	1

Work fully fashioned decreases each side every 6 rows __ time(s). If no number is given, do not work these rows.

	XS	S	M	L	1X	2X	3X	4X
7	6	6	6	6	6	6	6	6
6½	7	7	7	7	7	7	7	7
6	4	4	4	4	4	4	4	4
5½	5	5	5	5	5	5	5	5
5	3	3	3	3	3	3	3	3
4½	4	4	4	4	4	4	4	4
4	1	1	1	1	1	1	1	1
3½	4	4	4	4	4	4	4	4
3	2	2	2	2	2	2	2	2

You will have __ stitches remaining.

	XS	S	M	L	1X	2X	3X	4X
7	92	106	120	134	148	162	176	190
6½	84	96	110	122	136	148	162	174
6	78	90	102	114	126	138	150	162
5½	72	82	92	104	114	126	136	148
5	66	76	84	96	106	116	126	134
4½	58	66	76	86	94	102	112	120
4	52	60	68	76	84	92	100	108
3½	44	52	58	66	72	80	86	94
3	40	46	52	58	64	70	76	82

Continue even until the piece measures approximately 7"/18cm from the beginning, or 16½ (16½, 17, 17, 17, 17½, 17½, 18)"/41.5 (41.5, 43, 43, 43, 44.5, 44.5, 45.5)cm less than the desired finished length, ending after a right-side row.

Increase for the Bust

Work fully fashioned increases (see Notes) each side every 6 rows __ time(s).
If no number is given, do not work these rows.

	XS	S	M	L	1X	2X	3X	4X
7	1	1	1	1	1	1	1	1
6½	3	3	3	3	3	3	3	3
6	--	--	--	--	--	--	--	--
5½	2	2	2	2	2	2	2	2
5	--	--	--	--	--	--	--	--
4½	1	1	1	1	1	1	1	1
4	--	--	--	--	--	--	--	--
3½	1	1	1	1	1	1	1	1
3	--	--	--	--	--	--	--	--

Work fully fashioned increases each side every 8 rows __ times.

	XS	S	M	L	1X	2X	3X	4X
7	6	6	6	6	6	6	6	6
6½	4	4	4	4	4	4	4	4
6	6	6	6	6	6	6	6	6
5½	4	4	4	4	4	4	4	4
5	4	4	4	4	4	4	4	4
4½	4	4	4	4	4	4	4	4
4	2	2	2	2	2	2	2	2
3½	3	3	3	3	3	3	3	3
3	3	3	3	3	3	3	3	3

Work fully fashioned increases each side every 10 rows __ time(s). If no number is given, do not work these rows.

	XS	S	M	L	1X	2X	3X	4X
7	--	--	--	--	--	--	--	--
6½	--	--	--	--	--	--	--	--
6	--	--	--	--	--	--	--	--
5½	--	--	--	--	--	--	--	--
5	1	1	1	1	1	1	1	1
4½	--	--	--	--	--	--	--	--
4	2	2	2	2	2	2	2	2
3½	--	--	--	--	--	--	--	--
3	--	--	--	--	--	--	--	--

You will now have __ stitches.

	XS	S	M	L	1X	2X	3X	4X
7	106	120	134	148	162	176	190	204
6½	98	110	124	136	150	162	176	188
6	90	102	114	126	138	150	162	174
5½	84	94	104	116	126	138	148	160
5	76	86	94	106	116	126	136	144
4½	68	76	86	96	104	112	122	130
4	60	68	76	84	92	100	108	116
3½	52	60	66	74	80	88	94	102
3	46	52	58	64	70	76	82	88

Continue even until the piece measures approximately 14"/35.5cm from the beginning, or 9½ (9½, 10, 10, 10, 10½, 10½, 11)"/24 (24, 25.5, 25.5, 25.5, 26.5, 26.5, 28)cm less than the desired finished length, ending after a wrong-side row.

Shape the Armholes

Work same as for the straight silhouette with square indented construction (page 20).

You will have __ stitches remaining.

	XS	S	M	L	1X	2X	3X	4X
7	92	98	106	112	116	120	122	126
6½	84	92	98	104	108	110	114	118
6	78	84	90	96	100	102	106	108
5½	72	78	82	88	90	94	96	100
5	64	70	74	80	82	86	88	90
4½	58	64	68	72	74	76	78	82
4	52	56	60	64	66	68	70	72
3½	46	50	52	56	58	60	62	64
3	40	42	46	48	50	52	52	54

Continue even until the piece measures approximately 22¼ (22¼, 22¾, 22¾, 22¾, 23¼, 23¼, 23¾)"/56.5 (56.5, 58, 58, 58, 59, 59, 60.5)cm from the beginning, or 1¼"/3cm less than the desired finished length, ending after a wrong-side row.

Shape the Neck

Work same as for the straight silhouette with square indented construction (page 20).

Continue even until the piece measures approximately 22½ (22½, 23, 23, 23, 23½, 23½, 24)"/57 (57, 58.5, 58.5, 58.5, 59.5, 59.5, 61)cm from the beginning, or 1"/2.5cm less than the desired finished length, ending after a wrong-side row.

Shape the Shoulders

Work same as for the straight silhouette with square indented construction (page 20).

Shaped Silhouette with Set-In Construction

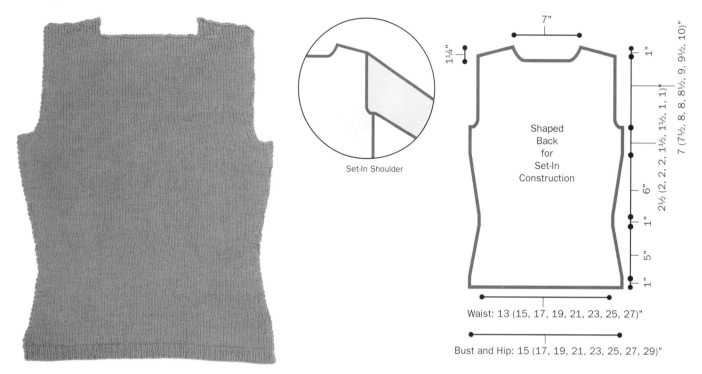

Set-In Shoulder

7"

1¼"

1"

Shaped
Back
for
Set-In
Construction

7 (7½, 8, 8, 8½, 1½, 1, 1)"

2½ (2, 2, 1½, 1½, 1, 1)"

6"

1"

1"

5"

1"

Waist: 13 (15, 17, 19, 21, 23, 25, 27)"

Bust and Hip: 15 (17, 19, 21, 23, 25, 27, 29)"

Finished Measurements

	XS	S	M	L	1X	2X	3X	4X
Bust	30"/76cm	34"/86.5cm	38"/96.5cm	42"/106.5cm	46"/117cm	50"/127cm	54"/137cm	58"/147.5cm
Waist	26"/66cm	30"/76cm	34"/86.5cm	38"/96.5cm	42"/106.5cm	46"/117cm	50"/127cm	54"/137cm
Hip	30"/76cm	34"/86.5cm	38"/96.5cm	42"/106.5cm	46"/117cm	50"/127cm	54"/137cm	58"/147.5cm
Length	23½"/59.5cm	23½"/59.5cm	24"/61cm	24"/61cm	24"/61cm	24½"/62cm	24½"/62cm	25"/63.5cm

Notes

- This pattern is written for K1P1 ribbed edges. Refer to pages 213–223 for information on how to customize the edge treatment.
- For fully fashioned decreases: On right-side rows, k1, ssk, knit to the last 3 stitches, k2tog, k1; on wrong-side rows, p1, p2tog, purl to the last 3 stitches, ssp (page 255), p1.
- For fully fashioned increases on right-side rows, k1, M1R (page 253), knit to the last stitch, M1L (page 253), k1.
- For fully fashioned neck decreases: On right-side rows, first half, knit to 3 stitches before the neck edge, k2tog, k1; second half, k1, ssk, work to the end of the row. On wrong-side rows, first half, purl to 3 stitches before the neck edge, ssp (page 255), p1; second half, p1, p2tog, work to the end of the row.

Back

Work same as for the shaped silhouette with square indented construction (page 35) until the piece measures approximately 14"/35.5cm from the beginning, or 9½ (9½, 10, 10, 10, 10½, 10½, 11)"/24 (24, 25.5, 25.5, 25.5, 26.5, 26.5, 28)cm less than the desired finished length, ending after a wrong-side row.

Continue even, if necessary, until the piece measures approximately 15½ (15, 15, 15, 14½, 14½, 14, 14)"/39.5 (38, 38, 38, 37, 37, 35.5, 35.5)cm from the beginning, or 8 (8½, 9, 9, 9½, 10, 10½, 11)"/20 (21.5, 23, 23, 24, 25, 26.5, 28)cm less than the desired finished length, ending after a wrong-side row.

Shape the Armholes

Work same as for the straight silhouette with set-in construction (page 25).

You will have __ stitches remaining.

	XS	S	M	L	1X	2X	3X	4X
7	92	98	106	112	116	120	122	126
6½	84	92	98	104	108	110	114	118
6	78	84	90	96	100	102	106	108
5½	72	78	82	88	90	94	96	100
5	64	70	74	80	82	86	88	90
4½	58	64	68	72	74	76	78	82
4	52	56	60	64	66	68	70	72
3½	46	50	52	56	58	60	62	64
3	40	42	46	48	50	52	52	54

Continue even until the piece measures approximately 22¼ (22¼, 22¾, 22¾, 22¾, 23¼, 23¼, 23¾)"/56.5 (56.5, 58, 58, 58, 59, 59, 60.5)cm from the beginning, or 1¼"/3cm less than the desired finished length, ending after a wrong-side row.

Shape the Neck

Work same as for the straight silhouette with square indented construction (page 20).

Continue even until the piece measures approximately 22½ (22½, 23, 23, 23, 23½, 23½, 24)"/57 (57, 58.5, 58.5, 58.5, 59.5, 59.5, 61)cm from the beginning, or 1"/2.5cm less than the desired finished length, ending after a wrong-side row.

Shape the Shoulders

Work same as for the straight silhouette with square indented construction (page 20).

Shaped Silhouette with Raglan Construction

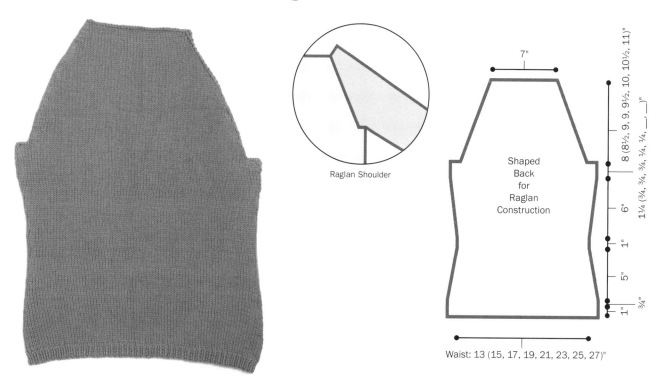

Raglan Shoulder

7"

8 (8½, 9, 9, 9½, 10, 10½, 11)"

1¼ (¾, ¾, ¾, ¼, ¼, —, —)"

Shaped
Back
for
Raglan
Construction

6"

1"

5"

1"

¾"

Waist: 13 (15, 17, 19, 21, 23, 25, 27)"

Finished Measurements

	XS	S	M	L	1X	2X	3X	4X
Bust	30"/76cm	34"/86.5cm	38"/96.5cm	42"/106.5cm	46"/117cm	50"/127cm	54"/137cm	58"/147.5cm
Waist	26"/66cm	30"/76cm	34"/86.5cm	38"/96.5cm	42"/106.5cm	46"/117cm	50"/127cm	54"/137cm
Hip	30"/76cm	34"/86.5cm	38"/96.5cm	42"/106.5cm	46"/117cm	50"/127cm	54"/137cm	58"/147.5cm
Length	24¼"/61.5cm	24¼"/61.5cm	24¾"/63cm	24¾"/63cm	24¾"/63cm	25¼"/64cm	25½"/65cm	26"/66cm

Notes

- The total finished length of this garment includes one-half of the width of the upper edge of the sleeves; the front and back pieces are 1¼"/3cm shorter than the total length of the garment.
- This pattern is written for K1P1 ribbed edges. Refer to pages 213–223 for information on how to customize the edge treatment.
- For fully fashioned decreases: On right-side rows, k1, ssk, knit to the last 3 stitches, k2tog, k1; on wrong-side rows, p1, p2tog, purl to the last 3 stitches, ssp (page 255), p1.
- For fully fashioned increases on right-side rows, k1, M1R (page 253), knit to the last stitch, M1L (page 253), k1.

Back

Work same as for the shaped silhouette with square indented construction (page 35) until the piece measures approximately 1"/2.5cm from the beginning.

Continue even until the piece measures approximately 1¾"/4.5cm from the beginning, or 22½ (22½, 23, 23, 23, 23½, 23¾, 24¼)"/57 (57, 58.5, 58.5, 58.5, 59.5, 60.5, 61.5)cm less than the desired finished length, ending after a wrong-side row.

Decrease for the Waist

Work same as for the shaped silhouette with square indented construction (page 35).

You will have __ stitches remaining.

	XS	S	M	L	1X	2X	3X	4X
7	92	106	120	134	148	162	176	190
6½	84	96	110	122	136	148	162	174
6	78	90	102	114	126	138	150	162
5½	72	82	92	104	114	126	136	148
5	66	76	84	96	106	116	126	134
4½	58	66	76	86	94	102	112	120
4	52	60	68	76	84	92	100	108
3½	44	52	58	66	72	80	86	94
3	40	46	52	58	64	70	76	82

Continue even until the piece measures approximately 7¾"/19.5cm from the beginning, or 16½ (16½, 17, 17, 17, 17½, 17¾, 18¼)"/42 (42, 43.5, 43.5, 43.5, 44.5, 45.5, 46.5)cm less than the desired finished length, ending after a right-side row.

Increase for the Bust

Work same as for the shaped silhouette with square indented construction (page 35).

You will now have __ stitches.

	XS	S	M	L	1X	2X	3X	4X
7	106	120	134	148	162	176	190	204
6½	98	110	124	136	150	162	176	188
6	90	102	114	126	138	150	162	174
5½	84	94	104	116	126	138	148	160
5	76	86	94	106	116	126	136	144
4½	68	76	86	96	104	112	122	130
4	60	68	76	84	92	100	108	116
3½	52	60	66	74	80	88	94	102
3	46	52	58	64	70	76	82	88

Continue even, if necessary, until the piece measures approximately 15 (14½, 14½, 14½, 14, 14, 13¾, 13¾)"/38 (37, 37, 37, 35.5, 35.5, 35, 35)cm from the beginning, or 9¼ (9¾, 10¼, 10¼, 10¾, 11¼, 11¾, 12¼)"/23.5 (24.5, 26, 26, 27.5, 28.5, 30, 31)cm less than the desired finished length, ending after a wrong-side row.

Shape the Armholes

Work same as for the straight silhouette with raglan construction (page 30).

You will have __ stitches remaining.

	XS	S	M	L	1X	2X	3X	4X
7	48	48	48	48	48	48	48	48
6½	46	46	46	46	46	46	46	46
6	42	42	42	42	42	42	42	42
5½	38	38	38	38	38	38	38	38
5	34	34	34	34	34	34	34	34
4½	32	32	32	32	32	32	32	32
4	28	28	28	28	28	28	28	28
3½	24	24	24	24	24	24	24	24
3	22	22	22	22	22	22	22	22

Work 1 row even, if indicated below. If no number is given, do not work this row.

	XS	S	M	L	1X	2X	3X	4X
7	--	1	1	--	--	--	--	--
6½	--	--	1	1	--	--	--	--
6	--	--	--	--	--	--	--	--
5½	--	--	--	--	--	--	--	--
5	--	--	1	1	--	--	--	--
4½	--	1	1	1	--	--	--	--
4	--	1	--	--	1	--	--	--
3½	--	1	1	1	--	--	1	1
3	--	--	--	--	--	--	--	--

Bind off all stitches.

Shaped Silhouette with Saddle Shoulder Construction

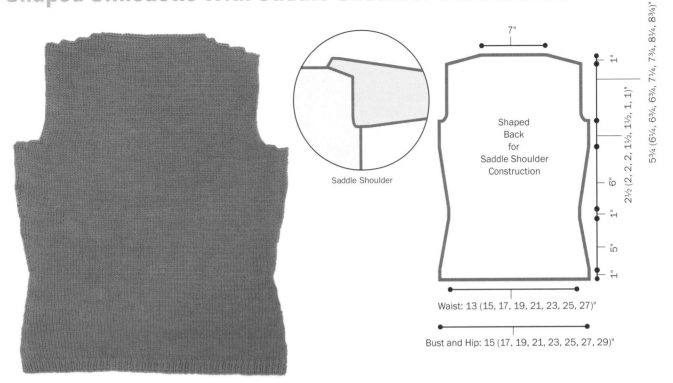

Saddle Shoulder

Shaped Back for Saddle Shoulder Construction

7"

1"

53⁄4 (61⁄4, 63⁄4, 63⁄4, 71⁄4, 73⁄4, 81⁄4, 83⁄4)"

21⁄2 (2, 2, 2, 11⁄2, 11⁄2, 1, 1)"

6"

1"

5"

1"

Waist: 13 (15, 17, 19, 21, 23, 25, 27)"

Bust and Hip: 15 (17, 19, 21, 23, 25, 27, 29)"

Finished Measurements

	XS	S	M	L	1X	2X	3X	4X
Bust	30"/76cm	34"/86.5cm	38"/96.5cm	42"/106.5cm	46"/117cm	50"/127cm	54"/137cm	58"/147.5cm
Waist	26"/66cm	30"/76cm	34"/86.5cm	38"/96.5cm	42"/106.5cm	46"/117cm	50"/127cm	54"/137cm
Hip	30"/76cm	34"/86.5cm	38"/96.5cm	42"/106.5cm	46"/117cm	50"/127cm	54"/137cm	58"/147.5cm
Length	23½"/59.5cm	23½"/59.5cm	24"/61cm	24"/61cm	24"/61cm	24½"/62cm	24½"/62cm	25"/63.5cm

Notes

- The total finished length of this garment includes one-half of the width of the upper edge of the sleeves; the front and back pieces are 1¼"/3cm shorter than the total length of the garment.
- This pattern is written for K1P1 ribbed edges. Refer to pages 213–223 for information on how to customize the edge treatment.
- For fully fashioned decreases: On right-side rows, k1, ssk, knit to the last 3 stitches, k2tog, k1; on wrong-side rows, p1, p2tog, purl to the last 3 stitches, ssp (page 255), p1.
- For fully fashioned increases on right-side rows, k1, M1R (page 253), knit to the last stitch, M1L (page 253), k1.
- For fully fashioned neck decreases: On right-side rows, first half, knit to 3 stitches before the neck edge, k2tog, k1; second half, k1, ssk, work to the end of the row. On wrong-side rows, first half, purl to 3 stitches before the neck edge, ssp (page 255), p1; second half, p1, p2tog, work to the end of the row.

Back

Work same as for the shaped silhouette with set-in construction (page 40) until the piece measures approximately 21¼ (21¼, 21¾, 21¾, 21¾, 22¼, 22¼, 22¾)"/54 (54, 55.5, 55.5, 55.5, 56.5, 56.5, 58)cm from the beginning, or 2¼"/5.5cm less than the desired finished length, ending after a wrong-side row.

You will have ___ stitches remaining.

	XS	S	M	L	1X	2X	3X	4X
7	92	98	106	112	116	120	122	126
6½	84	92	98	104	108	110	114	118
6	78	84	90	96	100	102	106	108
5½	72	78	82	88	90	94	96	100
5	64	70	74	80	82	86	88	90
4½	58	64	68	72	74	76	78	82
4	52	56	60	64	66	68	70	72
3½	46	50	52	56	58	60	62	64
3	40	42	46	48	50	52	52	54

Shape the Shoulders

Work same as for the straight silhouette with square indented construction (page 35).

A-Line Silhouette

The A-line silhouette is wider at the lower edge than it is at the bust. Its swingy shape suits most figures.

A-Line Silhouette with Square Indented Construction

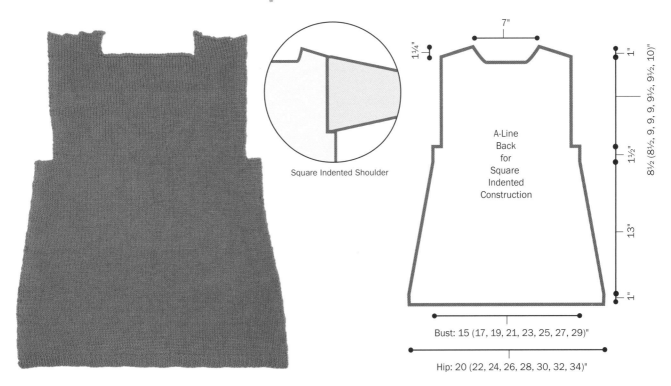

Square Indented Shoulder

A-Line
Back
for
Square
Indented
Construction

7"

1¼"

8½ (8½, 9, 9, 9½, 9½, 10)"

1"

1½"

13"

1"

Bust: 15 (17, 19, 21, 23, 25, 27, 29)"

Hip: 20 (22, 24, 26, 28, 30, 32, 34)"

Finished Measurements

	XS	S	M	L	1X	2X	3X	4X
Bust	30"/76cm	34"/86.5cm	38"/96.5cm	42"/106.5cm	46"/117cm	50"/127cm	54"/137cm	58"/147.5cm
Hip	40"/101.5cm	44"/112cm	48"/122cm	52"/132cm	56"/142cm	60"/152.5cm	64"/162.5cm	68"/172.5cm
Length	25"/63.5cm	25"/63.5cm	25½"/64.5cm	25½"/64.5cm	25½"/64.5cm	26"/66cm	26"/66cm	26½"/67.5cm

Notes

- This pattern is written for K1P1 ribbed edges. Refer to pages 213–223 for information on how to customize the edge treatment.
- For fully fashioned decreases: On right-side rows, k1, ssk, knit to the last 3 stitches, k2tog, k1; on wrong-side rows, p1, p2tog, purl to the last 3 stitches, ssp (page 255), p1.
- For fully fashioned neck decreases: On right-side rows, first half, knit to 3 stitches before the neck edge, k2tog, k1; second half, k1, ssk, work to the end of the row. On wrong-side rows, first half, purl to 3 stitches before the neck edge, ssp (page 255), p1; second half, p1, p2tog, work to the end of the row.

Back

Cast on __ stitches.

	XS	S	M	L	1X	2X	3X	4X
7	142	156	170	184	198	212	226	240
6½	130	142	156	168	182	194	208	220
6	120	132	144	156	168	180	192	204
5½	112	122	132	144	154	166	176	188
5	102	112	120	132	142	152	162	170
4½	90	98	108	118	126	134	144	152
4	80	88	96	104	112	120	128	136
3½	70	78	84	92	98	106	112	120
3	62	68	74	80	86	92	98	104

Begin K1P1 rib (page 215), and work even until the piece measures approximately 1"/2.5cm from the beginning, ending after a wrong-side row.

Decrease for the Bust

Begin stockinette stitch, and work fully fashioned decreases (see Notes) each side every 8 rows __ times.

	XS	S	M	L	1X	2X	3X	4X
7	5	5	5	5	5	5	5	5
6½	7	7	7	7	7	7	7	7
6	7	7	7	7	7	7	7	7
5½	7	7	7	7	7	7	7	7
5	6	6	6	6	6	6	6	6
4½	9	9	9	9	9	9	9	9
4	9	9	9	9	9	9	9	9
3½	5	5	5	5	5	5	5	5
3	2	3	3	3	3	3	3	3

Work fully fashioned decreases each side every 6 rows __ time(s).

	XS	S	M	L	1X	2X	3X	4X
7	13	13	13	13	13	13	13	13
6½	9	9	9	9	9	9	9	9
6	8	8	8	8	8	8	8	8
5½	7	7	7	7	7	7	7	7
5	7	7	7	7	7	7	7	7
4½	2	2	2	2	2	2	2	2
4	1	1	1	1	1	1	1	1
3½	4	4	4	4	4	4	4	4
3	6	6	6	6	6	6	6	6

You will now have __ stitches.

	XS	S	M	L	1X	2X	3X	4X
7	106	120	134	148	162	176	190	204
6½	98	110	124	136	150	162	176	188
6	90	102	114	126	138	150	162	174
5½	84	94	104	116	126	138	148	160
5	76	86	94	106	116	126	136	144
4½	68	76	86	96	104	112	122	130
4	60	68	76	84	92	100	108	116
3½	52	60	66	74	80	88	94	102
3	46	52	58	64	70	76	82	88

Continue even until the piece measures approximately 15½"/39.5cm from the beginning, or 9½ (9½, 10, 10, 10, 10½, 10½, 11)"/24 (24, 25, 25, 25, 26.5, 26.5, 28)cm less than the desired finished length, ending after a wrong-side row.

Shape the Armholes

Work same as for the straight silhouette with square indented construction (page 20).

You will have __ stitches remaining.

	XS	S	M	L	1X	2X	3X	4X
7	92	98	106	112	116	120	122	126
6½	84	92	98	104	108	110	114	118
6	78	84	90	96	100	102	106	108
5½	72	78	82	88	90	94	96	100
5	64	70	74	80	82	86	88	90
4½	58	64	68	72	74	76	78	82
4	52	56	60	64	66	68	70	72
3½	46	50	52	56	58	60	62	64
3	40	42	46	48	50	52	52	54

Continue even until the piece measures approximately 23¾ (23¾, 24¼, 24¼, 24¼, 24¾, 24¾, 25¼)"/60.5 (60.5, 61.5, 61.5, 61.5, 63, 63, 64.5)cm from the beginning, or 1¼"/3cm less than the desired finished length, ending after a wrong-side row.

Shape the Neck

Work same as for the straight silhouette with square indented construction (page 20).

You will have __ stitches remaining on each side.

	XS	S	M	L	1X	2X	3X	4X
7	22	25	29	32	34	36	37	39
6½	19	23	26	29	31	32	34	36
6	18	21	24	27	29	30	32	33
5½	17	20	22	25	26	28	29	31
5	15	18	20	23	24	26	27	28
4½	13	16	18	20	21	22	23	25
4	12	14	16	18	19	20	21	22
3½	11	13	14	16	17	18	19	20
3	9	10	12	13	14	15	15	16

Continue even, if necessary, until the piece measures approximately 24 (24, 24½, 24½, 24½, 25, 25, 25½)"/61 (61, 62, 62, 62, 63.5, 63.5, 65)cm from the beginning, or 1"/2.5cm less than the desired finished length, ending after a wrong-side row.

Shape the Shoulders

Work same as for the straight silhouette with square indented construction (page 20).

A-Line Silhouette with Set-In Construction

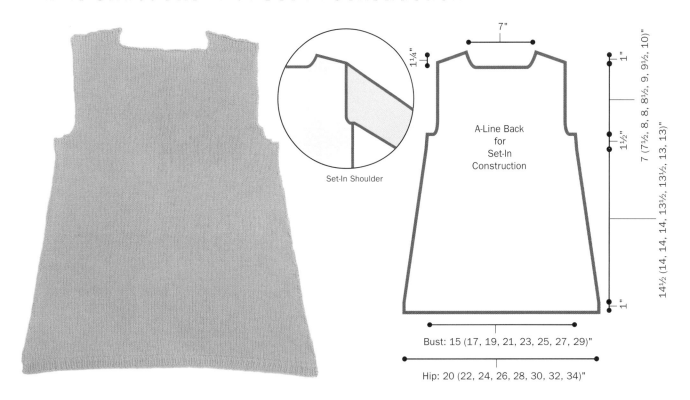

Set-In Shoulder

7"

1¼"

1"

1½"

A-Line Back for Set-In Construction

14½ (14, 14, 14, 13½, 13½, 13, 13)"

7 (7½, 8, 8, 8½, 9, 9½, 10)"

1"

Bust: 15 (17, 19, 21, 23, 25, 27, 29)"

Hip: 20 (22, 24, 26, 28, 30, 32, 34)"

Finished Measurements

	XS	S	M	L	1X	2X	3X	4X
Bust	30"/76cm	34"/86.5cm	38"/96.5cm	42"/106.5cm	46"/117cm	50"/127cm	54"/137cm	58"/147.5cm
Hip	40"/101.5cm	44"/112cm	48"/122cm	52"/132cm	56"/142cm	60"/152.5cm	64"/162.5cm	68"/172.5cm
Length	25"/63.5cm	25"/63.5cm	25½"/64.5cm	25½"/64.5cm	25½"/64.5cm	26"/66cm	26"/66cm	26½"/67.5cm

Notes

- This pattern is written for K1P1 ribbed edges. Refer to pages 213–223 for information on how to customize the edge treatment.
- For fully fashioned decreases: On right-side rows, k1, ssk, knit to the last 3 stitches, k2tog, k1; on wrong-side rows, p1, p2tog, purl to the last 3 stitches, ssp (page 255), p1.
- For fully fashioned neck decreases: On right-side rows, first half, knit to 3 stitches before the neck edge, k2tog, k1; second half, k1, ssk, work to the end of the row. On wrong-side rows, first half, purl to 3 stitches before the neck edge, ssp (page 255), p1; second half, p1, p2tog, work to the end of the row.

Back

Cast on __ stitches.

	XS	S	M	L	1X	2X	3X	4X
7	142	156	170	184	198	212	226	240
6½	130	142	156	168	182	194	208	220
6	120	132	144	156	168	180	192	204
5½	112	122	132	144	154	166	176	188
5	102	112	120	132	142	152	162	170
4½	90	98	108	118	126	134	144	152
4	80	88	96	104	112	120	128	136
3½	70	78	84	92	98	106	112	120
3	62	68	74	80	86	92	98	104

Begin K1P1 rib (page 215), and work even until the piece measures approximately 1"/2.5cm from the beginning, ending after a wrong-side row.

Decrease for the Bust

Begin stockinette stitch, and work fully fashioned decreases (see Notes) each side every 10 rows __ time(s). If no number is given, do not work these rows.

	XS	S	M	L	1X	2X	3X	4X
7	--	--	--	--	--	--	--	--
6½	--	--	--	--	--	--	--	--
6	--	--	--	--	--	--	--	--
5½	--	--	--	--	--	--	--	--
5	--	--	--	--	--	--	--	--
4½	3	2	2	2	--	--	--	--
4	4	2	2	2	1	1	--	--
3½	--	--	--	--	--	--	--	--
3	--	--	--	--	--	--	--	--

Work fully fashioned decreases each side every 8 rows __ times.

	XS	S	M	L	1X	2X	3X	4X
7	11	9	9	9	7	7	5	5
6½	14	12	12	12	9	9	7	7
6	13	11	11	11	9	9	7	7
5½	12	11	11	11	9	9	7	7
5	12	10	10	10	8	8	7	7
4½	8	9	9	9	11	11	9	9
4	6	8	8	8	9	9	9	9
3½	9	8	8	8	7	7	6	6
3	5	4	4	4	3	3	2	2

Work fully fashioned decreases each side every 6 rows __ time(s). If no number is given, do not work these rows.

	XS	S	M	L	1X	2X	3X	4X
7	7	9	9	9	11	11	13	13
6½	2	4	4	4	7	7	9	9
6	2	4	4	4	6	6	8	8
5½	2	3	3	3	5	5	7	7
5	1	3	3	3	5	5	6	6
4½	--	--	--	--	--	--	2	2
4	--	--	--	--	--	--	1	1
3½	--	1	1	1	2	2	3	3
3	3	4	4	4	5	5	6	6

You will have __ stitches remaining.

	XS	S	M	L	1X	2X	3X	4X
7	106	120	134	148	162	176	190	204
6½	98	110	124	136	150	162	176	188
6	90	102	114	126	138	150	162	174
5½	84	94	104	116	126	138	148	160
5	76	86	94	106	116	126	136	144
4½	68	76	86	96	104	112	122	130
4	60	68	76	84	92	100	108	116
3½	52	60	66	74	80	88	94	102
3	46	52	58	64	70	76	82	88

Continue even until the piece measures approximately 17 (16½, 16½, 16½, 16, 16, 15½, 15½)"/43 (42, 42, 42, 40.5, 40.5, 39.5, 39.5)cm from the beginning, or 8 (8½, 9, 9, 9½, 10, 10½, 11)"/20.5 (21.5, 23, 23, 24, 25.5, 26.5, 28)cm less than the desired finished length, ending after a wrong-side row.

Shape the Armholes

Work same as for the straight silhouette with set-in construction (page 25).

You will have __ stitches remaining.

	XS	S	M	L	1X	2X	3X	4X
7	92	98	106	112	116	120	122	126
6½	84	92	98	104	108	110	114	118
6	78	84	90	96	100	102	106	108
5½	72	78	82	88	90	94	96	100
5	64	70	74	80	82	86	88	90
4½	58	64	68	72	74	76	78	82
4	52	56	60	64	66	68	70	72
3½	46	50	52	56	58	60	62	64
3	40	42	46	48	50	52	52	54

Continue even until the piece measures approximately 23¾ (23¾, 24¼, 24¼, 24¼, 24¾, 24¾, 25¼)"/60.5 (60.5, 61.5, 61.5, 61.5, 63, 63, 64)cm from the beginning, or 1¼"/3cm less than the desired finished length, ending after a wrong-side row.

Shape the Neck

Work same as for the straight silhouette with square indented construction (page 20).

You will have __ stitches remaining on each side.

	XS	S	M	L	1X	2X	3X	4X
7	22	25	29	32	34	36	37	39
6½	19	23	26	29	31	32	34	36
6	18	21	24	27	29	30	32	33
5½	17	20	22	25	26	28	29	31
5	15	18	20	23	24	26	27	28
4½	13	16	18	20	21	22	23	25
4	12	14	16	18	19	20	21	22
3½	11	13	14	16	17	18	19	20
3	9	10	12	13	14	15	15	16

Continue even until the piece measures approximately 24 (24, 24½, 24½, 24½, 25, 25, 25½)"/61 (61, 62, 62, 62, 63.5, 63.5, 65)cm from the beginning, or 1"/2.5cm less than the desired finished length, ending after a wrong-side row.

Shape the Shoulders

Work same as for the straight silhouette with square indented construction (page 20).

A-Line Silhouette with Raglan Construction

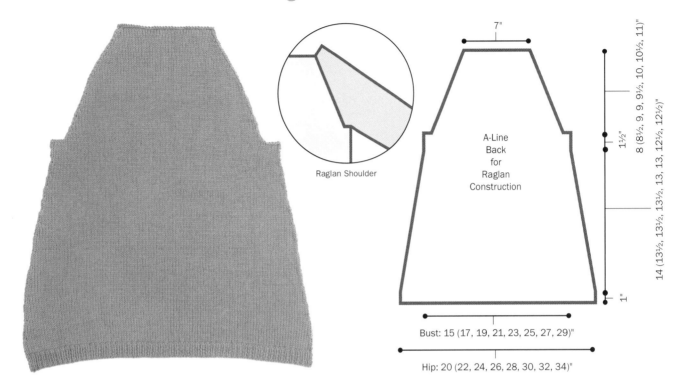

Raglan Shoulder

7"

A-Line
Back
for
Raglan
Construction

8 (8½, 9, 9, 9½, 10, 10½, 11)"

1½"

14 (13½, 13½, 13½, 13, 13, 12½, 12½)"

1"

Bust: 15 (17, 19, 21, 23, 25, 27, 29)"

Hip: 20 (22, 24, 26, 28, 30, 32, 34)"

Finished Measurements

	XS	S	M	L	1X	2X	3X	4X
Bust	30"/76cm	34"/86.5cm	38"/96.5cm	42"/106.5cm	46"/117cm	50"/127cm	54"/137cm	58"/147.5cm
Hip	40"/101.5cm	44"/112cm	48"/122cm	52"/132cm	56"/142cm	60"/152.5cm	64"/162.5cm	68"/172.5cm
Length	25¾"/65.5cm	25¾"/65.5cm	26¼"/66.5cm	26¼"/66.5cm	26¼"/66.5cm	26¾"/68cm	26¾"/68cm	27¼"/69cm

Notes

- The total finished length of this garment includes one-half of the width of the upper edge of the sleeves; the front and back pieces are 1¼"/3cm shorter than the total length of the garment.
- This pattern is written for K1P1 ribbed edges. Refer to pages 213–223 for information on how to customize the edge treatment.
- For fully fashioned decreases: On right-side rows, k1, ssk, knit to the last 3 stitches, k2tog, k1; on wrong-side rows, p1, p2tog, purl to the last 3 stitches, ssp (page 255), p1.

Back

Cast on __ stitches.

	XS	S	M	L	1X	2X	3X	4X
7	142	156	170	184	198	212	226	240
6½	130	142	156	168	182	194	208	220
6	120	132	144	156	168	180	192	204
5½	112	122	132	144	154	166	176	188
5	102	112	120	132	142	152	162	170
4½	90	98	108	118	126	134	144	152
4	80	88	96	104	112	120	128	136
3½	70	78	84	92	98	106	112	120
3	62	68	74	80	86	92	98	104

Begin K1P1 rib (page 215), and work even until the piece measures approximately 1"/2.5cm from the beginning, ending after a wrong-side row.

Decrease for the Bust

Begin stockinette stitch, and work fully fashioned decreases (see Notes) each side every 10 rows __ time(s). If no number is given, do not work these rows.

	XS	S	M	L	1X	2X	3X	4X
7	--	--	--	--	--	--	--	--
6½	--	--	--	--	--	--	--	--
6	--	--	--	--	--	--	--	--
5½	--	--	--	--	--	--	--	--
5	--	--	--	--	--	--	--	--
4½	2	--	--	--	--	--	--	--
4	2	1	1	1	--	--	--	--
3½	--	--	--	--	--	--	--	--
3	--	--	--	--	--	--	--	--

Work fully fashioned decreases each side every 8 rows __ time(s).

	XS	S	M	L	1X	2X	3X	4X
7	9	7	7	7	5	5	2	2
6½	12	9	9	9	7	7	5	5
6	11	9	9	9	7	7	5	5
5½	11	9	9	9	7	7	5	5
5	10	8	8	8	7	7	5	5
4½	9	11	11	11	9	9	7	7
4	8	9	9	9	9	9	8	8
3½	8	7	7	7	6	6	4	4
3	4	3	3	3	2	2	1	1

Work fully fashioned decreases each side every 6 rows __ time(s). If no number is given, do not work these rows.

	XS	S	M	L	1X	2X	3X	4X
7	9	11	11	11	13	13	16	16
6½	4	7	7	7	9	9	11	11
6	4	6	6	6	8	8	10	10
5½	3	5	5	5	7	7	9	9
5	3	5	5	5	6	6	8	8
4½	--	--	--	--	2	2	4	4
4	--	--	--	--	1	1	2	2
3½	1	2	2	2	3	3	5	5
3	4	5	5	5	6	6	7	7

You will have __ stitches remaining.

	XS	S	M	L	1X	2X	3X	4X
7	106	120	134	148	162	176	190	204
6½	98	110	124	136	150	162	176	188
6	90	102	114	126	138	150	162	174
5½	84	94	104	116	126	138	148	160
5	76	86	94	106	116	126	136	144
4½	68	76	86	96	104	112	122	130
4	60	68	76	84	92	100	108	116
3½	52	60	66	74	80	88	94	102
3	46	52	58	64	70	76	82	88

Continue even until the piece measures approximately 16½ (16, 16, 16, 15½, 15½, 15, 15)"/42 (40.5, 40.5, 40.5, 39.5, 39.5, 38, 38)cm from the beginning, or 9¼ (9¾, 10¼, 10¼, 10¾, 11¼, 11¾, 12¼)"/23.5 (25, 26, 26, 27, 28.5, 30, 31)cm less than the desired finished length, ending after a wrong-side row.

Shape the Armholes

Work same as for the straight silhouette with raglan construction (page 30).

You will have __ stitches remaining.

	XS	S	M	L	1X	2X	3X	4X
7	48	48	48	48	48	48	48	48
6½	46	46	46	46	46	46	46	46
6	42	42	42	42	42	42	42	42
5½	38	38	38	38	38	38	38	38
5	34	34	34	34	34	34	34	34
4½	32	32	32	32	32	32	32	32
4	28	28	28	28	28	28	28	28
3½	24	24	24	24	24	24	24	24
3	22	22	22	22	22	22	22	22

Work 1 row even, if indicated below. If no number is given, do not work this row.

	XS	S	M	L	1X	2X	3X	4X
7	--	1	1	--	--	--	--	--
6½	--	--	1	1	--	--	--	--
6	--	--	--	--	--	--	--	--
5½	--	--	--	--	--	--	--	--
5	--	--	1	1	--	--	--	--
4½	--	1	1	1	--	--	--	--
4	--	1	--	--	1	--	--	--
3½	--	1	1	1	--	--	1	1
3	--	--	--	--	--	--	--	--

Bind off all stitches.

A-Line Silhouette with Saddle Shoulder Construction

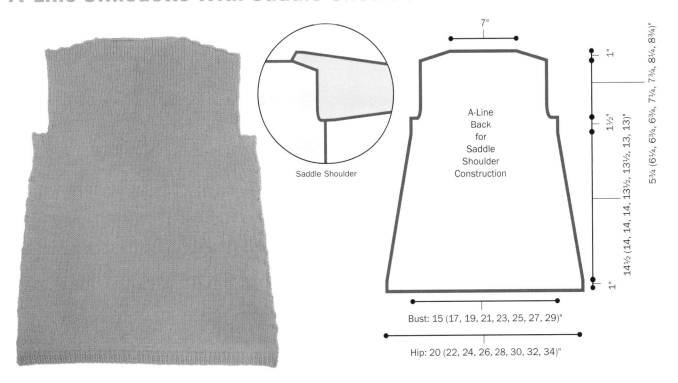

Saddle Shoulder

7"

A-Line
Back
for
Saddle
Shoulder
Construction

1"

1½"

5¾ (6¼, 6¾, 6¾, 7¼, 7¾, 8¼, 8¾)"

14½ (14, 14, 14, 13½, 13½, 13, 13)"

1"

Bust: 15 (17, 19, 21, 23, 25, 27, 29)"

Hip: 20 (22, 24, 26, 28, 30, 32, 34)"

Finished Measurements

	XS	S	M	L	1X	2X	3X	4X
Bust	30"/76cm	34"/86.5cm	38"/96.5cm	42"/106.5cm	46"/117cm	50"/127cm	54"/137cm	58"/147.5cm
Hip	40"/101.5cm	44"/112cm	48"/122cm	52"/132cm	56"/142cm	60"/152.5cm	64"/162.5cm	68"/172.5cm
Length	25"/63.5cm	25"/63.5cm	25½"/64.5cm	25½"/64.5cm	25½"/64.5cm	26"/66cm	26"/66cm	26½"/67.5cm

Notes

- The total finished length of this garment includes one-half of the width of the upper edge of the sleeves; the front and back pieces are 1¼"/3cm shorter than the total length of the garment.
- This pattern is written for K1P1 ribbed edges. Refer to pages 213–223 for information on how to customize the edge treatment.
- For fully fashioned decreases: On right-side rows, k1, ssk, knit to the last 3 stitches, k2tog, k1; on wrong-side rows, p1, p2tog, purl to the last 3 stitches, ssp (page 255), p1.

Back

Cast on __ stitches.

	XS	S	M	L	1X	2X	3X	4X
7	142	156	170	184	198	212	226	240
6½	130	142	156	168	182	194	208	220
6	120	132	144	156	168	180	192	204
5½	112	122	132	144	154	166	176	188
5	102	112	120	132	142	152	162	170
4½	90	98	108	118	126	134	144	152
4	80	88	96	104	112	120	128	136
3½	70	78	84	92	98	106	112	120
3	62	68	74	80	86	92	98	104

Begin K1P1 rib (page 215), and work even until the piece measures approximately 1"/2.5cm from the beginning, ending after a wrong-side row.

Decrease for the Bust

Work same as for the A-line silhouette with set-in construction (page 51).

You will have __ stitches remaining.

	XS	S	M	L	1X	2X	3X	4X
7	106	120	134	148	162	176	190	204
6½	98	110	124	136	150	162	176	188
6	90	102	114	126	138	150	162	174
5½	84	94	104	116	126	138	148	160
5	76	86	94	106	116	126	136	144
4½	68	76	86	96	104	112	122	130
4	60	68	76	84	92	100	108	116
3½	52	60	66	74	80	88	94	102
3	46	52	58	64	70	76	82	88

Continue even until the piece measures approximately 17 (16½, 16½, 16½, 16, 16, 15½, 15½)"/43 (42, 42, 42, 40.5, 40.5, 39.5, 39.5)cm from the beginning, or 8 (8½, 9, 9, 9½, 10, 10½, 11)"/20.5 (21.5, 23, 23, 24, 25.5, 26.5, 28)cm less than the desired finished length, ending after a wrong-side row.

Shape the Armholes

Work same as for the straight silhouette with set-in construction (page 25).

Continue even until the piece measures approximately 22¾ (22¾, 23¼, 23¼, 23¼, 23¾, 23¾, 24¼)"/58 (58, 59, 59, 59, 60.5, 60.5, 62)cm from the beginning, or 2¼"/5.5cm less than the desired finished length, ending after a wrong-side row.

Shape the Shoulders

Work same as for the straight silhouette with square indented construction (page 20). Bind off all stitches.

Tapered Silhouette

Shaped like an inverted triangle, this classic silhouette is perfect for casual as well as dressy looks.

Tapered Silhouette with Square Indented Construction

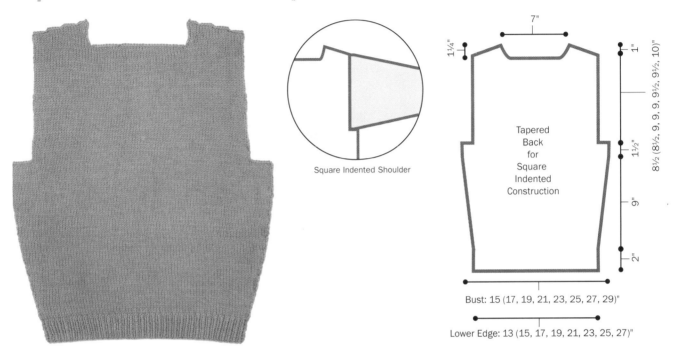

Square Indented Shoulder

Tapered Back for Square Indented Construction

7"

1¼"

8½ (8½, 9, 9, 9½, 9½, 10)"

1"

1½"

9"

2"

Bust: 15 (17, 19, 21, 23, 25, 27, 29)"

Lower Edge: 13 (15, 17, 19, 21, 23, 25, 27)"

Finished Measurements

	XS	S	M	L	1X	2X	3X	4X
Bust	30"/76cm	34"/86.5cm	38"/96.5cm	42"/106.5cm	46"/117cm	50"/127cm	54"/137cm	58"/147.5cm
Lower Edge	26"/66cm	30"/76cm	34"/86.5cm	38"/96.5cm	42"/107cm	46"/117cm	50"/127cm	54"/137cm
Length	22"/56cm	22"/56cm	22½"/57cm	22½"/57cm	22½"/57cm	23"/58.5cm	23"/58.5cm	23½"/59.5cm

Notes

- This pattern is written for K1P1 ribbed edges. Refer to pages 213–223 for information on how to customize the edge treatment.
- For fully fashioned increases: On right-side rows, k1, M1R (page 253), knit to the last stitch, M1L (page 253), k1.
- For fully fashioned neck decreases: On right-side rows, first half, knit to 3 stitches before the neck edge, k2tog, k1; second half, k1, ssk, work to the end of the row. On wrong-side rows, first half, purl to 3 stitches before the neck edge, ssp (page 255), p1; second half, p1, p2tog, work to the end of the row.

Back

Cast on __ stitches.

	XS	S	M	L	1X	2X	3X	4X
7	92	106	120	134	148	162	176	190
6½	84	96	110	122	136	148	162	174
6	78	90	102	114	126	138	150	162
5½	72	82	92	104	114	126	136	148
5	66	76	84	96	106	116	126	134
4½	58	66	76	86	94	102	112	120
4	52	60	68	76	84	92	100	108
3½	46	54	60	68	74	82	88	96
3	40	46	52	58	64	70	76	82

Begin K1P1 rib, and work even until the piece measures approximately 2"/5cm from the beginning, ending after a WS row.

Increase for the Bust

Begin stockinette stitch, and work fully fashioned increases (see Notes) each side every 16 rows once, if indicated below. If no number is given, do not work these rows.

	XS	S	M	L	1X	2X	3X	4X
7	--	--	--	--	--	--	--	--
6½	--	--	--	--	--	--	--	--
6	--	--	--	--	--	--	--	--
5½	--	--	--	--	--	--	--	--
5	--	--	--	--	--	--	--	--
4½	--	--	--	--	--	--	--	--
4	--	--	--	--	--	--	--	--
3½	1	1	1	1	1	1	1	1
3	--	--	--	--	--	--	--	--

Work fully fashioned increases each side every 14 rows __ time(s). If no number is given, do not work these rows.

	XS	S	M	L	1X	2X	3X	4X
7	--	--	--	--	--	--	--	--
6½	--	--	--	--	--	--	--	--
6	--	--	--	--	--	--	--	--
5½	--	--	--	--	--	--	--	--
5	1	1	1	1	1	1	1	1
4½	--	--	--	--	--	--	--	--
4	3	3	3	3	3	3	3	3
3½	2	2	2	2	2	2	2	2
3	--	--	--	--	--	--	--	--

Work fully fashioned increases each side every 12 rows __ time(s). If no number is given, do not work these rows.

	XS	S	M	L	1X	2X	3X	4X
7	5	5	5	5	5	5	5	5
6½	3	3	3	3	3	3	3	3
6	6	6	6	6	6	6	6	6
5½	4	4	4	4	4	4	4	4
5	4	4	4	4	4	4	4	4
4½	4	4	4	4	4	4	4	4
4	1	1	1	1	1	1	1	1
3½	--	--	--	--	--	--	--	--
3	3	3	3	3	3	3	3	3

Work fully fashioned increases each side every 10 rows __ time(s). If no number is given, do not work these rows.

	XS	S	M	L	1X	2X	3X	4X
7	2	2	2	2	2	2	2	2
6½	4	4	4	4	4	4	4	4
6	--	--	--	--	--	--	--	--
5½	2	2	2	2	2	2	2	2
5	--	--	--	--	--	--	--	--
4½	1	1	1	1	1	1	1	1
4	--	--	--	--	--	--	--	--
3½	--	--	--	--	--	--	--	--
3	--	--	--	--	--	--	--	--

You will now have __ stitches.

	XS	S	M	L	1X	2X	3X	4X
7	106	120	134	148	162	176	190	204
6½	98	110	124	136	150	162	176	188
6	90	102	114	126	138	150	162	174
5½	84	94	104	116	126	138	148	160
5	76	86	94	106	116	126	136	144
4½	68	76	86	96	104	112	122	130
4	60	68	76	84	92	100	108	116
3½	52	60	66	74	80	88	94	102
3	46	52	58	64	70	76	82	88

Continue even until the piece measures approximately 12½"/32cm from the beginning, or 9½ (9½, 10, 10, 10, 10½, 10½, 11)"/24 (24, 25, 25, 25, 26.5, 26.5, 27.5)cm less than the desired finished length, ending after a wrong-side row.

Shape the Armholes

Work same as for the straight silhouette with square indented construction (page 20).

You will have __ stitches remaining.

	XS	S	M	L	1X	2X	3X	4X
7	92	98	106	112	116	120	122	126
6½	84	92	98	104	108	110	114	118
6	78	84	90	96	100	102	106	108
5½	72	78	82	88	90	94	96	100
5	64	70	74	80	82	86	88	90
4½	58	64	68	72	74	76	78	82
4	52	56	60	64	66	68	70	72
3½	46	50	52	56	58	60	62	64
3	40	42	46	48	50	52	52	54

Continue even until the piece measures approximately 20¾ (20¾, 21¼, 21¼, 21¼, 21¾, 21¾, 22¼)"/53 (53, 54, 54, 54, 55.5, 55.5, 56.5)cm from the beginning, or 1¼"/3cm less than the desired finished length, ending after a wrong-side row.

Shape the Neck

Work same as for the straight silhouette with square indented construction (page 20).

You will have __ stitches remaining on each side.

	XS	S	M	L	1X	2X	3X	4X
7	22	25	29	32	34	36	37	39
6½	19	23	26	29	31	32	34	36
6	18	21	24	27	29	30	32	33
5½	17	20	22	25	26	28	29	31
5	15	18	20	23	24	26	27	28
4½	13	16	18	20	21	22	23	25
4	12	14	16	18	19	20	21	22
3½	11	13	14	16	17	18	19	20
3	9	10	12	13	14	15	15	16

Continue even, if necessary, until the piece measures approximately 21 (21, 21½, 21½, 21½, 22, 22, 22½)"/53.5 (53.5, 54.5, 54.5, 54.5, 56, 56, 57)cm from the beginning, or 1"/2.5cm less than the desired finished length, ending after a wrong-side row.

Shape the Shoulders

Work same as for the straight silhouette with square indented construction (page 20).

Tapered Silhouette with Set-In Construction

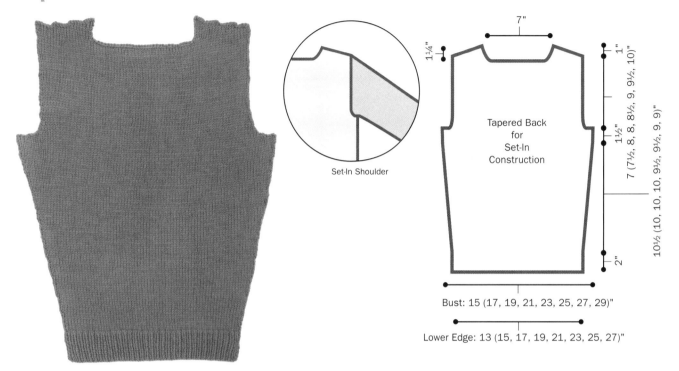

Set-In Shoulder

7"

1¼"

1½"

1"

1"

Tapered Back
for
Set-In
Construction

7 (7½, 8, 8, 8½, 9, 9½, 10)"

10½ (10, 10, 10, 9½, 9½, 9, 9)"

2"

Bust: 15 (17, 19, 21, 23, 25, 27, 29)"

Lower Edge: 13 (15, 17, 19, 21, 23, 25, 27)"

Finished Measurements

	XS	S	M	L	1X	2X	3X	4X
Bust	30"/76cm	34"/86.5cm	38"/96.5cm	42"/106.5cm	46"/117cm	50"/127cm	54"/137cm	58"/147.5cm
Lower Edge	26"/66cm	30"/76cm	34"/86.5cm	38"/96.5cm	42"/107cm	46"/117cm	50"/127cm	54"/137cm
Length	22"/56cm	22"/56cm	22½"/57cm	22½"/57cm	22½"/57cm	23"/58.5cm	23"/58.5cm	23½"/59.5cm

Notes

- This pattern is written for K1P1 ribbed edges. Refer to pages 213–223 for information on how to customize the edge treatment.
- For fully fashioned decreases: On right-side rows, k1, ssk, knit to the last 3 stitches, k2tog, k1; on wrong-side rows, p1, p2tog, purl to the last 3 stitches, ssp (page 255), p1.
- For fully fashioned increases: On right-side rows, k1, M1R (page 253), knit to the last stitch, M1L (page 253), k1.
- For fully fashioned neck decreases: On right-side rows, first half, knit to 3 stitches before the neck edge, k2tog, k1; second half, k1, ssk, work to the end of the row. On wrong-side rows, first half, purl to 3 stitches before the neck edge, ssp (page 255), p1; second half, p1, p2tog, work to the end of the row.

Back

Cast on __ stitches.

	XS	S	M	L	1X	2X	3X	4X
7	92	106	120	134	148	162	176	190
6½	84	96	110	122	136	148	162	174
6	78	90	102	114	126	138	150	162
5½	72	82	92	104	114	126	136	148
5	66	76	84	96	106	116	126	134
4½	58	66	76	86	94	102	112	120
4	52	60	68	76	84	92	100	108
3½	46	54	60	68	74	82	88	96
3	40	46	52	58	64	70	76	82

Begin K1P1 rib (page 215), and work even until the piece measures approximately 2"/5cm from the beginning, ending after a WS row.

Increase for the Bust

Begin stockinette stitch, and work fully fashioned increases (see Notes) each side every 18 rows __ time(s). If no number is given, do not work these rows.

	XS	S	M	L	1X	2X	3X	4X
7	--	--	--	--	--	--	--	--
6½	--	--	--	--	--	--	--	--
6	--	--	--	--	--	--	--	--
5½	--	--	--	--	--	--	--	--
5	--	--	--	--	--	--	--	--
4½	--	--	--	--	--	--	--	--
4	--	--	--	--	--	--	--	--
3½	2	1	1	1	--	--	--	--
3	--	--	--	--	--	--	--	--

Work fully fashioned increases each side every 16 rows __ time(s). If no number is given, do not work these rows.

	XS	S	M	L	1X	2X	3X	4X
7	--	--	--	--	--	--	--	--
6½	--	--	--	--	--	--	--	--
6	--	--	--	--	--	--	--	--
5½	--	--	--	--	--	--	--	--
5	2	--	--	--	--	--	--	--
4½	--	--	--	--	--	--	--	--
4	4	2	2	2	1	1	--	--
3½	1	2	2	2	3	3	2	2
3	--	--	--	--	--	--	--	--

Work fully fashioned increases each side every 14 rows __ time(s). If no number is given, do not work these rows.

	XS	S	M	L	1X	2X	3X	4X
7	5	3	3	3	1	1	--	--
6½	3	1	1	1	--	--	--	--
6	6	4	4	4	2	2	--	-
5½	3	2	2	2	--	--	--	--
5	3	5	5	5	3	3	2	2
4½	4	3	3	3	1	1	--	--
4	--	2	2	2	3	3	3	3
3½	--	--	--	--	--	--	1	1
3	3	2	2	2	1	1	--	--

Work fully fashioned increases each side every 12 rows __ time(s). If no number is given, do not work these rows.

	XS	S	M	L	1X	2X	3X	4X
7	2	4	4	4	6	6	6	6
6½	4	6	6	6	5	5	3	3
6	--	2	2	2	4	4	6	6
5½	3	4	4	4	5	5	4	4
5	--	--	--	--	2	2	3	3
4½	1	2	2	2	4	4	4	4
4	--	--	--	--	--	--	1	1
3½	--	--	--	--	--	--	--	--
3	--	1	1	1	2	2	3	3

Work fully fashioned increases each side every 10 rows __ time(s). If no number is given, do not work these rows.

	XS	S	M	L	1X	2X	3X	4X
7	--	--	--	--	--	--	1	1
6½	--	--	--	--	2	2	4	4
6	--	--	--	--	--	--	--	--
5½	--	--	--	--	1	1	2	2
5	--	--	--	--	--	--	--	--
4½	--	--	--	--	--	--	1	1
4	--	--	--	--	--	--	--	--
3½	--	--	--	--	--	--	--	--
3	--	--	--	--	--	--	--	--

You will now have __ stitches.

	XS	S	M	L	1X	2X	3X	4X
7	106	120	134	148	162	176	190	204
6½	98	110	124	136	150	162	176	188
6	90	102	114	126	138	150	162	174
5½	84	94	104	116	126	138	148	160
5	76	86	94	106	116	126	136	144
4½	68	76	86	96	104	112	122	130
4	60	68	76	84	92	100	108	116
3½	52	60	66	74	80	88	94	102
3	46	52	58	64	70	76	82	88

Continue even until the piece measures approximately 14 (13½, 13½, 13½, 13, 13, 12½, 12½)"/35.5 (34.5, 34.5, 34.5, 33, 33, 32, 31.5)cm from the beginning, or 8 (8½, 9, 9, 9½, 10, 10½, 11)"/20.5 (21.5, 22.5, 22.5, 24, 25.5, 26.5, 28)cm less than the desired finished length, ending after a wrong-side row.

Shape the Armholes

Work same as for the straight silhouette with set-in construction (page 25).

You will have __ stitches remaining.

	XS	S	M	L	1X	2X	3X	4X
7	92	98	106	112	116	120	122	126
6½	84	92	98	104	108	110	114	118
6	78	84	90	96	100	102	106	108
5½	72	78	82	88	90	94	96	100
5	64	70	74	80	82	86	88	90
4½	58	64	68	72	74	76	78	82
4	52	56	60	64	66	68	70	72
3½	46	50	52	56	58	60	62	64
3	40	42	46	48	50	52	52	54

Continue even until the piece measures approximately 20¾ (20¾, 21¼, 21¼, 21¼, 21¾, 21¾, 22¼)"/53 (53, 54, 54, 54, 55.5, 55.5, 56.5)cm from the beginning, or 1¼"/3cm less than the desired finished length, ending after a wrong-side row.

Shape the Neck

Work same as for the straight silhouette with square indented construction (page 20).

You will have __ stitches remaining on each side.

	XS	S	M	L	1X	2X	3X	4X
7	22	25	29	32	34	36	37	39
6½	19	23	26	29	31	32	34	36
6	18	21	24	27	29	30	32	33
5½	17	20	22	25	26	28	29	31
5	15	18	20	23	24	26	27	28
4½	13	16	18	20	21	22	23	25
4	12	14	16	18	19	20	21	22
3½	11	13	14	16	17	18	19	20
3	9	10	12	13	14	15	15	16

Continue even, if necessary, until the piece measures approximately 21 (21, 21½, 21½, 21½, 22, 22, 22½)"/53.5 (53.5, 54.5, 54.5, 54.5, 56, 56, 57)cm from the beginning, or 1"/2.5cm less than the desired finished length, ending after a wrong-side row.

Shape the Shoulders

Work same as for the straight silhouette with square indented construction (page 20).

Tapered Silhouette with Raglan Construction

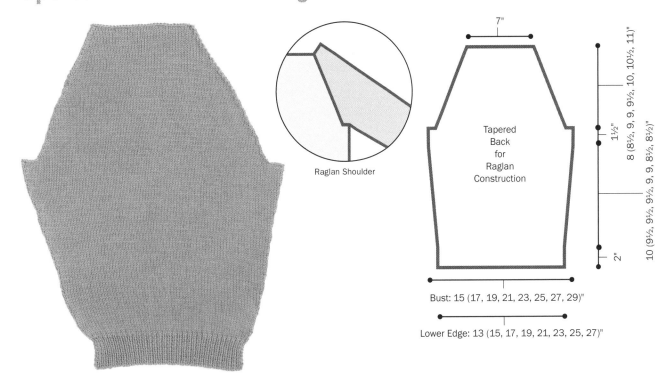

Raglan Shoulder

7"

Tapered Back for Raglan Construction

8 (8½, 9, 9, 9½, 10, 10½, 11)"

1½"

10 (9½, 9½, 9½, 9, 9, 8½, 8½)"

2"

Bust: 15 (17, 19, 21, 23, 25, 27, 29)"

Lower Edge: 13 (15, 17, 19, 21, 23, 25, 27)"

Finished Measurements

	XS	S	M	L	1X	2X	3X	4X
Bust	30"/76cm	34"/86.5cm	38"/96.5cm	42"/106.5cm	46"/117cm	50"/127cm	54"/137cm	58"/147.5cm
Lower Edge	26"/66cm	30"/76cm	34"/86.5cm	38"/96.5cm	42"/107cm	46"/117cm	50"/127cm	54"/137cm
Length	22¾"/58cm	22¾"/58cm	23¼"/59cm	23¼"/59cm	23¼"/59cm	23¾"/60.5cm	23¾"/60.5cm	24¼"/61.5cm

Notes

- The total finished length of this garment includes one-half of the width of the upper edge of the sleeves; the front and back pieces are 1¼"/3cm shorter than the total length of the garment.
- This pattern is written for K1P1 ribbed edges. Refer to pages 213–223 for information on how to customize the edge treatment.
- For fully fashioned decreases: On right-side rows, k1, ssk, knit to the last 3 stitches, k2tog, k1; on wrong-side rows, p1, p2tog, purl to the last 3 stitches, ssp (page 255), p1.
- For fully fashioned increases on right-side rows, k1, M1R (page 253), knit to the last stitch, M1L (page 253), k1.

Back

Cast on __ stitches.

	XS	S	M	L	1X	2X	3X	4X
7	92	106	120	134	148	162	176	190
6½	84	96	110	122	136	148	162	174
6	78	90	102	114	126	138	150	162
5½	72	82	92	104	114	126	136	148
5	66	76	84	96	106	116	126	134
4½	58	66	76	86	94	102	112	120
4	52	60	68	76	84	92	100	108
3½	46	54	60	68	74	82	88	96
3	40	46	52	58	64	70	76	82

Begin K1P1 rib (page 215), and work even until the piece measures approximately 2"/5cm from the beginning, ending after a WS row.

Increase for the Bust

Begin stockinette stitch, and work fully fashioned increases (see Notes) each side every 18 rows once, if indicated below. If no number is given, do not work these rows.

	XS	S	M	L	1X	2X	3X	4X
7	--	--	--	--	--	--	--	--
6½	--	--	--	--	--	--	--	--
6	--	--	--	--	--	--	--	--
5½	--	--	--	--	--	--	--	--
5	--	--	--	--	--	--	--	--
4½	--	--	--	--	--	--	--	--
4	--	--	--	--	--	--	--	--
3½	1	--	--	--	--	--	--	--
3	--	--	--	--	--	--	--	--

Work fully fashioned increases each side every 16 rows __ time(s). If no number is given, do not work these rows.

	XS	S	M	L	1X	2X	3X	4X
7	--	--	--	--	--	--	--	--
6½	--	--	--	--	--	--	--	--
6	--	--	--	--	--	--	--	--
5½	--	--	--	--	--	--	--	--
5	--	--	--	--	--	--	--	--
4½	--	--	--	--	--	--	--	--
4	2	1	1	1	--	--	--	--
3½	2	3	3	3	2	2	--	--
3	--	--	--	--	--	--	--	--

Work fully fashioned increases each side every 14 rows __ time(s). If no number is given, do not work these rows.

	XS	S	M	L	1X	2X	3X	4X
7	3	1	1	1	--	--	--	--
6½	1	--	--	--	--	--	--	--
6	4	2	2	2	--	--	--	--
5½	2	--	--	--	--	--	--	--
5	5	3	3	3	2	2	--	--
4½	3	1	1	1	--	--	--	--
4	2	1	1	1	--	--	--	--
3½	--	--	--	--	1	1	3	3
3	2	1	1	1	--	--	--	--

Work fully fashioned increases each side every 12 rows __ time(s). If no number is given, do not work these rows.

	XS	S	M	L	1X	2X	3X	4X
7	4	6	6	6	6	6	3	3
6½	6	5	5	5	3	3	1	1
6	2	4	4	4	6	6	4	4
5½	4	5	5	5	4	4	2	2
5	--	2	2	2	3	3	5	5
4½	2	4	4	4	4	4	3	3
4	2	3	3	3	3	3	2	2
3½	--	--	--	--	--	--	--	--
3	1	2	2	2	3	3	2	2

Work fully fashioned increases each side every 10 rows __ time(s). If no number is given, do not work these rows.

	XS	S	M	L	1X	2X	3X	4X
7	--	--	--	--	1	1	4	4
6½	--	2	2	2	4	4	6	6
6	--	--	--	--	--	--	2	2
5½	--	1	1	1	2	2	4	4
5	--	--	--	--	--	--	--	--
4½	--	--	--	--	1	1	2	2
4	--	--	--	--	1	1	2	2
3½	--	--	--	--	--	--	--	--
3	--	--	--	--	--	--	1	1

You will now have __ stitches.

	XS	S	M	L	1X	2X	3X	4X
7	106	120	134	148	162	176	190	204
6½	98	110	124	136	150	162	176	188
6	90	102	114	126	138	150	162	174
5½	84	94	104	116	126	138	148	160
5	76	86	94	106	116	126	136	144
4½	68	76	86	96	104	112	122	130
4	60	68	76	84	92	100	108	116
3½	52	60	66	74	80	88	94	102
3	46	52	58	64	70	76	82	88

Continue even until the piece measures approximately 13½ (13, 13, 13, 12½, 12½, 12, 12)"/34.5 (33, 33, 33, 32, 32, 30.5, 30.5)cm from the beginning, or 9¼ (9¾, 10¼, 10¼, 10¾, 11¼, 11¾, 12¼)"/23.5 (25, 26, 26, 27.5, 28.5, 30, 31)cm less than the desired finished length, ending after a wrong-side row.

Shape the Armholes

Work same as for the straight silhouette with raglan construction (page 30).

You will have __ stitches remaining.

	XS	S	M	L	1X	2X	3X	4X
7	48	48	48	48	48	48	48	48
6½	46	46	46	46	46	46	46	46
6	42	42	42	42	42	42	42	42
5½	38	38	38	38	38	38	38	38
5	34	34	34	34	34	34	34	34
4½	32	32	32	32	32	32	32	32
4	28	28	28	28	28	28	28	28
3½	24	24	24	24	24	24	24	24
3	22	22	22	22	22	22	22	22

Work 1 row even, if indicated below. If no number is given, do not work this row.

	XS	S	M	L	1X	2X	3X	4X
7	--	1	1	--	--	--	--	--
6½	--	--	1	1	--	--	--	--
6	--	--	--	--	--	--	--	--
5½	--	--	--	--	--	--	--	--
5	--	--	1	1	--	--	--	--
4½	--	1	1	1	--	--	--	--
4	--	1	--	--	1	--	--	--
3½	--	1	1	1	--	--	1	1
3	--	--	--	--	--	--	--	--

Bind off all stitches.

Tapered Silhouette with Saddle Shoulder Construction

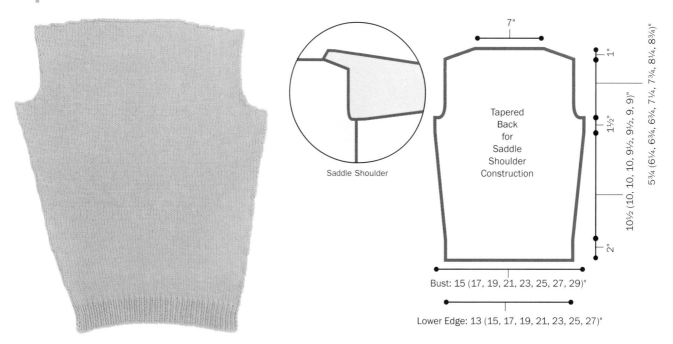

Saddle Shoulder

Tapered
Back
for
Saddle
Shoulder
Construction

7"

1"

1½"

10½ (10, 10, 10, 9½, 9½, 9, 9)"

5¾ (6¼, 6¾, 6¾, 7¼, 7¾, 8¼, 8¾)"

2"

Bust: 15 (17, 19, 21, 23, 25, 27, 29)"

Lower Edge: 13 (15, 17, 19, 21, 23, 25, 27)"

Finished Measurements

	XS	S	M	L	1X	2X	3X	4X
Bust	30"/76cm	34"/86.5cm	38"/96.5cm	42"/106.5cm	46"/117cm	50"/127cm	54"/137cm	58"/147.5cm
Lower Edge	26"/66cm	30"/76cm	34"/86.5cm	38"/96.5cm	42"/107cm	46"/117cm	50"/127cm	54"/137cm
Length	22"/56cm	22"/56cm	22½"/57cm	22½"/57cm	22½"/57cm	23"/58.5cm	23"/58.5cm	23½"/59.5cm

Notes

- The total finished length of this garment includes one-half of the width of the upper edge of the sleeves; the front and back pieces are 1¼"/3cm shorter than the total length of the garment.
- This pattern is written for K1P1 ribbed edges. Refer to pages 213–223 for information on how to customize the edge treatment.
- For fully fashioned decreases: On right-side rows, k1, ssk, knit to the last 3 stitches, k2tog, k1; on wrong-side rows, p1, p2tog, purl to the last 3 stitches, ssp (page 255), p1.
- For fully fashioned increases on right-side rows, k1, M1R (page 253), knit to the last stitch, M1L (page 253), k1.

Back

Cast on __ stitches.

	XS	S	M	L	1X	2X	3X	4X
7	92	106	120	134	148	162	176	190
6½	84	96	110	122	136	148	162	174
6	78	90	102	114	126	138	150	162
5½	72	82	92	104	114	126	136	148
5	66	76	84	96	106	116	126	134
4½	58	66	76	86	94	102	112	120
4	52	60	68	76	84	92	100	108
3½	46	54	60	68	74	82	88	96
3	40	46	52	58	64	70	76	82

Begin K1P1 rib (page 215), and work even until the piece measures approximately 2"/5cm from the beginning, ending after a wrong-side row.

Increase for the Bust

Work same as for the tapered silhouette with set-in construction (pages 213–223).

You will now have __ stitches.

	XS	S	M	L	1X	2X	3X	4X
7	106	120	134	148	162	176	190	204
6½	98	110	124	136	150	162	176	188
6	90	102	114	126	138	150	162	174
5½	84	94	104	116	126	138	148	160
5	76	86	94	106	116	126	136	144
4½	68	76	86	96	104	112	122	130
4	60	68	76	84	92	100	108	116
3½	52	60	66	74	80	88	94	102
3	46	52	58	64	70	76	82	88

Continue even until the piece measures approximately 14 (13½, 13½, 13½, 13, 13, 12½, 12½)"/35.5 (34.5, 34.5, 34.5, 33, 33, 32, 32)cm from the beginning, or 8 (8½, 9, 9, 9½, 10, 10½, 11)"/20.5 (21.5, 23, 23, 24, 25.5, 26.5, 28)cm less than the desired finished length, ending after a wrong-side row.

Shape the Armholes

Work same as for the straight silhouette with set-in construction (page 25).

You will have __ stitches remaining.

	XS	S	M	L	1X	2X	3X	4X
7	92	98	106	112	116	120	122	126
6½	84	92	98	104	108	110	114	118
6	78	84	90	96	100	102	106	108
5½	72	78	82	88	90	94	96	100
5	64	70	74	80	82	86	88	90
4½	58	64	68	72	74	76	78	82
4	52	56	60	64	66	68	70	72
3½	46	50	52	56	58	60	62	64
3	40	42	46	48	50	52	52	54

Continue even until the piece measures approximately 19¾ (19¾, 20¼, 20¼, 20¼, 20¾, 20¾, 21¼)"/50 (50, 51.5, 51.5, 51.5, 52.5, 52.5, 54)cm from the beginning, or 2¼"/5.5cm less than the desired finished length, ending after a wrong-side row.

Shape the Shoulders

Work same as for the straight silhouette with square indented construction (page 20).

Bind off all stitches.

Empire Waist Silhouette

Universally flattering, this shape features a horizontal band just under the bust. Choose one of the textures from the Edge Treatments on pages 213–223 to create your own custom look!

Empire Waist Silhouette with Square Indented Construction

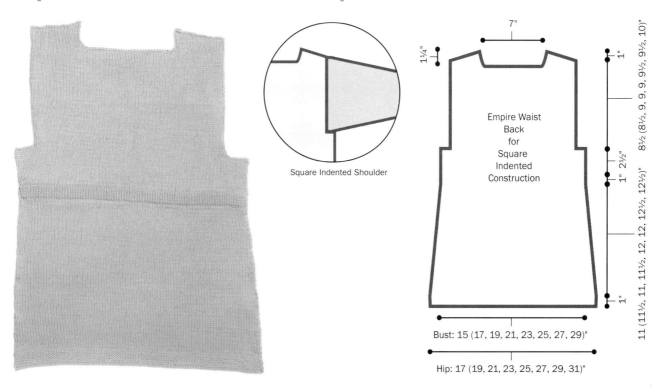

Square Indented Shoulder

Empire Waist Back for Square Indented Construction

7"

1¼"

1"

8½ (8½, 9, 9, 9, 9½, 9½, 10)"

1" 2½"

1" 2½"

11 (11½, 11, 11½, 12, 12, 12½, 12½)"

1"

Bust: 15 (17, 19, 21, 23, 25, 27, 29)"

Hip: 17 (19, 21, 23, 25, 27, 29, 31)"

Finished Measurements

	XS	S	M	L	1X	2X	3X	4X
Bust	30"/76cm	34"/86.5cm	38"/96.5cm	42"/106.5cm	46"/117cm	50"/127cm	54"/137cm	58"/147.5cm
Hip	34"/86.5cm	38"/96.5cm	42"/106.5cm	46"/117cm	50"/127cm	54"/137cm	58"/147.5cm	62"/157.5cm
Length	25"/63.5cm	25½"/64.5cm	25½"/64.5cm	26"/66cm	26½"/67.5cm	27"/68.5cm	27½"/70cm	28"/71cm

Notes

- This pattern is written for garter stitch lower edges and a garter stitch empire waistband. Refer to pages 213–223 for information on how to customize these details.
- For fully fashioned increases on right-side rows, k1, M1R (page 253), knit to the last stitch, M1L (page 253), k1.
- For fully fashioned neck decreases: On right-side rows, first half, knit to 3 stitches before the neck edge, k2tog, k1; second half, k1, ssk, work to the end of the row. On wrong-side rows, first half, purl to 3 stitches before the neck edge, ssp (page 255), p1; second half, p1, p2tog, work to the end of the row.
- For best results, work the empire waistband with knitting needles two sizes smaller than those required for the main fabric.

Back

Empire Waistband (knitted sideways)

Cast on __ stitches.

	XS	S	M	L	1X	2X	3X	4X
7	9	9	9	9	9	9	9	9
6½	9	9	9	9	9	9	9	9
6	8	8	8	8	8	8	8	8
5½	8	8	8	8	8	8	8	8
5	7	7	7	7	7	7	7	7
4½	7	7	7	7	7	7	7	7
4	6	6	6	6	6	6	6	6
3½	6	6	6	6	6	6	6	6
3	5	5	5	5	5	5	5	5

Begin garter stitch pattern, and work even until the piece measures approximately 15 (17, 19, 21, 23, 25, 27, 29)"/38 (43, 48.5, 53.5, 58.5, 63.5, 68.5, 73.5)cm from the beginning, ending after a wrong-side row.

Bind off all stitches in the pattern.

Lower Body

With the right side facing and the main size knitting needles, pick up and knit __ stitches along one long edge of the empire waistband.

	XS	S	M	L	1X	2X	3X	4X
7	106	120	134	148	162	176	190	204
6½	98	110	124	136	150	162	176	188
6	90	102	114	126	138	150	162	174
5½	84	94	104	116	126	138	148	160
5	76	86	94	106	116	126	136	144
4½	68	76	86	96	104	112	122	130
4	60	68	76	84	92	100	108	116
3½	52	60	66	74	80	88	94	102
3	46	52	58	64	70	76	82	88

Begin stockinette stitch, and work fully fashioned increases (see Notes) each side every 12 rows __ time(s). If no number is given, do not work these rows.

	XS	S	M	L	1X	2X	3X	4X
7	4	2	4	2	--	--	--	--
6½	7	4	7	4	2	2	--	--
6	2	--	2	--	--	--	--	--
5½	5	3	5	3	1	1	--	--
5	--	--	--	--	--	--	--	--
4½	3	1	3	1	--	--	--	--
4	--	--	--	--	--	--	--	--
3½	3	2	3	2	1	1	--	--
3	1	--	1	--	--	--	--	--

Work fully fashioned increases each side every 14 rows __ time(s). If no number is given, do not work these rows.

	XS	S	M	L	1X	2X	3X	4X
7	3	5	3	5	7	7	4	4
6½	--	3	--	3	5	5	7	7
6	4	6	4	6	4	4	2	2
5½	1	3	1	3	5	5	5	5
5	5	3	5	3	2	2	--	--
4½	2	4	2	4	4	4	3	3
4	2	1	2	1	--	--	--	--
3½	1	2	1	2	3	3	3	3
3	2	3	2	3	2	2	1	1

Work fully fashioned increases each side every 16 rows __ time(s). If no number is given, do not work these rows.

	XS	S	M	L	1X	2X	3X	4X
7	--	--	--	--	--	--	3	3
6½	--	--	--	--	--	--	--	--
6	--	--	--	--	2	2	4	4
5½	--	--	--	--	--	--	1	1
5	--	2	--	2	3	3	5	5
4½	--	--	--	--	1	1	2	2
4	2	3	2	3	3	3	2	2
3½	--	--	--	--	--	--	1	1
3	--	--	--	--	1	1	2	2

Work fully fashioned increases each side every 18 rows __ time(s). If no number is given, do not work these rows.

	XS	S	M	L	1X	2X	3X	4X
7	--	--	--	--	--	--	--	--
6½	--	--	--	--	--	--	--	--
6	--	--	--	--	--	--	--	--
5½	--	--	--	--	--	--	--	--
5	--	--	--	--	--	--	--	--
4½	--	--	--	--	--	--	--	--
4	--	--	--	--	1	1	2	2
3½	--	--	--	--	--	--	--	--
3	--	--	--	--	--	--	--	--

You will now have __ stitches.

	XS	S	M	L	1X	2X	3X	4X
7	120	134	148	162	176	190	204	218
6½	112	124	138	150	164	176	190	202
6	102	114	126	138	150	162	174	186
5½	96	106	116	128	138	150	160	172
5	86	96	104	116	126	136	146	154
4½	78	86	96	106	114	122	132	140
4	68	76	84	92	100	108	116	124
3½	60	68	74	82	88	96	102	110
3	52	58	64	70	76	82	88	94

Continue even, if necessary, until the piece measures approximately 11 (11½, 11, 11½, 12, 12, 12½, 12½)"/28 (29, 28, 29, 30.5, 30.5, 32, 32)cm from the beginning of the lower body, or 13 (13, 13½, 13½, 13½, 14, 14, 14½)"/33 (33, 34.5, 34.5, 34.5, 35.5, 35.5, 37)cm less than the desired finished length, ending after a wrong-side row.

Lower Edging
Work even in garter stitch pattern for 1"/2.5cm.

Bind off all stitches in the pattern.

Upper Body

With the right side facing and the main size knitting needles, pick up and knit __ stitches along the other long edge of the empire waistband.

	XS	S	M	L	1X	2X	3X	4X
7	106	120	134	148	162	176	190	204
6½	98	110	124	136	150	162	176	188
6	90	102	114	126	138	150	162	174
5½	84	94	104	116	126	138	148	160
5	76	86	94	106	116	126	136	144
4½	68	76	86	96	104	112	122	130
4	60	68	76	84	92	100	108	116
3½	52	60	66	74	80	88	94	102
3	46	52	58	64	70	76	82	88

Begin stockinette stitch, and work even for 2½"/6.5cm, or until the piece measures 9½ (9½, 10, 10, 10, 10½, 10½, 11)"/24 (24, 25.5, 25.5, 25.5, 26.5, 26.5, 28)cm less than the desired finished length, ending after a wrong-side row.

Shape the Armholes

Work same as for the straight silhouette with square indented construction (page 20).

You will have __ stitches remaining.

	XS	S	M	L	1X	2X	3X	4X
7	92	98	106	112	116	120	122	126
6½	84	92	98	104	108	110	114	118
6	78	84	90	96	100	102	106	108
5½	72	78	82	88	90	94	96	100
5	64	70	74	80	82	86	88	90
4½	58	64	68	72	74	76	78	82
4	52	56	60	64	66	68	70	72
3½	46	50	52	56	58	60	62	64
3	40	42	46	48	50	52	52	54

Continue even until the piece measures approximately 23¾ (24¼, 24¼, 24¾, 25¼, 25¾, 26¼, 26¾)"/60.5 (61.5, 61.5, 63, 64, 65.5, 66.5, 68)cm from the beginning, or 1¼"/3cm less than the desired finished length, ending after a wrong-side row.

Shape the Neck

Work same as for the straight silhouette with square indented construction (page 20).

You will have __ stitches remaining on each side.

	XS	S	M	L	1X	2X	3X	4X
7	22	25	29	32	34	36	37	39
6½	19	23	26	29	31	32	34	36
6	18	21	24	27	29	30	32	33
5½	17	20	22	25	26	28	29	31
5	15	18	20	23	24	26	27	28
4½	13	16	18	20	21	22	23	25
4	12	14	16	18	19	20	21	22
3½	11	13	14	16	17	18	19	20
3	9	10	12	13	14	15	15	16

Continue even, if necessary, until the piece measures approximately 24 (24½, 24½, 25, 25½, 26, 26½, 27)"/61 (62, 62, 63.5, 65, 66, 67.5, 68.5)cm from the beginning, or 1"/2.5cm less than the desired finished length, ending after a wrong-side row.

Shape the Shoulders

Work same as for the straight silhouette with square indented construction (page 20).

Empire Waist Silhouette with Set-In Construction

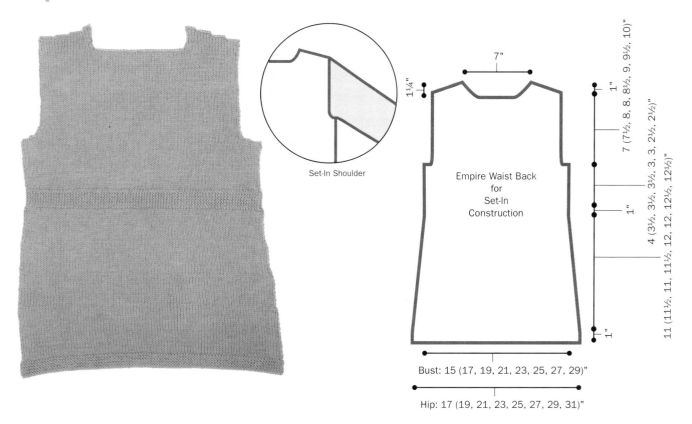

Set-In Shoulder

1 1/4"

7"

7 (7 1/2, 8, 8, 8 1/2, 9, 9 1/2, 10)"

1"

Empire Waist Back
for
Set-In
Construction

4 (3 1/2, 3 1/2, 3 1/2, 3, 3, 2 1/2, 2 1/2)"

1"

11 (11 1/2, 11, 11 1/2, 12, 12, 12 1/2, 12 1/2)"

1"

Bust: 15 (17, 19, 21, 23, 25, 27, 29)"

Hip: 17 (19, 21, 23, 25, 27, 29, 31)"

Finished Measurements

	XS	S	M	L	1X	2X	3X	4X
Bust	30"/76cm	34"/86.5cm	38"/96.5cm	42"/106.5cm	46"/117cm	50"/127cm	54"/137cm	58"/147.5cm
Hip	34"/86.5cm	38"/96.5cm	42"/106.5cm	46"/117cm	50"/127cm	54"/137cm	58"/147.5cm	62"/157.5cm
Length	25"/63.5cm	25 1/2"/64.5cm	25 1/2"/64.5cm	26"/66cm	26 1/2"/67.5cm	27"/68.5cm	27 1/2"/70cm	28"/71cm

Notes

- This pattern is written for garter stitch lower edges and empire waistband. Refer to pages 213–223 for information on how to customize these details.
- For fully fashioned increases on right-side rows, k1, M1R (page 253), knit to the last stitch, M1L (page 253), k1.
- For fully fashioned neck decreases: On right-side rows, first half, knit to 3 stitches before the neck edge, k2tog, k1; second half, k1, ssk, work to the end of the row. On wrong-side rows, first half, purl to 3 stitches before the neck edge, ssp (page 255), p1; second half, p1, p2tog, work to the end of the row.
- For best results, work the empire waistband with knitting needles two sizes smaller than those required for the main fabric.

Back

Empire Waistband (knitted sideways)

Work same as for the empire waist silhouette with square indented construction (page 79).

Lower Body

With the right side facing and the main size knitting needles, pick up and knit __ stitches along one long edge of the empire waistband.

	XS	S	M	L	1X	2X	3X	4X
7	106	120	134	148	162	176	190	204
6½	98	110	124	136	150	162	176	188
6	90	102	114	126	138	150	162	174
5½	84	94	104	116	126	138	148	160
5	76	86	94	106	116	126	136	144
4½	68	76	86	96	104	112	122	130
4	60	68	76	84	92	100	108	116
3½	52	60	66	74	80	88	94	102
3	46	52	58	64	70	76	82	88

Work the lower body same as for the empire waist silhouette with square indented construction (page 79) until the piece measures approximately 11 (11½, 11, 11½, 12, 12, 12½, 12½)"/28 (29, 28, 29, 30.5, 30.5, 32, 32)cm from the beginning of the lower body, or 13 (13, 13½, 13½, 13½, 14, 14, 14½)"/33 (33, 34.5, 34.5, 34.5, 35.5, 35.5, 37)cm less than the desired finished length, ending after a wrong-side row.

You will now have __ stitches.

	XS	S	M	L	1X	2X	3X	4X
7	120	134	148	162	176	190	204	218
6½	112	124	138	150	164	176	190	202
6	102	114	126	138	150	162	174	186
5½	96	106	116	128	138	150	160	172
5	86	96	104	116	126	136	146	154
4½	78	86	96	106	114	122	132	140
4	68	76	84	92	100	108	116	124
3½	60	68	74	82	88	96	102	110
3	52	58	64	70	76	82	88	94

Lower Edging

Work same as for the empire waist silhouette with square indented construction (page 79).

Upper Body

With the right side facing and the main size knitting needles, pick up and knit __ stitches along the other long edge of the empire waistband.

	XS	S	M	L	1X	2X	3X	4X
7	106	120	134	148	162	176	190	204
6½	98	110	124	136	150	162	176	188
6	90	102	114	126	138	150	162	174
5½	84	94	104	116	126	138	148	160
5	76	86	94	106	116	126	136	144
4½	68	76	86	96	104	112	122	130
4	60	68	76	84	92	100	108	116
3½	52	60	66	74	80	88	94	102
3	46	52	58	64	70	76	82	88

Begin stockinette stitch, and work even for 4 (3½, 3½, 3½, 3, 3, 2½, 2½)"/10 (9, 9, 9, 7.5, 7.5, 6.5, 6.5)cm, or until the piece measures 8 (8½, 9, 9, 9½, 10, 10½, 11)"/20.5 (21.5, 23, 23, 24, 25.5, 26.5, 28)cm less than the desired finished length, ending after a wrong-side row.

Shape the Armholes

Work same as for the straight silhouette with set-in construction (page 25).

You will have __ stitches remaining.

	XS	S	M	L	1X	2X	3X	4X
7	92	98	106	112	116	120	122	126
6½	84	92	98	104	108	110	114	118
6	78	84	90	96	100	102	106	108
5½	72	78	82	88	90	94	96	100
5	64	70	74	80	82	86	88	90
4½	58	64	68	72	74	76	78	82
4	52	56	60	64	66	68	70	72
3½	46	50	52	56	58	60	62	64
3	40	42	46	48	50	52	52	54

Continue even until the piece measures approximately 23¾ (24¼, 24¼, 24¾, 25¼, 25¾, 26¼, 26¾)"/60.5 (61.5, 61.5, 63, 64, 65.5, 66.5, 68)cm from the beginning, or 1¼"/3cm less than the desired finished length, ending after a wrong-side row.

Shape the Neck

Work same as for the straight silhouette with square indented construction (page 20).

You will have __ stitches remaining on each side.

	XS	S	M	L	1X	2X	3X	4X
7	22	25	29	32	34	36	37	39
6½	19	23	26	29	31	32	34	36
6	18	21	24	27	29	30	32	33
5½	17	20	22	25	26	28	29	31
5	15	18	20	23	24	26	27	28
4½	13	16	18	20	21	22	23	25
4	12	14	16	18	19	20	21	22
3½	11	13	14	16	17	18	19	20
3	9	10	12	13	14	15	15	16

Continue even, if necessary, until the piece measures approximately 24 (24½, 24½, 25, 25½, 26, 26½, 27)"/61 (62, 62, 63.5, 65, 66, 67.5, 68.5)cm from the beginning, or 1"/2.5cm less than the desired finished length, ending after a wrong-side row.

Shape the Shoulders

Work same as for the straight silhouette with square indented construction (page 20).

Empire Waist Silhouette with Raglan Construction

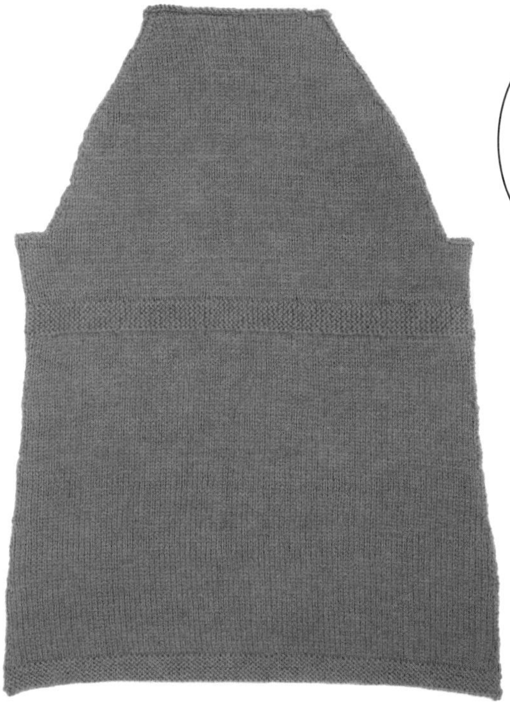

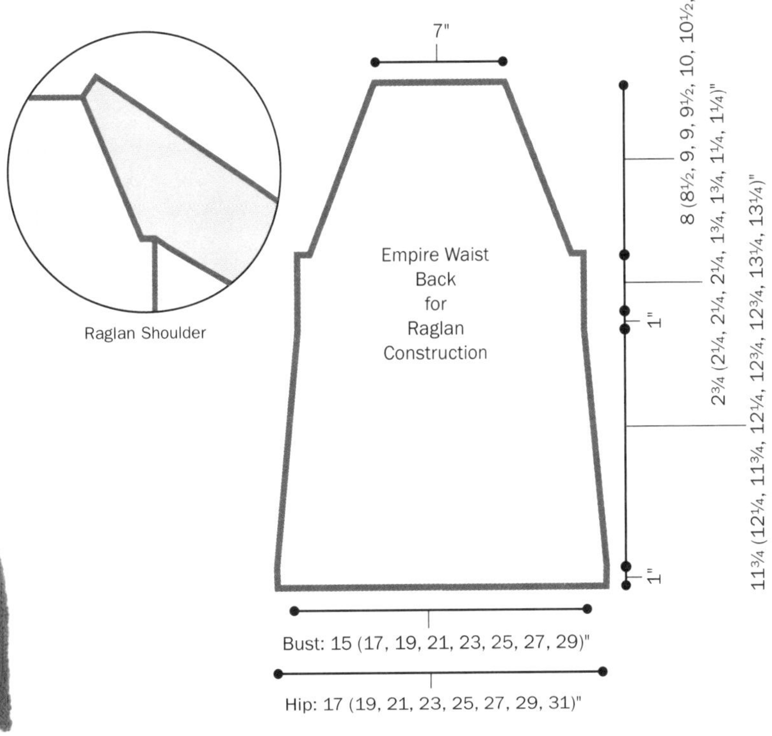
Raglan Shoulder
7"
Empire Waist
Back
for
Raglan
Construction
8 (8½, 9, 9, 9½, 10, 10½, 11)"
2¾ (2¼, 2¼, 2¼, 1¾, 1¾, 1¼, 1¼)"
11¾ (12¼, 11¾, 12¼, 12¾, 12¾, 13¼, 13¼)"
1"
1"
Bust: 15 (17, 19, 21, 23, 25, 27, 29)"
Hip: 17 (19, 21, 23, 25, 27, 29, 31)"

Finished Measurements

	XS	S	M	L	1X	2X	3X	4X
Bust	30"/76cm	34"/86.5cm	38"/96.5cm	42"/106.5cm	46"/117cm	50"/127cm	54"/137cm	58"/147.5cm
Hip	34"/86.5cm	38"/96.5cm	42"/106.5cm	46"/117cm	50"/127cm	54"/137cm	58"/147.5cm	62"/157.5cm
Length	25¾"/65.5cm	26¼"/66.5cm	26¼"/66.5cm	26¾"/68cm	27¼"/69cm	27¾"/70.5cm	28¼"/72cm	28¾"/73cm

Notes

- The total finished length of this garment includes one-half of the width of the upper edge of the sleeves; the front and back pieces are 1¼"/3cm shorter than the total length of the garment.
- This pattern is written for garter stitch lower edges and empire waistband. Refer to pages 213–223 for information on how to customize these details.
- For fully fashioned increases on right-side rows, k1, M1R (page 253), knit to the last stitch, M1L (page 253), k1.
- For best results, work the empire waistband with knitting needles two sizes smaller than those required for the main fabric.

Back

Empire Waistband (knitted sideways)
Work same as for the empire waist silhouette with square indented construction (page 79).

Lower Body
With the right side facing and the main size knitting needles, pick up and knit __ stitches along one long edge of the empire waistband.

	XS	S	M	L	1X	2X	3X	4X
7	106	120	134	148	162	176	190	204
6½	98	110	124	136	150	162	176	188
6	90	102	114	126	138	150	162	174
5½	84	94	104	116	126	138	148	160
5	76	86	94	106	116	126	136	144
4½	68	76	86	96	104	112	122	130
4	60	68	76	84	92	100	108	116
3½	52	60	66	74	80	88	94	102
3	46	52	58	64	70	76	82	88

Begin stockinette stitch, and work fully fashioned increases (see Notes) each side every 12 rows __ time(s). If no number is given, do not work these rows.

	XS	S	M	L	1X	2X	3X	4X
7	1	--	1	--	--	--	--	--
6½	3	1	3	1	--	--	--	--
6	--	--	--	--	--	--	--	--
5½	2	--	2	--	--	--	--	--
5	--	--	--	--	--	--	--	--
4½	--	--	--	--	--	--	--	--
4	--	--	--	--	--	--	--	--
3½	1	--	1	--	--	--	--	--
3	--	--	--	--	--	--	--	--

Work fully fashioned increases each side every 14 rows __ time(s). If no number is given, do not work these rows.

	XS	S	M	L	1X	2X	3X	4X
7	6	5	6	5	3	3	1	1
6½	4	6	4	6	6	6	4	4
6	5	3	5	3	1	1	--	--
5½	4	6	4	6	4	4	2	2
5	2	1	2	1	--	--	--	--
4½	5	3	5	3	2	2	--	--
4	--	--	--	--	--	--	--	--
3½	3	4	3	4	3	3	2	2
3	2	1	2	1	--	--	--	--

Work fully fashioned increases each side every 16 rows __ time(s). If no number is given, do not work these rows.

	XS	S	M	L	1X	2X	3X	4X
7	--	2	--	2	4	4	6	6
6½	--	--	--	--	1	1	3	3
6	1	3	1	3	5	5	5	5
5½	--	--	--	--	2	2	4	4
5	3	4	3	4	4	4	2	2
4½	--	2	--	2	3	3	5	5
4	4	2	4	2	1	1	--	--
3½	--	--	--	--	1	1	2	2
3	1	2	1	2	3	3	2	2

Work fully fashioned increases each side every 18 rows __ time(s). If no number is given, do not work these rows.

	XS	S	M	L	1X	2X	3X	4X
7	--	--	--	--	--	--	--	--
6½	--	--	--	--	--	--	--	--
6	--	--	--	--	--	--	1	1
5½	--	--	--	--	--	--	--	--
5	--	--	--	--	1	1	3	3
4½	--	--	--	--	--	--	--	--
4	--	2	--	2	3	3	3	3
3½	--	--	--	--	--	--	--	--
3	--	--	--	--	--	--	1	1

Work fully fashioned increases each side every 20 rows once, if indicated below.
If no number is given, do not work these rows.

	XS	S	M	L	1X	2X	3X	4X
7	--	--	--	--	--	--	--	--
6½	--	--	--	--	--	--	--	--
6	--	--	--	--	--	--	--	--
5½	--	--	--	--	--	--	--	--
5	--	--	--	--	--	--	--	--
4½	--	--	--	--	--	--	--	--
4	--	--	--	--	--	--	1	1
3½	--	--	--	--	--	--	--	--
3	--	--	--	--	--	--	--	--

You will now have __ stitches.

	XS	S	M	L	1X	2X	3X	4X
7	120	134	148	162	176	190	204	218
6½	112	124	138	150	164	176	190	202
6	102	114	126	138	150	162	174	186
5½	96	106	116	128	138	150	160	172
5	86	96	104	116	126	136	146	154
4½	78	86	96	106	114	122	132	140
4	68	76	84	92	100	108	116	124
3½	60	68	74	82	88	96	102	110
3	52	58	64	70	76	82	88	94

Continue even, if necessary, until the piece measures approximately 11¾ (12¼, 11¾, 12¼, 12¾, 12¾, 13¼, 13¼)"/30 (31, 30, 31, 32.5, 32.5, 33.5, 33.5)cm from the beginning of the lower body, or 12 (12, 12½, 12½, 12½, 13, 13, 13½)"/30.5 (30.5, 32, 32, 32, 33, 33, 34.5)cm less than the desired finished length, ending after a wrong-side row.

Lower Edging
Work same as for the empire waist silhouette with square indented construction (page 79).

Upper Body

With the right side facing and the main size knitting needles, pick up and knit __ stitches along the other long edge of the empire waistband.

	XS	S	M	L	1X	2X	3X	4X
7	106	120	134	148	162	176	190	204
6½	98	110	124	136	150	162	176	188
6	90	102	114	126	138	150	162	174
5½	84	94	104	116	126	138	148	160
5	76	86	94	106	116	126	136	144
4½	68	76	86	96	104	112	122	130
4	60	68	76	84	92	100	108	116
3½	52	60	66	74	80	88	94	102
3	46	52	58	64	70	76	82	88

Begin stockinette stitch, and work even for 2¾ (2¼, 2¼, 2¼, 1¾, 1¾, 1¼, 1¼)"/7 (5.5, 5.5, 5.5, 4.5, 4.5, 3, 3)cm from the beginning of the upper body, or until the piece measures 9¼ (9¾, 10¼, 10¼, 10¾, 11¼, 11¾, 12¼)"/23.5 (25, 26, 26, 27.5, 28.5, 30, 31)cm less than the desired finished length, ending after a wrong-side row.

Shape the Armholes

Work same as for the straight silhouette with raglan construction (page 30).

You will have __ stitches remaining.

	XS	S	M	L	1X	2X	3X	4X
7	48	48	48	48	48	48	48	48
6½	46	46	46	46	46	46	46	46
6	42	42	42	42	42	42	42	42
5½	38	38	38	38	38	38	38	38
5	34	34	34	34	34	34	34	34
4½	32	32	32	32	32	32	32	32
4	28	28	28	28	28	28	28	28
3½	24	24	24	24	24	24	24	24
3	22	22	22	22	22	22	22	22

Work 1 row even, if indicated below. If no number is given, do not work this row.

	XS	S	M	L	1X	2X	3X	4X
7	--	1	1	--	--	--	--	--
6½	--	--	1	1	--	--	--	--
6	--	--	--	--	--	--	--	--
5½	--	--	--	--	--	--	--	--
5	--	--	1	1	--	--	--	--
4½	--	1	1	1	--	--	--	--
4	--	1	--	--	1	--	--	--
3½	--	1	1	1	--	--	1	1
3	--	--	--	--	--	--	--	--

Bind off all stitches.

Empire Waist Silhouette with Saddle Shoulder Construction

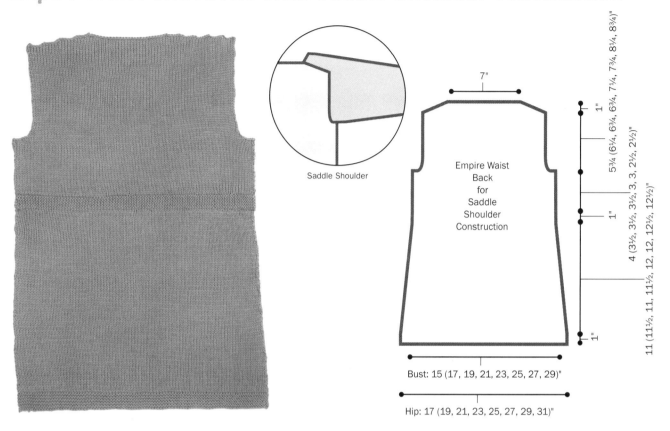

Saddle Shoulder

7"

Empire Waist
Back
for
Saddle
Shoulder
Construction

1"

5¾ (6¼, 6¾, 6¾, 7¼, 7¾, 8¼, 8¾)"

4 (3½, 3½, 3½, 3, 3, 2½, 2½)"

1"

11 (11½, 11, 11½, 12, 12, 12½, 12½)"

1"

Bust: 15 (17, 19, 21, 23, 25, 27, 29)"

Hip: 17 (19, 21, 23, 25, 27, 29, 31)"

Finished Measurements

	XS	S	M	L	1X	2X	3X	4X
Bust	30"/76cm	34"/86.5cm	38"/96.5cm	42"/106.5cm	46"/117cm	50"/127cm	54"/137cm	58"/147.5cm
Hip	34"/86.5cm	38"/96.5cm	42"/106.5cm	46"/117cm	50"/127cm	54"/137cm	58"/147.5cm	62"/157.5cm
Length	25"/63.5cm	25½"/64.5cm	25½"/64.5cm	26"/66cm	26½"/67.5cm	27"/68.5cm	27½"/70cm	28"/71cm

Notes

- The total finished length of this garment includes one-half of the width of the upper edge of the sleeves; the front and back pieces are 1¼"/3cm shorter than the total length of the garment.
- This pattern is written for garter stitch lower edges and empire waistband. Refer to pages 213–223 for information on how to customize these details.
- For fully fashioned increases on right-side rows, k1, M1R (page 253), knit to the last stitch, M1L (page 253), k1.
- For best results, work the empire waistband with knitting needles two sizes smaller than those required for the main fabric.

Back

Empire Waistband (knitted sideways)

Work same as for the empire waist silhouette with square indented construction (page 79).

Lower Body

Work same as for the empire waist silhouette with set-in construction (page 85).

Continue even, if necessary, until the piece measures approximately 11 (11½, 11, 11½, 12, 12, 12½, 12½)"/28 (29, 28, 29, 30.5, 30.5, 32, 32)cm from the beginning of the lower body, or 12 (12, 12½, 12½, 12½, 13, 13, 13½)"/30.5 (30.5, 32, 32, 32, 33, 33, 34.5)cm less than the desired finished length, ending after a wrong-side row.

Lower Edging

Work same as for the empire waist silhouette with square indented construction (page 79).

Upper Body

With the right side facing and the main size knitting needles, pick up and knit __ stitches along the other long edge of the empire waistband.

	XS	S	M	L	1X	2X	3X	4X
7	106	120	134	148	162	176	190	204
6½	98	110	124	136	150	162	176	188
6	90	102	114	126	138	150	162	174
5½	84	94	104	116	126	138	148	160
5	76	86	94	106	116	126	136	144
4½	68	76	86	96	104	112	122	130
4	60	68	76	84	92	100	108	116
3½	52	60	66	74	80	88	94	102
3	46	52	58	64	70	76	82	88

Begin stockinette stitch, and work even for 4 (3½, 3½, 3½, 3, 3, 2½, 2½)"/10 (9, 9, 9, 7.5, 7.5, 6.5, 6.5)cm, or until the piece measures 8 (8½, 9, 9, 9½, 10, 10½, 11)"/20.5 (21.5, 23, 23, 24, 25.5, 26.5, 28)cm less than the desired finished length, ending after a wrong-side row.

Shape the Armholes

Work same as for the straight silhouette with set-in construction (page 25).

You will have __ stitches remaining.

	XS	S	M	L	1X	2X	3X	4X
7	92	98	106	112	116	120	122	126
6½	84	92	98	104	108	110	114	118
6	78	84	90	96	100	102	106	108
5½	72	78	82	88	90	94	96	100
5	64	70	74	80	82	86	88	90
4½	58	64	68	72	74	76	78	82
4	52	56	60	64	66	68	70	72
3½	46	50	52	56	58	60	62	64
3	40	42	46	48	50	52	52	54

Continue even until the piece measures approximately 22¾ (23¼, 23¼, 23¾, 24¼, 24¾, 25¼, 25¾)"/58 (59, 59, 60.5, 61.5, 63, 64, 65.5)cm from the beginning, or 2¼"/5.5cm less than the desired finished length, ending after a wrong-side row.

Shape the Shoulders

Work same as for the straight silhouette with square indented construction (page 20).

FRONTS

Use this section to knit the front of your garment.
The front pieces are all based on the back silhouettes, with
changes only at the neckline to create round, scoop, V, placket,
or slit openings. Choose the one that has the icon to match
the neckline shape (pages 195–212) you wish to make.

NECKLINES AND RAGLANS

When shaping the front neckline for raglan construction, be sure to maintain the raglan armhole decreases as you work the neck shaping. Once the neckline shaping is complete, continue to work the raglan decreases until no stitches remain. The armhole depth of the front and back should match perfectly.

NECK OPENING SIZE

The modular patterns in this book are all written for an average-size adult neck. It is easy, however, to adjust the finished size of the neck opening. Just use one of the following methods when working your desired neck treatment:

1. For a slightly larger neck opening, do not bind off the center front and center back neck stitches; instead, slip the stitches onto holders to be picked up later. Without the bind-off edge, the neck opening will have a little more "give."

2. To make your neck opening a little larger or smaller, invisibly increase or decrease the number of stitches in your neckline treatment after picking up stitches.

FRONT NECKLINE DEPTHS

Each neckline treatment requires a different front neck drop. This table suggests the typical drop of the front neck opening for several neck shapes and finishing treatments.

Neckline Shape and Treatment	Typical Front Neck Drop
Round Necklines	
Crewneck	2½"–3"/6.5cm–7.5cm
Mock Turtleneck	2½"–3"/6.5cm–7.5cm
Turtleneck	1½"/4cm
Johnny Collar	2½"–3"/6.5cm–7.5cm
Hood	2½"–4"/6.5cm–10cm
Lace Collar	2½"–3½"/6.5cm–8.5cm
Split Ribbed Collar	2½"–3"/6.5cm–7.5cm
Scoop Necklines	
Classic Scoop Neck with Garter Trim	4"–7"/10cm–17.5cm
Cowl Neck	4"–5½"/10cm–14cm
V Necklines	
Mitered V-Neck	6½"–13"/16.5cm–32.5cm
Crossover V-Neck	6½"–13"/16.5cm–32.5cm
Square Necklines	
Square Neckline with Mitered Ribbed Trim	5"–7"/12.5cm–17.5cm
Square Neckline with Garter Stitch Trim	5"–7"/12.5cm–17.5cm
Shawl Collar	7"–9"/17.5cm–22.5cm
Placket Necklines	
Buttoned Crewneck with Collar	Placket opening depth: 7"–10"/17.5cm–25cm Round neck opening depth: 2½"–3"/6.5–7.5cm
Buttoned Henley	Placket opening depth: 7–10"/17.5cm–25cm Round neck opening depth: 2½"–3"/6.5–7.5cm
Buttoned High Neck	Placket opening depth: 7"–10"/17.5cm–25cm Round neck opening depth: 2½"–3"/6.5–7.5cm
Slit Necklines	
Zippered High Neck	Slit opening depth: 3½"–6½"/9cm–16.5cm Round neck opening depth: 2½"–3"/6.5–7.5cm
Slit Neckline with Collar	Slit opening depth: 4½"–6½"/11.5cm–16.5cm Round neck opening depth: 2½"–3"/6.5–7.5cm
Zip Neck with Collar	Slit opening depth: 4½"–6½"/11.5cm–16.5cm Round neck opening depth: 2½"–3"/6.5–7.5cm

Round Neckline

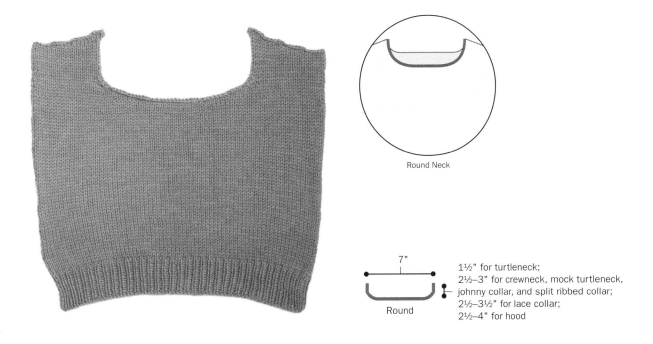

Round Neck

7"

Round

1½" for turtleneck;
2½–3" for crewneck, mock turtleneck, johnny collar, and split ribbed collar;
2½–3½" for lace collar;
2½–4" for hood

Notes

- For fully fashioned neck decreases: On right-side rows, first half, knit to 3 stitches before the neck edge, k2tog, k1; second half, k1, ssk, work to the end of the row. On wrong-side rows, first half, purl to 3 stitches before the neck edge, ssp (page 255), p1; second half, p1, p2tog, work to the end of the row.
- When using raglan construction, continue the raglan armhole shaping same as for the back while working the front neck shaping.
- For garments with saddle shoulders, begin the shoulder shaping when the piece measures approximately 1"/2.5cm less than the desired finished length, and work the shoulder shaping and the remaining front neck shaping at the same time.

Front

Work same as for the back (pages 19–97) until the piece measures the appropriate length for your desired neckline treatment (pages 195–212), ending after a wrong-side row.

Shape the Neck

Place markers on both sides of the middle __ stitches.

	XS	S	M	L	1X	2X	3X	4X
7	20	20	20	20	20	20	20	20
6½	18	18	18	18	18	18	18	18
6	16	16	16	16	16	16	16	16
5½	14	14	14	14	14	14	14	14
5	12	12	12	12	12	12	12	12
4½	12	12	12	12	12	12	12	12
4	10	10	10	10	10	10	10	10
3½	10	10	10	10	10	10	10	10
3	10	10	10	10	10	10	10	10

Knit across to the first marker, join a second ball of yarn, and bind off the stitches between the markers, then knit across to the end of the row.

Work both sides at once with separate balls of yarn, and bind off __ stitches each neck edge once.

	XS	S	M	L	1X	2X	3X	4X
7	5	5	5	5	5	5	5	5
6½	5	5	5	5	5	5	5	5
6	5	5	5	5	5	5	5	5
5½	5	5	5	5	5	5	5	5
5	5	5	5	5	5	5	5	5
4½	4	4	4	4	4	4	4	4
4	4	4	4	4	4	4	4	4
3½	3	3	3	3	3	3	3	3
3	3	3	3	3	3	3	3	3

Work both sides at once with separate balls of yarn, and bind off __ stitches each neck edge once.

	XS	S	M	L	1X	2X	3X	4X
7	3	3	3	3	3	3	3	3
6½	4	4	4	4	4	4	4	4
6	3	3	3	3	3	3	3	3
5½	3	3	3	3	3	3	3	3
5	3	3	3	3	3	3	3	3
4½	3	3	3	3	3	3	3	3
4	2	2	2	2	2	2	2	2
3½	2	2	2	2	2	2	2	2
3	2	2	2	2	2	2	2	2

Work both sides at once with separate balls of yarn, and work fully fashioned decreases (see Notes) each neck edge every row __ time(s).

	XS	S	M	L	1X	2X	3X	4X
7	5	5	5	5	5	5	5	5
6½	4	4	4	4	4	4	4	4
6	4	4	4	4	4	4	4	4
5½	3	3	3	3	3	3	3	3
5	2	2	2	2	2	2	2	2
4½	2	2	2	2	2	2	2	2
4	3	3	3	3	3	3	3	3
3½	2	2	2	2	2	2	2	2
3	1	1	1	1	1	1	1	1

Work both sides at once with separate balls of yarn, and work fully fashioned decreases each neck edge every other row once, if indicated below. If no number is given, do not work these rows.

	XS	S	M	L	1X	2X	3X	4X
7	1	1	1	1	1	1	1	1
6½	1	1	1	1	1	1	1	1
6	1	1	1	1	1	1	1	1
5½	1	1	1	1	1	1	1	1
5	1	1	1	1	1	1	1	1
4½	1	1	1	1	1	1	1	1
4	--	--	--	--	--	--	--	--
3½	--	--	--	--	--	--	--	--
3	--	--	--	--	--	--	--	--

You will have __ stitches remaining on each side, *except* when using raglan or saddle shoulder construction.

	XS	S	M	L	1X	2X	3X	4X
7	22	25	29	32	34	36	37	39
6½	19	23	26	29	31	32	34	36
6	18	21	24	27	29	30	32	33
5½	17	20	22	25	26	28	29	31
5	15	18	20	23	24	26	27	28
4½	13	16	18	20	21	22	23	25
4	12	14	16	18	19	20	21	22
3½	11	13	14	16	17	18	19	20
3	9	10	12	13	14	15	15	16

Complete same as for the back for your desired silhouette.

Scoop Neckline

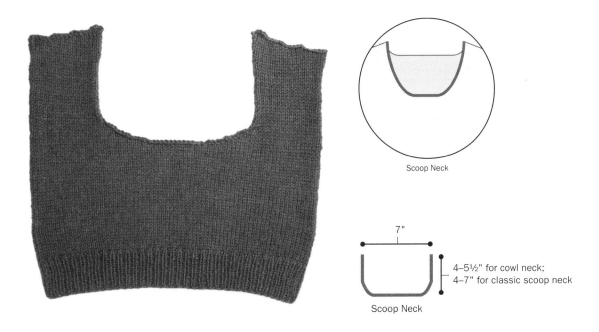

Scoop Neck

7"

4–5½" for cowl neck;
4–7" for classic scoop neck

Scoop Neck

Notes

- For fully fashioned neck decreases: On right-side rows, first half, knit to 3 stitches before the neck edge, k2tog, k1; second half, k1, ssk, work to the end of the row. On wrong-side rows, first half, purl to 3 stitches before the neck edge, ssp (page 255), p1; second half, p1, p2tog, work to the end of the row.
- When using raglan construction, continue the raglan armhole shaping same as for the back while working the front neck shaping.

Front

Work same as for the back (pages 19–97) until the piece measures the appropriate length for your desired neckline treatment (pages 195–212), ending after a wrong-side row.

Shape the Neck

Place markers on both sides of the middle ___ stitches.

	XS	S	M	L	1X	2X	3X	4X
7	20	20	20	20	20	20	20	20
6½	18	18	18	18	18	18	18	18
6	16	16	16	16	16	16	16	16
5½	14	14	14	14	14	14	14	14
5	12	12	12	12	12	12	12	12
4½	12	12	12	12	12	12	12	12
4	10	10	10	10	10	10	10	10
3½	10	10	10	10	10	10	10	10
3	10	10	10	10	10	10	10	10

Knit across to the first marker, join a second ball of yarn, and bind off the stitches between the markers, then knit across to the end of the row.

Work both sides at once with separate balls of yarn, and bind off __ stitches each neck edge once.

	XS	S	M	L	1X	2X	3X	4X
7	4	4	4	4	4	4	4	4
6½	4	4	4	4	4	4	4	4
6	4	4	4	4	4	4	4	4
5½	4	4	4	4	4	4	4	4
5	4	4	4	4	4	4	4	4
4½	4	4	4	4	4	4	4	4
4	3	3	3	3	3	3	3	3
3½	3	3	3	3	3	3	3	3
3	3	3	3	3	3	3	3	3

Work both sides at once with separate balls of yarn, and bind off __ stitches each neck edge once.

	XS	S	M	L	1X	2X	3X	4X
7	4	4	4	4	4	4	4	4
6½	4	4	4	4	4	4	4	4
6	3	3	3	3	3	3	3	3
5½	3	3	3	3	3	3	3	3
5	3	3	3	3	3	3	3	3
4½	3	3	3	3	3	3	3	3
4	3	3	3	3	3	3	3	3
3½	3	3	3	3	3	3	3	3
3	2	2	2	2	2	2	2	2

Work both sides at once with separate balls of yarn, and bind off __ stitches
each neck edge once. If no number is given, do not work these rows.

	XS	S	M	L	1X	2X	3X	4X
7	3	3	3	3	3	3	3	3
6½	3	3	3	3	3	3	3	3
6	3	3	3	3	3	3	3	3
5½	2	2	2	2	2	2	2	2
5	2	2	2	2	2	2	2	2
4½	2	2	2	2	2	2	2	2
4	2	2	2	2	2	2	2	2
3½	--	--	--	--	--	--	--	--
3	--	--	--	--	--	--	--	--

Work both sides at once with separate balls of yarn, and work fully fashioned decreases (see Notes) each neck edge every row once.

Work both sides at once with separate balls of yarn, and work fully fashioned decreases
each neck edge every other row __ time(s). If no number is given, do not work these rows.

	XS	S	M	L	1X	2X	3X	4X
7	3	3	3	3	3	3	3	3
6½	3	3	3	3	3	3	3	3
6	3	3	3	3	3	3	3	3
5½	3	3	3	3	3	3	3	3
5	2	2	2	2	2	2	2	2
4½	1	1	1	1	1	1	1	1
4	1	1	1	1	1	1	1	1
3½	1	1	1	1	1	1	1	1
3	1	1	1	1	1	1	1	1

You will have __ stitches remaining on each side, *except* when using raglan or saddle shoulder construction.

	XS	S	M	L	1X	2X	3X	4X
7	22	25	29	32	34	36	37	39
6½	19	23	26	29	31	32	34	36
6	18	21	24	27	29	30	32	33
5½	17	20	22	25	26	28	29	31
5	15	18	20	23	24	26	27	28
4½	13	16	18	20	21	22	23	25
4	12	14	16	18	19	20	21	22
3½	11	13	14	16	17	18	19	20
3	9	10	12	13	14	15	15	16

Complete same as for the back for your desired silhouette.

V Neckline

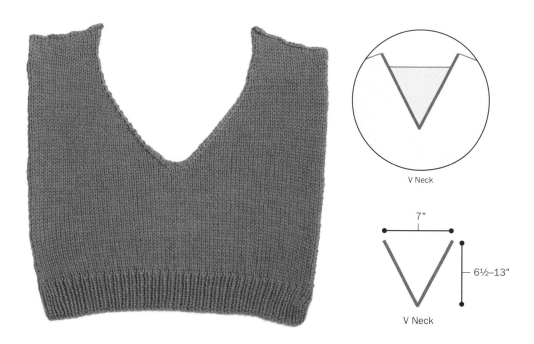

V Neck

7"

6½–13"

V Neck

Notes

- When using raglan construction, continue the raglan armhole shaping same as for the back while working the front neck shaping.
- For garments with saddle shoulders, begin the shoulder shaping when the piece measures approximately 1"/2.5cm less than the desired finished length, and work shoulder shaping and the remaining front neck shaping at the same time.

Front

Work same as for the back (pages 19–97) until the piece measures the appropriate length for your desired neckline treatment (pages 195–212), ending after a wrong-side row.

Shape the Neck

Place a marker between the 2 middle stitches.

Next row (RS) (Decrease Row): Work across until 3 stitches before the marker, k2tog, k1; join a second ball of yarn, slip the marker, k1, ssk, and work across to end the row.

Working both sides with separate balls of yarn, repeat the decrease row every other row __ times more.

	XS	S	M	L	1X	2X	3X	4X
7	23	23	23	23	23	23	23	23
6½	22	22	22	22	22	22	22	22
6	19	19	19	19	19	19	19	19
5½	17	17	17	17	17	17	17	17
5	14	14	14	14	14	14	14	14
4½	14	14	14	14	14	14	14	14
4	11	11	11	11	11	11	11	11
3½	10	10	10	10	10	10	10	10
3	10	10	10	10	10	10	10	10

Working both sides with separate balls of yarn, repeat the decrease row every 4 rows __ time(s). If no number is given, do not work these rows.

	XS	S	M	L	1X	2X	3X	4X
7	--	--	--	--	--	--	--	--
6½	--	--	--	--	--	--	--	--
6	1	1	1	1	1	1	1	1
5½	1	1	1	1	1	1	1	1
5	2	2	2	2	2	2	2	2
4½	1	1	1	1	1	1	1	1
4	2	2	2	2	2	2	2	2
3½	1	1	1	1	1	1	1	1
3	--	--	--	--	--	--	--	--

You will have __ stitches remaining on each side, *except* when using raglan or saddle shoulder construction.

	XS	S	M	L	1X	2X	3X	4X
7	22	25	29	32	34	36	37	39
6½	19	23	26	29	31	32	34	36
6	18	21	24	27	29	30	32	33
5½	17	20	22	25	26	28	29	31
5	15	18	20	23	24	26	27	28
4½	13	16	18	20	21	22	23	25
4	12	14	16	18	19	20	21	22
3½	11	13	14	16	17	18	19	20
3	9	10	12	13	14	15	15	16

Complete same as for the back for your desired silhouette.

Square Neckline

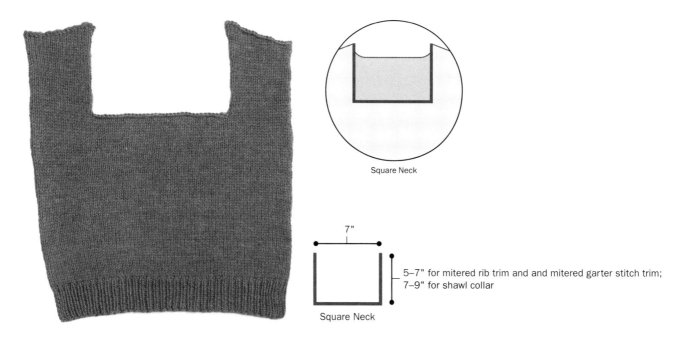

Square Neck

7"

5–7" for mitered rib trim and and mitered garter stitch trim; 7–9" for shawl collar

Square Neck

Notes

- When using raglan construction, continue the raglan armhole shaping same as for the back while working the front neck shaping.
- Work same as for the back (pages 19–97) until the piece measures the appropriate length for your desired neckline treatment (pages 195–212), ending after a wrong-side row.

Shape the Neck

Place markers on both sides of the middle ___ stitches.

	XS	S	M	L	1X	2X	3X	4X
7	48	48	48	48	48	48	48	48
6½	46	46	46	46	46	46	46	46
6	42	42	42	42	42	42	42	42
5½	38	38	38	38	38	38	38	38
5	34	34	34	34	34	34	34	34
4½	32	32	32	32	32	32	32	32
4	28	28	28	28	28	28	28	28
3½	24	24	24	24	24	24	24	24
3	22	22	22	22	22	22	22	22

Knit across to the first marker, join a second ball of yarn, and bind off the stitches between the markers, then knit across to end the row.

You will have __ stitches remaining on each side, *except* when using raglan or saddle shoulder construction.

	XS	S	M	L	1X	2X	3X	4X
7	22	25	29	32	34	36	37	39
6½	19	23	26	29	31	32	34	36
6	18	21	24	27	29	30	32	33
5½	17	20	22	25	26	28	29	31
5	15	18	20	23	24	26	27	28
4½	13	16	18	20	21	22	23	25
4	12	14	16	18	19	20	21	22
3½	11	13	14	16	17	18	19	20
3	9	10	12	13	14	15	15	16

Complete same as for the back for your desired silhouette.

Placket Neckline

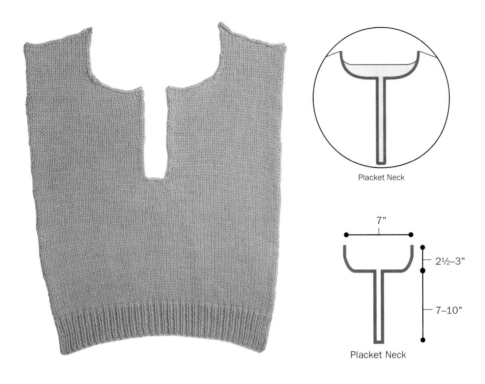

Placket Neck

7"

2½–3"

7–10"

Placket Neck

Notes

- For fully fashioned neck decreases: On right-side rows, first half, knit to 3 stitches before the neck edge, k2tog, k1; second half, k1, ssk, work to the end of the row. On wrong-side rows, first half, purl to 3 stitches before the neck edge, ssp (page 255), p1; second half, p1, p2tog, work to the end of the row.
- When using raglan construction, continue the raglan armhole shaping same as for the back while working the front neck shaping.
- For garments with saddle shoulders, begin the shoulder shaping when the piece measures approximately 1"/2.5cm less than the desired finished length, and work the shoulder shaping and the remaining front neck shaping at the same time.

Front

Work same as for the back (pages 19–97) until the piece measures the appropriate length for your desired neckline treatment (pages 195–212), ending after a wrong-side row.

Divide for the Placket

Place markers on both sides of the middle __ stitches.

	XS	S	M	L	1X	2X	3X	4X
7	8	8	8	8	8	8	8	8
6½	6	6	6	6	6	6	6	6
6	6	6	6	6	6	6	6	6
5½	6	6	6	6	6	6	6	6
5	6	6	6	6	6	6	6	6
4½	4	4	4	4	4	4	4	4
4	4	4	4	4	4	4	4	4
3½	4	4	4	4	4	4	4	4
3	4	4	4	4	4	4	4	4

Knit across to the first marker, join a second ball of yarn, and bind off the stitches between the markers, then knit across to end the row.

Work even on both sides at once with separate balls of yarn until the piece measures approximately 2½"/6.5cm less than the desired finished length, ending after a wrong-side row.

Shape the Neck

Work both sides at once with separate balls of yarn, and bind off __ stitches each neck edge once.

	XS	S	M	L	1X	2X	3X	4X
7	6	6	6	6	6	6	6	6
6½	6	6	6	6	6	6	6	6
6	5	5	5	5	5	5	5	5
5½	5	5	5	5	5	5	5	5
5	4	4	4	4	4	4	4	4
4½	4	4	4	4	4	4	4	4
4	4	4	4	4	4	4	4	4
3½	3	3	3	3	3	3	3	3
3	3	3	3	3	3	3	3	3

Work both sides at once with separate balls of yarn, and bind off __ stitches each neck edge once.

	XS	S	M	L	1X	2X	3X	4X
7	5	5	5	5	5	5	5	5
6½	5	5	5	5	5	5	5	5
6	5	5	5	5	5	5	5	5
5½	4	4	4	4	4	4	4	4
5	4	4	4	4	4	4	4	4
4½	4	4	4	4	4	4	4	4
4	3	3	3	3	3	3	3	3
3½	3	3	3	3	3	3	3	3
3	3	3	3	3	3	3	3	3

Work both sides at once with separate balls of yarn, and bind off __ stitches each neck edge once.

	XS	S	M	L	1X	2X	3X	4X
7	3	3	3	3	3	3	3	3
6½	4	4	4	4	4	4	4	4
6	3	3	3	3	3	3	3	3
5½	3	3	3	3	3	3	3	3
5	3	3	3	3	3	3	3	3
4½	3	3	3	3	3	3	3	3
4	2	2	2	2	2	2	2	2
3½	2	2	2	2	2	2	2	2
3	2	2	2	2	2	2	2	2

Work both sides at once with separate balls of yarn, and work fully fashioned decreases (see Notes) at each neck edge every row __ time(s).

	XS	S	M	L	1X	2X	3X	4X
7	5	5	5	5	5	5	5	5
6½	4	4	4	4	4	4	4	4
6	4	4	4	4	4	4	4	4
5½	3	3	3	3	3	3	3	3
5	2	2	2	2	2	2	2	2
4½	2	2	2	2	2	2	2	2
4	3	3	3	3	3	3	3	3
3½	2	2	2	2	2	2	2	2
3	1	1	1	1	1	1	1	1

Work both sides at once with separate balls of yarn, and work fully fashioned decreases (see Notes) at each neck edge every other row once, if indicated below. If no number is given, do not work these rows.

	XS	S	M	L	1X	2X	3X	4X
7	1	1	1	1	1	1	1	1
6½	1	1	1	1	1	1	1	1
6	1	1	1	1	1	1	1	1
5½	1	1	1	1	1	1	1	1
5	1	1	1	1	1	1	1	1
4½	1	1	1	1	1	1	1	1
4	--	--	--	--	--	--	--	--
3½	--	--	--	--	--	--	--	--
3	--	--	--	--	--	--	--	--

You will have __ stitches remaining on each side, *except* when using raglan or saddle shoulder construction.

	XS	S	M	L	1X	2X	3X	4X
7	22	25	29	32	34	36	37	39
6½	19	23	26	29	31	32	34	36
6	18	21	24	27	29	30	32	33
5½	17	20	22	25	26	28	29	31
5	15	18	20	23	24	26	27	28
4½	13	16	18	20	21	22	23	25
4	12	14	16	18	19	20	21	22
3½	11	13	14	16	17	18	19	20
3	9	10	12	13	14	15	15	16

Complete same as for the back for your desired silhouette.

Slit Neckline

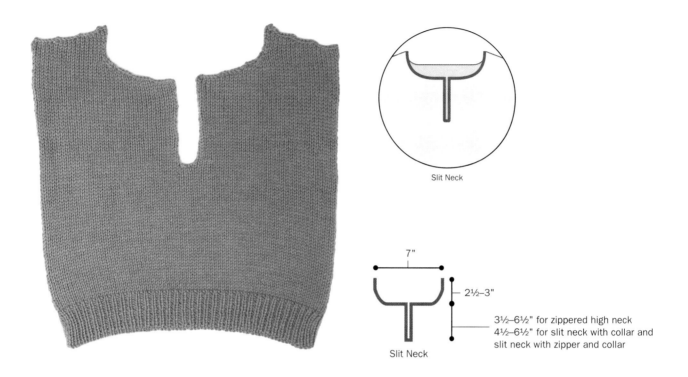

Slit Neck

7"

2½–3"

3½–6½" for zippered high neck
4½–6½" for slit neck with collar and
slit neck with zipper and collar

Slit Neck

Notes
- For fully fashioned neck decreases: On right-side rows, first half, knit to 3 stitches before the neck edge, k2tog, k1; second half, k1, ssk, work to the end of the row. On wrong-side rows, first half, purl to 3 stitches before the neck edge, ssp (page 255), p1; second half, p1, p2tog, work to the end of the row.
- When using raglan construction, continue the raglan armhole shaping same as for the back while working the front neck shaping.

Front
Work same as for the back (pages 19–97) until the piece measures the appropriate length for your desired neckline treatment (pages 195–212), ending after a wrong-side row.

Shape the Placket
Place markers on both sides of the middle 2 stitches.

Knit across to the first marker, join a second ball of yarn, and bind off the stitches between the markers, then knit across to end the row.

Work even on both sides at once with separate balls of yarn until the piece measures approximately 2½"/6.5cm less than the desired finished length, ending after a wrong-side row.

Shape the Neck

Work both sides at once with separate balls of yarn, and bind off __ stitches each neck edge once.

	XS	S	M	L	1X	2X	3X	4X
7	9	9	9	9	9	9	9	9
6½	8	8	8	8	8	8	8	8
6	7	7	7	7	7	7	7	7
5½	6	6	6	6	6	6	6	6
5	5	5	5	5	5	5	5	5
4½	5	5	5	5	5	5	5	5
4	4	4	4	4	4	4	4	4
3½	4	4	4	4	4	4	4	4
3	4	4	4	4	4	4	4	4

Work both sides at once with separate balls of yarn, and bind off __ stitches each neck edge once.

	XS	S	M	L	1X	2X	3X	4X
7	5	5	5	5	5	5	5	5
6½	5	5	5	5	5	5	5	5
6	5	5	5	5	5	5	5	5
5½	5	5	5	5	5	5	5	5
5	5	5	5	5	5	5	5	5
4½	4	4	4	4	4	4	4	4
4	4	4	4	4	4	4	4	4
3½	3	3	3	3	3	3	3	3
3	3	3	3	3	3	3	3	3

Work both sides at once with separate balls of yarn, and bind off __ stitches each neck edge once.

	XS	S	M	L	1X	2X	3X	4X
7	3	3	3	3	3	3	3	3
6½	4	4	4	4	4	4	4	4
6	3	3	3	3	3	3	3	3
5½	3	3	3	3	3	3	3	3
5	3	3	3	3	3	3	3	3
4½	3	3	3	3	3	3	3	3
4	2	2	2	2	2	2	2	2
3½	2	2	2	2	2	2	2	2
3	2	2	2	2	2	2	2	2

Work both sides at once with separate balls of yarn, and work fully fashioned decreases (see Notes) at each neck edge every row ___ time(s).

	XS	S	M	L	1X	2X	3X	4X
7	5	5	5	5	5	5	5	5
6½	4	4	4	4	4	4	4	4
6	4	4	4	4	4	4	4	4
5½	3	3	3	3	3	3	3	3
5	2	2	2	2	2	2	2	2
4½	2	2	2	2	2	2	2	2
4	3	3	3	3	3	3	3	3
3½	2	2	2	2	2	2	2	2
3	1	1	1	1	1	1	1	1

Work both sides at once with separate balls of yarn, and work fully fashioned decreases (see Notes) at each neck edge every other row once, if indicated below. If no number is given, do not work these rows.

	XS	S	M	L	1X	2X	3X	4X
7	1	1	1	1	1	1	1	1
6½	1	1	1	1	1	1	1	1
6	1	1	1	1	1	1	1	1
5½	1	1	1	1	1	1	1	1
5	1	1	1	1	1	1	1	1
4½	1	1	1	1	1	1	1	1
4	--	--	--	--	--	--	--	--
3½	--	--	--	--	--	--	--	--
3	--	--	--	--	--	--	--	--

You will have ___ stitches remaining on each side, *except* when using raglan or saddle shoulder construction.

	XS	S	M	L	1X	2X	3X	4X
7	22	25	29	32	34	36	37	39
6½	19	23	26	29	31	32	34	36
6	18	21	24	27	29	30	32	33
5½	17	20	22	25	26	28	29	31
5	15	18	20	23	24	26	27	28
4½	13	16	18	20	21	22	23	25
4	12	14	16	18	19	20	21	22
3½	11	13	14	16	17	18	19	20
3	9	10	12	13	14	15	15	16

Complete same as for the back for your desired silhouette.

SLEEVES

Find the perfect sleeve in this section. Just be certain
that the armhole construction icon matches the one for
the armhole construction for your back piece.

Square Indented Construction

Square Indented—Classic Long Sleeve

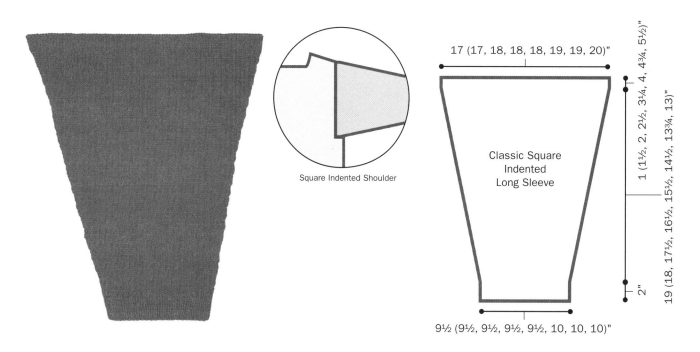

Square Indented Shoulder

17 (17, 18, 18, 18, 19, 19, 20)"

Classic Square
Indented
Long Sleeve

1 (1½, 2, 2½, 3¼, 4, 4¾, 5½)"

19 (18, 17½, 16½, 15½, 15½, 14½, 13¾, 13)"

2"

9½ (9½, 9½, 9½, 9½, 10, 10, 10)"

Finished Measurements

	XS	S	M	L	1X	2X	3X	4X
Length from Underarm	22"/56cm	21½"/54.5cm	21½"/54.5cm	21"/53.5cm	20¾"/52.5cm	20½"/52cm	20½"/52cm	20½"/52cm
Width at Lower Edge	9½"/24cm	9½"/24cm	9½"/24cm	9½"/24cm	9½"/24cm	10"/25.5cm	10"/25.5cm	10"/25.5cm
Width at Upper Arm	17"/43cm	17"/43cm	18"/45.5cm	18"/45.5cm	18"/45.5cm	19"/48.5cm	19"/48.5cm	20"/51cm

Notes
- This pattern is written for K1P1 ribbed edges. Refer to pages 213–223 for information on how to customize the edge treatment.
- For fully fashioned increases on right-side rows, k1, M1R (page 253), knit to the last stitch, M1L (page 253), k1.

Sleeve

Cast on __ stitches.

	XS	S	M	L	1X	2X	3X	4X
7	64	64	64	68	68	70	70	70
6½	58	58	58	62	62	66	66	66
6	54	54	54	56	56	60	60	60
5½	50	50	50	52	52	56	56	56
5	44	44	44	48	48	50	50	50
4½	40	40	40	42	42	44	44	44
4	36	36	36	38	38	40	40	40
3½	32	32	32	34	34	36	36	36
3	28	28	28	28	28	30	30	30

Begin K1P1 rib (page 215), and work even until the piece measures approximately 2"/5cm.

Begin stockinette stitch, and work fully fashioned increases (see Notes) each side every other row __ time(s). If no number is given, do not work these rows.

	XS	S	M	L	1X	2X	3X	4X
7	--	--	--	--	--	--	--	12
6½	--	--	--	--	--	--	--	9
6	--	--	--	--	--	--	--	8
5½	--	--	--	--	--	--	--	5
5	--	--	--	--	--	--	--	5
4½	--	--	--	--	--	--	--	4
4	--	--	--	--	--	--	--	1
3½	--	--	--	--	--	--	--	2
3	--	--	--	--	--	--	--	4

Work fully fashioned increases each side every 4 rows __ time(s). If no number is given, do not work these rows.

	XS	S	M	L	1X	2X	3X	4X
7	--	3	14	13	17	28	31	23
6½	--	2	13	11	15	26	29	23
6	--	--	11	12	16	23	26	22
5½	--	--	10	10	14	18	21	22
5	--	--	8	5	9	18	21	20
4½	--	--	6	7	10	16	19	19
4	--	--	2	2	5	11	13	19
3½	--	--	2	1	3	9	11	15
3	--	--	4	6	8	13	13	11

Work fully fashioned increases each side every 6 rows __ time(s). If no number is given, do not work these rows.

	XS	S	M	L	1X	2X	3X	4X
7	27	25	17	16	12	3	--	--
6½	23	24	16	16	12	3	--	--
6	20	24	16	14	10	4	1	--
5½	17	21	15	14	10	6	3	--
5	18	21	15	16	12	5	2	--
4½	11	14	15	13	10	5	2	--
4	7	10	16	15	12	7	5	--
3½	9	11	13	13	11	6	4	--
3	10	12	9	7	5	1	1	--

Work fully fashioned increases each side every 8 rows __ time(s). If no number is given, do not work these rows.

	XS	S	M	L	1X	2X	3X	4X
7	1	--	--	--	--	--	--	--
6½	3	--	--	--	--	--	--	--
6	4	--	--	--	--	--	--	--
5½	5	1	--	--	--	--	--	--
5	3	--	--	--	--	--	--	--
4½	7	4	--	--	--	--	--	--
4	9	6	--	--	--	--	--	--
3½	5	3	--	--	--	--	--	--
3	2	--	--	--	--	--	--	--

You will now have __ stitches.

	XS	S	M	L	1X	2X	3X	4X
7	120	120	126	126	126	132	132	140
6½	110	110	116	116	116	124	124	130
6	102	102	108	108	108	114	114	120
5½	94	94	100	100	100	104	104	110
5	86	86	90	90	90	96	96	100
4½	76	76	82	82	82	86	86	90
4	68	68	72	72	72	76	76	80
3½	60	60	62	62	62	66	66	70
3	52	52	54	54	54	58	58	60

Continue even until the piece measures approximately 22 (21½, 21½, 21, 20¾, 20½, 20½, 20½)"/56 (54.5, 54.5, 53.5, 52.5, 52, 52, 52)cm from the beginning, or the desired length, ending after a wrong-side row.

Bind off all stitches.

Square Indented—Classic Three-Quarter Sleeve

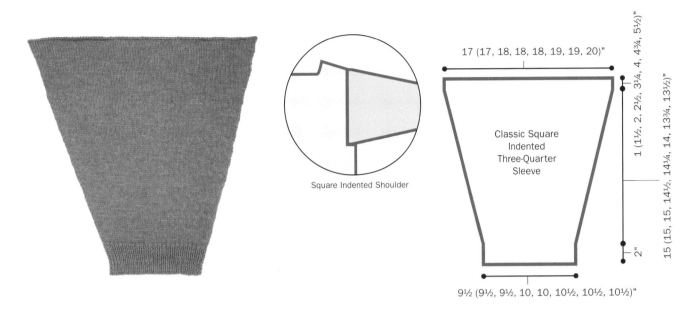

17 (17, 18, 18, 18, 19, 19, 20)"

1 (1½, 2, 2½, 3¼, 3¾, 4, 4¾, 5½)"

15 (15, 15, 14½, 14¼, 14, 13¾, 13½)"

Classic Square
Indented
Three-Quarter
Sleeve

2"

9½ (9½, 9½, 10, 10, 10½, 10½, 10½)"

Square Indented Shoulder

Finished Measurements

	XS	S	M	L	1X	2X	3X	4X
Length from Underarm	18"/45.5cm	18½"/47cm	19"/48.5cm	19"/48.5cm	19½"/49.5cm	20"/51cm	20½"/52cm	21"/53.5cm
Width at Lower Edge	9½"/24cm	9½"/24cm	9½"/24cm	10"/25.5cm	10"/25.5cm	10½"/26.5cm	10½"/26.5cm	10½"/26.5cm
Width at Upper Arm	17"/43cm	17"/43cm	18"/45.5cm	18"/45.5cm	18"/45.5cm	19"/48.5cm	19"/48.5cm	20"/51cm

Notes
- This pattern is written for K1P1 ribbed edges. Refer to pages 213–223 for information on how to customize the edge treatment.
- For fully fashioned increases on right-side rows, k1, M1R (page 253), knit to the last stitch, M1L (page 253), k1.

Sleeve

Cast on __ stitches.

	XS	S	M	L	1X	2X	3X	4X
7	66	66	66	70	70	74	74	74
6½	62	62	62	64	64	68	68	68
6	58	58	58	60	60	64	64	64
5½	52	52	52	54	54	58	58	58
5	48	48	48	50	50	52	52	52
4½	42	42	42	46	46	48	48	48
4	38	38	38	40	40	42	42	42
3½	34	34	34	36	36	38	38	38
3	28	28	28	30	30	32	32	32

Begin K1P1 rib (page 215), and work even until the piece measures approximately 2"/5cm.

Begin stockinette stitch, and work fully fashioned increases (see Notes) each side every other row __ time(s). If no number is given, do not work these rows.

	XS	S	M	L	1X	2X	3X	4X
7	--	--	--	--	--	--	--	6
6½	--	--	--	--	--	--	--	5
6	--	--	--	--	--	--	--	2
5½	--	--	--	--	--	--	--	2
5	--	--	--	--	--	--	--	1
4½	--	--	--	--	--	--	--	--
4	--	--	--	--	--	--	--	--
3½	--	--	--	--	--	--	--	--
3	--	--	--	--	--	--	--	1

Work fully fashioned increases each side every 4 rows __ times. If no number is given, do not work these rows.

	XS	S	M	L	1X	2X	3X	4X
7	14	14	23	19	20	24	26	27
6½	9	9	18	17	18	25	26	26
6	6	6	15	14	15	19	20	26
5½	7	7	16	15	16	17	18	24
5	5	5	11	10	11	18	18	23
4½	3	3	12	7	8	12	13	20
4	--	--	6	5	6	9	10	17
3½	2	2	5	3	4	7	8	15
3	6	6	9	7	8	11	12	13

Work fully fashioned increases each side every 6 rows __ time(s). If no number is given, do not work these rows.

	XS	S	M	L	1X	2X	3X	4X
7	13	13	7	9	8	5	3	--
6½	15	15	9	9	8	3	2	--
6	16	16	10	10	9	6	5	--
5½	14	14	8	8	7	6	5	--
5	14	14	10	10	9	4	4	--
4½	14	14	8	11	10	7	6	1
4	15	15	11	11	10	8	7	2
3½	11	11	9	10	9	7	6	1
3	6	6	4	5	4	2	1	--

You will now have __ stitches.

	XS	S	M	L	1X	2X	3X	4X
7	120	120	126	126	126	132	132	140
6½	110	110	116	116	116	124	124	130
6	102	102	108	108	108	114	114	120
5½	94	94	100	100	100	104	104	110
5	86	86	90	90	90	96	96	100
4½	76	76	82	82	82	86	86	90
4	68	68	72	72	72	76	76	80
3½	60	60	62	62	62	66	66	70
3	52	52	54	54	54	58	58	60

Continue even until the piece measures approximately 18 (18½, 19, 19, 19½, 20, 20½, 21)"/45.5 (47, 48.5, 48.5, 49.5, 51, 52, 53.5)cm from the beginning, or the desired length, ending after a wrong-side row.

Bind off all stitches.

Square Indented—Classic Short Sleeve

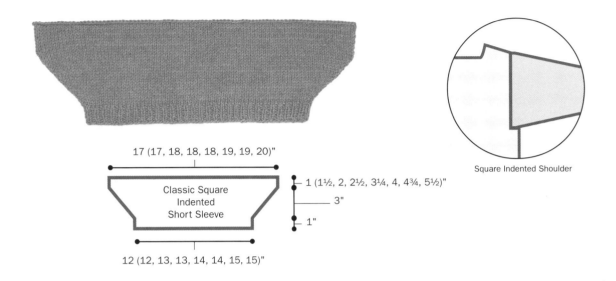

17 (17, 18, 18, 18, 19, 19, 20)"

Classic Square Indented Short Sleeve

1 (1½, 2, 2½, 3¼, 4, 4¾, 5½)"

3"

1"

12 (12, 13, 13, 14, 14, 15, 15)"

Square Indented Shoulder

Finished Measurements

	XS	S	M	L	1X	2X	3X	4X
Length from Underarm	5"/12.5cm	5½"/14cm	6"/15cm	6½"/16.5cm	7¼"/18.5cm	8"/20.5cm	8¾"/22cm	9½"/24cm
Width at Lower Edge	12"/30.5cm	12"/30.5cm	13"/33cm	13"/33cm	14"/35.5cm	14"/35.5cm	15"/38cm	15"/38cm
Width at Upper Arm	17"/43cm	17"/43cm	18"/45.5cm	18"/45.5cm	18"/45.5cm	19"/48.5cm	19"/48.5cm	20"/51cm

Notes

- This pattern is written for K1P1 ribbed edges. Refer to pages 213–223 for information on how to customize the edge treatment.
- For fully fashioned increases: On right-side rows, k1, M1R (page 253), knit to the last stitch, M1L (page 253), k1; on wrong-side rows, p1, M1 purlwise (page 253), purl to the last stitch, M1 purlwise, p1.

Sleeve

Cast on __ stitches.

	XS	S	M	L	1X	2X	3X	4X
7	84	84	92	92	98	98	104	104
6½	78	78	84	84	92	92	98	98
6	72	72	78	78	84	84	90	90
5½	66	66	72	72	78	78	82	82
5	60	60	64	64	70	70	74	74
4½	54	54	58	58	64	64	68	68
4	48	48	52	52	56	56	60	60
3½	42	42	46	46	50	50	52	52
3	36	36	40	40	42	42	46	46

Begin K1P1 rib (page 215), and work even until the piece measures approximately 1"/2.5cm.

Begin stockinette stitch, and work fully fashioned increases (see Notes) each side every row __ times.
If no number is given, do not work these rows.

	XS	S	M	L	1X	2X	3X	4X
7	10	10	8	8	2	8	2	10
6½	6	6	6	6	--	6	--	6
6	6	6	6	6	--	6	--	6
5½	6	6	6	6	--	4	--	6
5	6	6	6	6	--	6	2	6
4½	2	2	4	4	--	2	--	2
4	2	2	2	2	--	2	--	2
3½	4	4	2	2	--	2	--	4
3	4	4	2	2	--	4	--	2

Work fully fashioned increases each side every other row __ times.

	XS	S	M	L	1X	2X	3X	4X
7	8	8	9	9	12	9	12	8
6½	10	10	10	10	11	10	13	10
6	9	9	9	9	12	9	12	9
5½	8	8	8	8	11	9	11	8
5	7	7	7	7	10	7	9	7
4½	9	9	8	8	8	9	8	9
4	8	8	8	8	7	8	7	8
3½	5	5	6	6	5	6	7	5
3	4	4	5	5	6	4	6	5

Work fully fashioned increases each side every 4 rows once, if indicated below.
If no number is given, do not work these rows.

	XS	S	M	L	1X	2X	3X	4X
7	--	--	--	--	--	--	--	--
6½	--	--	--	--	1	--	--	--
6	--	--	--	--	--	--	--	--
5½	--	--	--	--	--	--	--	--
5	--	--	--	--	--	--	--	--
4½	--	--	--	--	1	--	1	--
4	--	--	--	--	1	--	1	--
3½	--	--	--	--	1	--	--	--
3	--	--	--	--	--	--	--	--

You will now have __ stitches.

	XS	S	M	L	1X	2X	3X	4X
7	120	120	126	126	126	132	132	140
6½	110	110	116	116	116	124	124	130
6	102	102	108	108	108	114	114	120
5½	94	94	100	100	100	104	104	110
5	86	86	90	90	90	96	96	100
4½	76	76	82	82	82	86	86	90
4	68	68	72	72	72	76	76	80
3½	60	60	62	62	62	66	66	70
3	52	52	54	54	54	58	58	60

Continue even until the piece measures approximately 5 (5½, 6, 6½, 7¼, 8, 8¾, 9½)"/12.5 (14, 15, 16.5, 18.5, 20.5, 22, 24)cm from the beginning, or the desired length, ending after a wrong-side row.

Bind off all stitches.

Set-In Construction

Set-In—Classic Long Sleeve

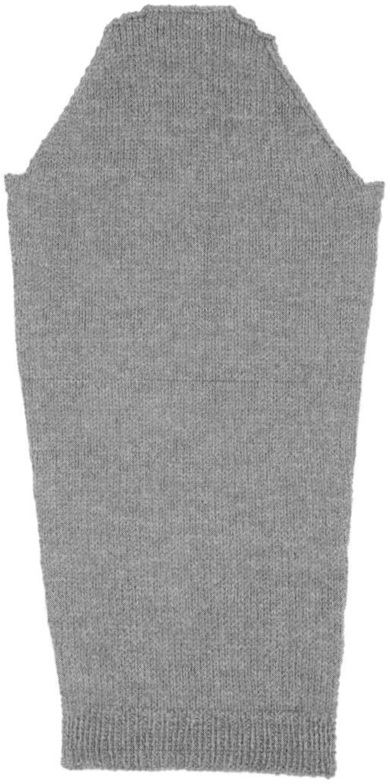

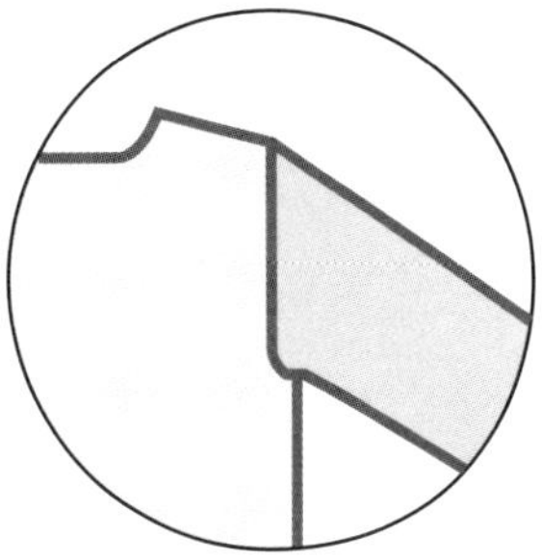

Set-In Shoulder

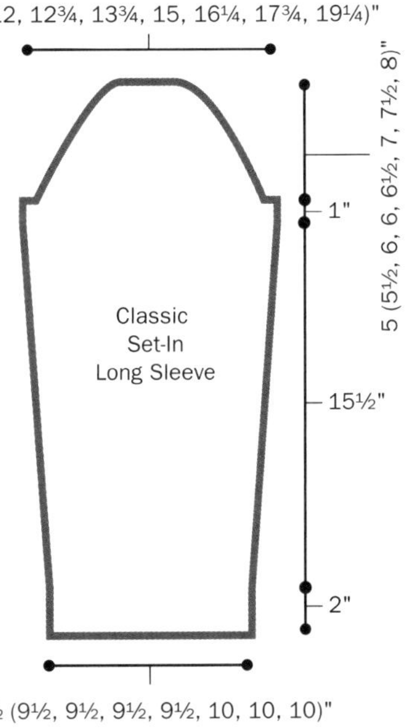
11½ (12, 12¾, 13¾, 15, 16¼, 17¾, 19¼)"
5 (5½, 6, 6, 6½, 7, 7½, 8)"
1"
Classic
Set-In
Long Sleeve
15½"
2"
9½ (9½, 9½, 9½, 9½, 10, 10, 10)"

Finished Measurements

	XS	S	M	L	1X	2X	3X	4X
Length from Underarm	18½"/47cm	18½"/47cm	18½"/47cm	18½"/47cm	18½"/47cm	18½"/47cm	18½"/47cm	18½"/47cm
Width at Lower Edge	9½"/24cm	9½"/24cm	9½"/24cm	9½"/24cm	9½"/24cm	10"/25.5cm	10"/25.5cm	10"/25.5cm
Width at Upper Arm	11½"/29cm	12"/30.5cm	12¾"/32.5cm	13¾"/35cm	15"/38cm	16¼"/ 41.5cm	17¾"/45cm	19¼"/49cm

Notes

- This pattern is written for K1P1 ribbed edges. Refer to pages 213–223 for information on how to customize the edge treatment.
- For fully fashioned decreases: On right-side rows, k1, ssk, knit to the last 3 stitches, k2tog, k1; on wrong-side rows, p1, p2tog, purl to the last 3 stitches, ssp (page 255), p1.
- For fully fashioned increases: On right-side rows, k1, M1R (page 253), knit to the last stitch, M1L (page 253), k1.

Sleeve

Cast on __ stitches.

	XS	S	M	L	1X	2X	3X	4X
7	64	64	64	66	66	70	70	70
6½	58	58	58	62	62	66	66	66
6	54	54	54	58	58	60	60	60
5½	50	50	50	52	52	56	56	56
5	44	44	44	48	48	50	50	50
4½	40	40	40	42	42	46	46	46
4	36	36	36	38	38	40	40	40
3½	32	32	32	34	34	36	36	36
3	28	28	28	28	28	30	30	30

Begin K1P1 rib (page 215), and work even until the piece measures approximately 2"/5cm.

Begin stockinette stitch, and work fully fashioned increases (see Notes) each side every 4 rows __ time(s). If no number is given, do not work these rows.

	XS	S	M	L	1X	2X	3X	4X
7	--	--	--	--	--	--	11	29
6½	--	--	--	--	--	--	9	24
6	--	--	--	--	--	--	7	22
5½	--	--	--	--	--	--	5	17
5	--	--	--	--	--	--	3	15
4½	--	--	--	--	--	--	1	13
4	--	--	--	--	--	--	2	11
3½	--	--	--	--	--	--	--	9
3	--	--	--	--	--	--	5	11

Work fully fashioned increases each side every 6 rows __ times. If no number is given, do not work these rows.

	XS	S	M	L	1X	2X	3X	4X
7	--	--	--	--	10	18	16	4
6½	--	--	--	--	6	14	16	6
6	--	--	--	--	2	14	16	6
5½	--	--	--	--	2	10	16	8
5	--	--	--	--	2	10	16	8
4½	--	--	--	--	2	6	16	8
4	--	--	--	--	--	6	14	8
3½	--	--	--	--	--	5	13	7
3	--	--	--	--	5	9	7	3

Work fully fashioned increases each side every 8 rows __ time(s). If no number is given, do not work these rows.

	XS	S	M	L	1X	2X	3X	4X
7	--	--	--	5	10	4	--	--
6½	--	--	--	4	12	6	--	--
6	--	--	--	--	14	5	--	--
5½	--	--	--	2	13	7	--	--
5	--	--	--	--	12	6	--	--
4½	--	--	--	--	11	8	--	--
4	--	--	--	--	9	7	--	--
3½	--	--	--	--	6	6	--	--
3	--	--	--	4	4	1	--	--

Work fully fashioned increases each side every 10 rows __ times. If no number is given, do not work these rows.

	XS	S	M	L	1X	2X	3X	4X
7	--	--	8	10	--	--	--	--
6½	--	--	6	10	--	--	--	--
6	--	--	4	10	--	--	--	--
5½	--	--	2	10	--	--	--	--
5	--	--	6	6	--	--	--	--
4½	--	--	4	10	--	--	--	--
4	--	--	--	8	2	--	--	--
3½	--	--	3	3	3	--	--	--
3	--	--	--	3	--	--	--	--

Work fully fashioned increases each side every 12 rows __ time(s). If no number is given, do not work these rows.

	XS	S	M	L	1X	2X	3X	4X
7	--	--	5	--	--	--	--	--
6½	--	4	6	--	--	--	--	--
6	--	1	7	2	--	--	--	--
5½	--	--	8	--	--	--	--	--
5	--	2	4	4	--	--	--	--
4½	--	--	5	--	--	--	--	--
4	--	--	3	1	--	--	--	--
3½	--	--	4	4	--	--	--	--
3	--	--	4	--	--	--	--	--

Work fully fashioned increases each side every 14 rows __ time(s). If no number is given, do not work these rows.

	XS	S	M	L	1X	2X	3X	4X
7	--	10	--	--	--	--	--	--
6½	6	6	--	--	--	--	--	--
6	2	8	--	--	--	--	--	--
5½	--	6	--	--	--	--	--	--
5	2	6	--	--	--	--	--	--
4½	--	6	--	--	--	--	--	--
4	--	2	4	--	--	--	--	--
3½	--	1	--	--	--	--	--	--
3	--	1	1	--	--	--	--	--

Work fully fashioned increases each side every 16 rows __ time(s). If no number is given, do not work these rows.

	XS	S	M	L	1X	2X	3X	4X
7	2	--	--	--	--	--	--	--
6½	3	--	--	--	--	--	--	--
6	6	--	--	--	--	--	--	--
5½	5	2	--	--	--	--	--	--
5	5	--	--	--	--	--	--	--
4½	4	1	--	--	--	--	--	--
4	--	4	--	--	--	--	--	--
3½	--	4	--	--	--	--	--	--
3	--	3	--	--	--	--	--	--

Work fully fashioned increases each side every 18 rows __ time(s). If no number is given, do not work these rows.

	XS	S	M	L	1X	2X	3X	4X
7	6	--	--	--	--	--	--	--
6½	--	--	--	--	--	--	--	--
6	--	--	--	--	--	--	--	--
5½	2	--	--	--	--	--	--	--
5	--	--	--	--	--	--	--	--
4½	2	--	--	--	--	--	--	--
4	4	--	--	--	--	--	--	--
3½	1	--	--	--	--	--	--	--
3	--	--	--	--	--	--	--	--

Work fully fashioned increases each side every 20 rows __ time(s). If no number is given, do not work these rows.

	XS	S	M	L	1X	2X	3X	4X
7	--	--	--	--	--	--	--	--
6½	--	--	--	--	--	--	--	--
6	--	--	--	--	--	--	--	--
5½	--	--	--	--	--	--	--	--
5	--	--	--	--	--	--	--	--
4½	--	--	--	--	--	--	--	--
4	1	--	--	--	--	--	--	--
3½	3	--	--	--	--	--	--	--
3	2	--	--	--	--	--	--	--

Work fully fashioned increases each side every 22 rows once, if indicated below.
If no number is given, do not work these rows.

	XS	S	M	L	1X	2X	3X	4X
7	--	--	--	--	--	--	--	--
6½	--	--	--	--	--	--	--	--
6	--	--	--	--	--	--	--	--
5½	--	--	--	--	--	--	--	--
5	--	--	--	--	--	--	--	--
4½	--	--	--	--	--	--	--	--
4	--	--	--	--	--	--	--	--
3½	--	--	--	--	--	--	--	--
3	1	--	--	--	--	--	--	--

You will now have __ stitches.

	XS	S	M	L	1X	2X	3X	4X
7	80	84	90	96	106	114	124	136
6½	76	78	82	90	98	106	116	126
6	70	72	76	82	90	98	106	116
5½	64	66	70	76	82	90	98	106
5	58	60	64	68	76	82	88	96
4½	52	54	58	62	68	74	80	88
4	46	48	50	56	60	66	72	78
3½	40	42	46	48	52	58	62	68
3	34	36	38	42	46	50	54	58

Continue even until the piece measures approximately 18½"/47cm from the beginning, or the desired length to the armhole, ending after a wrong-side row.

Shape the Cap

Bind off __ stitches at the beginning of the next 2 rows.

	XS	S	M	L	1X	2X	3X	4X
7	3	4	4	5	5	6	9	10
6½	3	4	4	5	6	7	9	10
6	3	3	4	4	5	6	8	8
5½	2	3	3	4	4	5	7	7
5	2	3	3	4	4	5	6	6
4½	2	3	3	3	4	4	5	5
4	2	2	2	3	3	4	5	6
3½	2	2	2	3	3	4	5	5
3	2	2	2	3	3	4	4	5

Work fully fashioned decreases (see Notes) each side every 4 rows once, if indicated below.
If no number is given, do not work these rows.

	XS	S	M	L	1X	2X	3X	4X
7	--	--	--	--	--	--	--	--
6½	--	1	1	--	--	--	--	--
6	--	--	--	--	--	--	--	--
5½	--	--	--	--	--	--	--	--
5	--	1	--	--	--	--	--	--
4½	--	--	--	--	--	--	--	--
4	--	--	--	--	--	--	--	--
3½	--	--	--	--	--	--	--	--
3	--	--	--	--	--	--	--	--

Work fully fashioned decreases each side every other row __ times.

	XS	S	M	L	1X	2X	3X	4X
7	18	21	22	20	21	22	25	24
6½	17	18	20	20	21	22	24	24
6	15	18	20	18	19	20	22	21
5½	14	17	19	17	18	19	21	20
5	13	14	17	16	16	18	20	19
4½	12	14	16	14	15	16	17	16
4	11	13	14	13	14	15	16	17
3½	8	10	10	10	11	11	13	12
3	6	7	8	7	7	8	8	9

Work fully fashioned decreases each side every row __ time(s). If no number is given, do not work these rows.

	XS	S	M	L	1X	2X	3X	4X
7	2	--	2	6	10	12	11	17
6½	2	--	--	4	6	8	9	13
6	3	1	--	5	7	9	9	15
5½	3	--	--	4	6	8	8	13
5	2	--	--	2	6	6	6	11
4½	2	--	--	4	5	7	8	13
4	1	--	--	3	4	5	6	7
3½	2	1	3	3	4	6	5	9
3	1	1	1	3	5	5	7	7

Work 1 row even, if indicated below. If no number is given, do not work this row.

	XS	S	M	L	1X	2X	3X	4X
7	--	1	1	1	--	--	--	--
6½	--	--	--	--	--	1	--	--
6	--	--	1	--	--	--	--	--
5½	--	--	--	--	--	--	--	--
5	--	--	1	1	1	--	--	--
4½	--	1	--	--	--	--	--	--
4	--	--	1	--	--	--	--	--
3½	--	--	--	--	--	--	--	--
3	--	--	--	--	--	--	--	--

You will have __ stitches remaining.

	XS	S	M	L	1X	2X	3X	4X
7	34	34	34	34	34	34	34	34
6½	32	32	32	32	32	32	32	32
6	28	28	28	28	28	28	28	28
5½	26	26	26	26	26	26	26	26
5	24	24	24	24	24	24	24	24
4½	20	20	20	20	20	20	20	20
4	18	18	18	18	18	18	18	18
3½	16	16	16	16	16	16	16	16
3	16	16	16	16	16	16	16	16

Bind off __ stitches at the beginning of the next 4 rows.

	XS	S	M	L	1X	2X	3X	4X
7	4	4	4	4	4	4	4	4
6½	4	4	4	4	4	4	4	4
6	3	3	3	3	3	3	3	3
5½	3	3	3	3	3	3	3	3
5	3	3	3	3	3	3	3	3
4½	2	2	2	2	2	2	2	2
4	2	2	2	2	2	2	2	2
3½	2	2	2	2	2	2	2	2
3	2	2	2	2	2	2	2	2

You will have __ stitches remaining.

	XS	S	M	L	1X	2X	3X	4X
7	18	18	18	18	18	18	18	18
6½	16	16	16	16	16	16	16	16
6	16	16	16	16	16	16	16	16
5½	14	14	14	14	14	14	14	14
5	12	12	12	12	12	12	12	12
4½	12	12	12	12	12	12	12	12
4	10	10	10	10	10	10	10	10
3½	8	8	8	8	8	8	8	8
3	8	8	8	8	8	8	8	8

Bind off all stitches.

Set-In—Classic Three-Quarter Sleeve

Set-In Shoulder

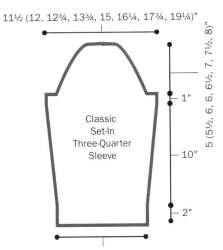

11½ (12, 12¾, 13¾, 15, 16¼, 17¾, 19¼)"

5 (5½, 6, 6, 6½, 7, 7½, 8)"

1"

Classic
Set-In
Three-Quarter
Sleeve

10"

2"

9½ (9½, 9½, 10, 10, 10½, 10½, 10½)"

Finished Measurements

	XS	S	M	L	1X	2X	3X	4X
Length from Underarm	13"/33cm	13"/33cm	13"/33cm	13"/33cm	13"/33cm	13"/33cm	13"/33cm	13"/33cm
Width at Lower Edge	9½"/24cm	9½"/24cm	9½"/24cm	10"/25.5cm	10"/25.5cm	10½"/26.5cm	10½"/26.5cm	10½"/26.5cm
Width at Upper Arm	11½"/29cm	12"/30.5cm	12¾"/32.5cm	13¾"/35cm	15"/38cm	16¼"/41.5cm	17¾"/45cm	19¼"/49cm

Notes
- This pattern is written for K1P1 ribbed edges. Refer to pages 213–223 for information on how to customize the edge treatment.
- For fully fashioned decreases: On right-side rows, k1, ssk, knit to the last 3 stitches, k2tog, k1; on wrong-side rows, p1, p2tog, purl to the last 3 stitches, ssp (page 255), p1.
- For fully fashioned increases: On right-side rows, k1, M1R (page 253), knit to the last stitch, M1L (page 253), k1.

Sleeve

Cast on __ stitches.

	XS	S	M	L	1X	2X	3X	4X
7	66	66	66	70	70	74	74	74
6½	62	62	62	66	66	68	68	68
6	58	58	58	60	60	64	64	64
5½	52	52	52	54	54	58	58	58
5	48	48	48	50	50	52	52	52
4½	42	42	42	46	46	48	48	48
4	38	38	38	40	40	42	42	42
3½	34	34	34	36	36	38	38	38
3	28	28	28	30	30	32	32	32

Begin K1P1 rib (page 215), and work even until the piece measures approximately 2"/5cm.

Begin stockinette stitch, and work fully fashioned increases (see Notes) each side every other row __ time(s). If no number is given, do not work these rows.

	XS	S	M	L	1X	2X	3X	4X
7	--	--	--	--	--	--	5	17
6½	--	--	--	--	--	--	6	16
6	--	--	--	--	--	--	2	12
5½	--	--	--	--	--	--	3	11
5	--	--	--	--	--	--	1	9
4½	--	--	--	--	--	--	--	8
4	--	--	--	--	--	--	--	6
3½	--	--	--	--	--	--	--	5
3	--	--	--	--	--	--	2	6

Work fully fashioned increases each side every 4 rows __ time(s). If no number is given, do not work these rows.

	XS	S	M	L	1X	2X	3X	4X
7	--	--	--	--	9	15	20	14
6½	--	--	--	--	6	15	18	13
6	--	--	--	--	5	11	19	14
5½	--	--	--	--	5	11	17	13
5	--	--	--	--	4	10	17	13
4½	--	--	--	--	1	7	16	12
4	--	--	--	--	--	6	15	12
3½	--	--	--	--	--	5	11	10
3	--	--	--	--	4	7	9	7

Work fully fashioned increases each side every 6 rows __ time(s). If no number is given, do not work these rows.

	XS	S	M	L	1X	2X	3X	4X
7	--	--	3	7	9	5	--	--
6½	--	--	--	6	10	4	--	--
6	--	--	--	4	10	6	--	--
5½	--	--	--	7	9	5	--	--
5	--	--	--	1	9	5	--	--
4½	--	--	--	--	10	6	--	--
4	--	--	--	2	10	6	--	--
3½	--	--	--	--	7	5	1	--
3	--	--	--	4	4	2	--	--

Work fully fashioned increases each side every 8 rows __ time(s). If no number is given, do not work these rows.

	XS	S	M	L	1X	2X	3X	4X
7	--	--	9	6	--	--	--	--
6½	--	--	8	6	--	--	--	--
6	--	--	5	7	--	--	--	--
5½	--	--	8	4	--	--	--	--
5	--	--	5	8	--	--	--	--
4½	--	--	8	8	--	--	--	--
4	--	--	--	6	--	--	--	--
3½	--	--	5	5	1	--	--	--
3	--	--	5	2	--	--	--	--

Work fully fashioned increases each side every 10 rows __ time(s). If no number is given, do not work these rows.

	XS	S	M	L	1X	2X	3X	4X
7	--	9	--	--	--	--	--	--
6½	--	6	2	--	--	--	--	--
6	--	2	4	--	--	--	--	--
5½	--	5	1	--	--	--	--	--
5	--	1	3	--	--	--	--	--
4½	--	4	--	--	--	--	--	--
4	--	--	6	--	--	--	--	--
3½	--	--	1	1	--	--	--	--
3	--	4	--	--	--	--	--	--

Work fully fashioned increases each side every 12 rows __ time(s). If no number is given, do not work these rows.

	XS	S	M	L	1X	2X	3X	4X
7	4	--	--	--	--	--	--	--
6½	7	2	--	--	--	--	--	--
6	2	5	--	--	--	--	--	--
5½	5	2	--	--	--	--	--	--
5	--	5	--	--	--	--	--	--
4½	3	2	--	--	--	--	--	--
4	--	5	--	--	--	--	--	--
3½	--	3	--	--	--	--	--	--
3	1	--	--	--	--	--	--	--

Work fully fashioned increases each side every 14 rows __ time(s). If no number is given, do not work these rows.

	XS	S	M	L	1X	2X	3X	4X
7	3	--	--	--	--	--	--	--
6½	--	--	--	--	--	--	--	--
6	4	--	--	--	--	--	--	--
5½	1	--	--	--	--	--	--	--
5	5	--	--	--	--	--	--	--
4½	2	--	--	--	--	--	--	--
4	2	--	--	--	--	--	--	--
3½	--	1	--	--	--	--	--	--
3	2	--	--	--	--	--	--	--

Work fully fashioned increases each side every 16 rows twice, if indicated below.
If no number is given, do not work these rows.

	XS	S	M	L	1X	2X	3X	4X
7	--	--	--	--	--	--	--	--
6½	--	--	--	--	--	--	--	--
6	--	--	--	--	--	--	--	--
5½	--	--	--	--	--	--	--	--
5	--	--	--	--	--	--	--	--
4½	--	--	--	--	--	--	--	--
4	2	--	--	--	--	--	--	--
3½	2	--	--	--	--	--	--	--
3	--	--	--	--	--	--	--	--

Work fully fashioned increases each side every 18 rows once, if indicated below.
If no number is given, do not work these rows.

	XS	S	M	L	1X	2X	3X	4X
7	--	--	--	--	--	--	--	--
6½	--	--	--	--	--	--	--	--
6	--	--	--	--	--	--	--	--
5½	--	--	--	--	--	--	--	--
5	--	--	--	--	--	--	--	--
4½	--	--	--	--	--	--	--	--
4	--	--	--	--	--	--	--	--
3½	1	--	--	--	--	--	--	--
3	--	--	--	--	--	--	--	--

You will now have __ stitches.

	XS	S	M	L	1X	2X	3X	4X
7	80	84	90	96	106	114	124	136
6½	76	78	82	90	98	106	116	126
6	70	72	76	82	90	98	106	116
5½	64	66	70	76	82	90	98	106
5	58	60	64	68	76	82	88	96
4½	52	54	58	62	68	74	80	88
4	46	48	50	56	60	66	72	78
3½	40	42	46	48	52	58	62	68
3	34	36	38	42	46	50	54	58

Continue even until the piece measures approximately 13"/33cm from the beginning, or the desired length to the armhole, ending after a wrong-side row.

Shape the Cap

Work same as for the set-in classic long sleeve (page 129).

You will have __ stitches remaining.

	XS	S	M	L	1X	2X	3X	4X
7	18	18	18	18	18	18	18	18
6½	16	16	16	16	16	16	16	16
6	16	16	16	16	16	16	16	16
5½	14	14	14	14	14	14	14	14
5	12	12	12	12	12	12	12	12
4½	12	12	12	12	12	12	12	12
4	10	10	10	10	10	10	10	10
3½	8	8	8	8	8	8	8	8
3	8	8	8	8	8	8	8	8

Bind off all stitches.

Set-In—Classic Short Sleeve

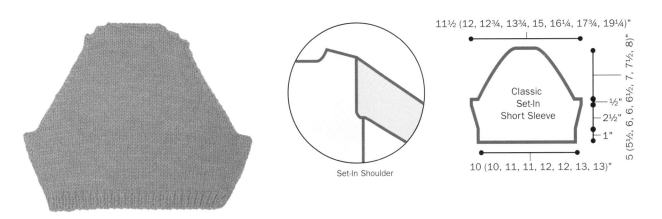

11½ (12, 12¾, 13¾, 15, 16¼, 17¾, 19¼)"

5 (5½, 6, 6, 6½, 7, 7½, 8)"

½"
2½"
1"

Classic
Set-In
Short Sleeve

10 (10, 11, 11, 12, 12, 13, 13)"

Set-In Shoulder

Finished Measurements

	XS	S	M	L	1X	2X	3X	4X
Length from Underarm	4"/10cm	4"/10cm	4"/10cm	4"/10cm	4"/10cm	4"/10cm	4"/10cm	4"/10cm
Width at Lower Edge	10"/25.5cm	10"/25.5cm	11"/28cm	11"/28cm	12"/30.5cm	12"/30.5cm	13"/33cm	13"/33cm
Width at Upper Arm	11½"/29cm	12"/30.5cm	12¾"/32.5cm	13¾"/35cm	15"/38cm	16¼"/41.5cm	17¾"/45cm	19¼"/49cm

Notes

- This pattern is written for K1P1 ribbed edges. Refer to pages 213–223 for information on how to customize the edge treatment.
- For fully fashioned decreases: On right-side rows, k1, ssk, knit to the last 3 stitches, k2tog, k1; on wrong-side rows, p1, p2tog, purl to the last 3 stitches, ssp (page 255), p1.
- For fully fashioned increases: On right-side rows, k1, M1R (page 253), knit to the last stitch, M1L (page 253), k1.

Sleeve

Cast on __ stitches.

	XS	S	M	L	1X	2X	3X	4X
7	70	70	78	78	84	84	92	92
6½	66	66	72	72	78	78	84	84
6	60	60	66	66	72	72	78	78
5½	56	56	60	60	66	66	72	72
5	50	50	56	56	60	60	66	66
4½	46	46	50	50	54	54	58	58
4	40	40	44	44	48	48	52	52
3½	36	36	38	38	42	42	46	46
3	30	30	34	34	36	36	40	40

Begin K1P1 rib (page 215), and work even until the piece measures approximately 1"/2.5cm.

Begin stockinette stitch, and work fully fashioned increases (see Notes) each side every row __ times.
If no number is given, do not work these rows.

	XS	S	M	L	1X	2X	3X	4X
7	--	--	--	--	--	8	10	22
6½	--	--	--	--	--	6	10	20
6	--	--	--	--	--	6	8	18
5½	--	--	--	--	--	6	8	16
5	--	--	--	--	--	6	6	14
4½	--	--	--	--	--	4	6	14
4	--	--	--	--	--	4	6	12
3½	--	--	--	--	--	4	4	10
3	--	--	--	--	--	4	4	8

Work fully fashioned increases each side every other row __ time(s).
If no number is given, do not work these rows.

	XS	S	M	L	1X	2X	3X	4X
7	--	3	1	7	11	7	6	--
6½	--	1	--	7	9	8	6	1
6	--	2	--	6	8	7	6	1
5½	--	1	1	7	7	6	5	1
5	--	2	--	4	8	5	5	1
4½	--	--	--	4	6	6	5	1
4	--	1	--	5	5	5	4	1
3½	--	--	2	4	4	4	4	1
3	--	1	--	3	5	3	3	1

Work fully fashioned increases each side every 4 rows __ time(s). If no number is given, do not work these rows.

	XS	S	M	L	1X	2X	3X	4X
7	4	4	5	2	--	--	--	--
6½	4	5	4	2	1	--	--	--
6	5	4	5	2	1	--	--	--
5½	3	4	4	1	1	--	--	--
5	4	3	4	2	--	--	--	--
4½	1	4	4	2	1	--	--	--
4	2	3	2	1	1	--	--	--
3½	--	3	2	1	1	--	--	--
3	1	2	1	1	--	--	--	--

Work fully fashioned increases each side every 6 rows __ time(s). If no number is given, do not work these rows.

	XS	S	M	L	1X	2X	3X	4X
7	1	--	--	--	--	--	--	--
6½	1	--	1	--	--	--	--	--
6	--	--	--	--	--	--	--	--
5½	1	--	--	--	--	--	--	--
5	--	--	--	--	--	--	--	--
4½	2	--	--	--	--	--	--	--
4	1	--	1	--	--	--	--	--
3½	2	--	--	--	--	--	--	--
3	1	--	1	--	--	--	--	--

You will now have __ stitches.

	XS	S	M	L	1X	2X	3X	4X
7	80	84	90	96	106	114	124	136
6½	76	78	82	90	98	106	116	126
6	70	72	76	82	90	98	106	116
5½	64	66	70	76	82	90	98	106
5	58	60	64	68	76	82	88	96
4½	52	54	58	62	68	74	80	88
4	46	48	50	56	60	66	72	78
3½	40	42	46	48	52	58	62	68
3	34	36	38	42	46	50	54	58

Continue even until the piece measures approximately 4"/10cm from the beginning, or the desired length to the armhole, ending after a wrong-side row.

Shape the Cap

Work same as for the set-in classic long sleeve (page 129).

You will have __ stitches remaining.

	XS	S	M	L	1X	2X	3X	4X
7	18	18	18	18	18	18	18	18
6½	16	16	16	16	16	16	16	16
6	16	16	16	16	16	16	16	16
5½	14	14	14	14	14	14	14	14
5	12	12	12	12	12	12	12	12
4½	12	12	12	12	12	12	12	12
4	10	10	10	10	10	10	10	10
3½	8	8	8	8	8	8	8	8
3	8	8	8	8	8	8	8	8

Bind off all stitches.

Set-In—Classic Cap Sleeve

Set-In Shoulder

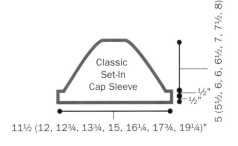

Classic Set-In Cap Sleeve

5 (5½, 6, 6, 6½, 7, 7½, 8)"

½"
½"

11½ (12, 12¾, 13¾, 15, 16¼, 17¾, 19¼)"

Finished Measurements

	XS	S	M	L	1X	2X	3X	4X
Length from Underarm	1"/2.5cm	1"/2.5cm	1"/2.5cm	1"/2.5cm	1"/2.5cm	1"/2.5cm	1"/2.5cm	1"/2.5cm
Width at Lower Edge	11½"/93.5cm	12"/30.5cm	12¾"/32.5cm	13¾"/35cm	15"/38cm	16¼"/41.5cm	17¾"/45cm	19¼"/49cm
Width at Upper Arm	11½"/29cm	12"/30.5cm	12¾"/32.5cm	13¾"/35cm	15"/38cm	16¼"/41.5cm	17¾"/45cm	19¼"/49cm

Notes

- This pattern is written for K1P1 ribbed edges. Refer to pages 213–223 for information on how to customize the edge treatment.
- For fully fashioned decreases: On right-side rows, k1, ssk, knit to the last 3 stitches, k2tog, k1; on wrong-side rows, p1, p2tog, purl to the last 3 stitches, ssp (page 255), p1.

Sleeve

Cast on __ stitches.

	XS	S	M	L	1X	2X	3X	4X
7	80	84	90	96	106	114	124	136
6½	76	78	82	90	98	106	116	126
6	70	72	76	82	90	98	106	116
5½	64	66	70	76	82	90	98	106
5	58	60	64	68	76	82	88	96
4½	52	54	58	62	68	74	80	88
4	46	48	50	56	60	66	72	78
3½	40	42	46	48	52	58	62	68
3	34	36	38	42	46	50	54	58

Begin K1P1 rib (page 215), and work even until the piece measures approximately ½"/1.5cm from the beginning.

Begin stockinette stitch, and work even until the piece measures approximately 1"/2.5cm from the beginning, or the desired length to the armhole, ending after a wrong-side row.

Shape the Cap

Work same as for the set-in classic long sleeve (page 129).

You will have __ stitches remaining.

	XS	S	M	L	1X	2X	3X	4X
7	18	18	18	18	18	18	18	18
6½	16	16	16	16	16	16	16	16
6	16	16	16	16	16	16	16	16
5½	14	14	14	14	14	14	14	14
5	12	12	12	12	12	12	12	12
4½	12	12	12	12	12	12	12	12
4	10	10	10	10	10	10	10	10
3½	8	8	8	8	8	8	8	8
3	8	8	8	8	8	8	8	8

Bind off all stitches.

Set-In—Bell Long Sleeve

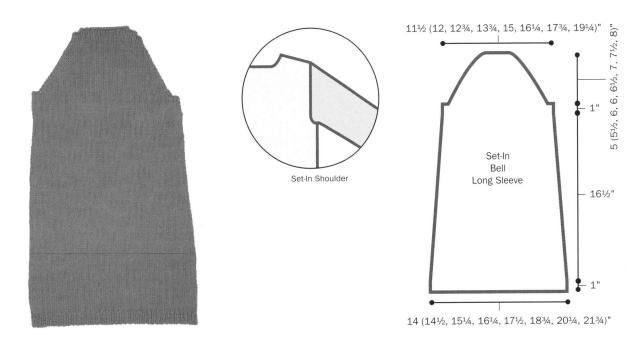

Set-In Shoulder

11½ (12, 12¾, 13¾, 15, 16¼, 17¾, 19¼)"

5 (5½, 6, 6, 6½, 7, 7½, 8)"

1"

Set-In
Bell
Long Sleeve

16½"

1"

14 (14½, 15¼, 16¼, 17½, 18¾, 20¼, 21¾)"

Finished Measurements

	XS	S	M	L	1X	2X	3X	4X
Length from Underarm	18½"/47cm	18½"/47cm	18½"/47cm	18½"/47cm	18½"/47cm	18½"/47cm	18½"/47cm	18½"/47cm
Width at Lower Edge	14"/35.5cm	14½"/37cm	15¼"/38.5cm	16¼"/41.5cm	17½"/44.5cm	18¾"/47.5cm	20¼"/51.5cm	21¾"/55cm
Width at Upper Arm	11½"/29cm	12"/30.5cm	12¾"/32.5cm	13¾"/35cm	15"/38cm	16¼"/41.5cm	17¾"/45cm	19¼"/49cm

Notes
- This pattern is written for K1P1 ribbed edges. Refer to pages 213–223 for information on how to customize the edge treatment.
- For fully fashioned decreases: On right-side rows, k1, ssk, knit to the last 3 stitches, k2tog, k1; on wrong-side rows, p1, p2tog, purl to the last 3 stitches, ssp (page 255), p1.

Sleeve

Cast on __ stitches.

	XS	S	M	L	1X	2X	3X	4X
7	98	102	108	114	122	132	142	152
6½	92	94	100	106	114	122	132	142
6	84	88	92	98	106	112	122	130
5½	78	80	84	90	96	104	112	120
5	70	72	76	82	88	94	102	108
4½	64	66	70	74	78	84	92	98
4	56	58	62	66	70	76	82	88
3½	48	50	54	56	62	66	70	76
3	42	44	46	48	52	56	60	66

Begin K1P1 rib (page 215), and work even until the piece measures approximately 1"/2.5cm.

Begin stockinette stitch, and work fully fashioned decreases (see Notes) each side every 8 rows 4 times, if indicated below. If no number is given, do not work these rows.

	XS	S	M	L	1X	2X	3X	4X
7	--	--	--	--	--	--	--	--
6½	--	--	--	--	--	--	--	--
6	--	--	--	--	--	--	--	--
5½	--	--	--	--	--	--	--	--
5	--	--	--	--	--	--	--	--
4½	--	--	--	--	--	--	--	--
4	--	--	--	--	--	--	--	--
3½	--	--	--	--	4	--	--	--
3	--	--	--	--	--	--	--	--

Work fully fashioned decreases each side every 10 rows __ time(s).
If no number is given, do not work these rows.

	XS	S	M	L	1X	2X	3X	4X
7	--	--	--	--	--	--	--	--
6½	--	--	--	--	--	--	--	--
6	--	--	--	--	--	--	--	--
5½	--	--	--	--	--	--	--	--
5	--	--	--	--	--	--	--	--
4½	--	--	--	--	--	--	--	--
4	--	--	--	--	--	--	--	--
3½	3	3	3	3	1	3	3	3
3	--	--	--	--	--	--	--	--

Work fully fashioned decreases each side every 12 rows once, if indicated below.
If no number is given, do not work these rows.

	XS	S	M	L	1X	2X	3X	4X
7	--	--	--	--	--	--	--	--
6½	--	--	--	--	--	--	--	--
6	--	--	--	--	--	--	--	--
5½	--	--	--	--	--	--	--	--
5	--	--	--	--	--	--	--	--
4½	--	--	--	--	--	--	--	--
4	--	--	--	--	--	--	--	--
3½	1	1	1	1	--	1	1	1
3	--	--	--	--	--	--	--	--

Work fully fashioned decreases each side every 14 rows __ times. If no number is given, do not work these rows.

	XS	S	M	L	1X	2X	3X	4X
7	--	--	--	--	--	--	--	--
6½	--	--	2	--	--	--	--	--
6	--	--	--	--	--	--	--	--
5½	--	--	--	--	--	--	--	--
5	--	--	--	--	--	--	--	--
4½	3	3	3	3	--	--	3	--
4	--	--	--	--	--	--	--	--
3½	--	--	--	--	--	--	--	--
3	--	--	--	--	--	--	--	--

Work fully fashioned decreases each side every 16 rows __ time(s).
If no number is given, do not work these rows.

	XS	S	M	L	1X	2X	3X	4X
7	7	7	7	7	--	7	7	--
6½	2	2	7	2	2	2	2	2
6	--	6	6	6	6	--	6	--
5½	1	1	1	1	1	1	1	1
5	--	--	--	5	--	--	5	--
4½	3	3	3	3	--	--	3	--
4	--	--	5	--	--	--	--	--
3½	--	--	--	--	--	--	--	--
3	3	3	3	--	--	--	--	3

Work fully fashioned decreases each side every 18 rows __ time(s).
If no number is given, do not work these rows.

	XS	S	M	L	1X	2X	3X	4X
7	2	2	2	2	6	2	2	6
6½	6	6	--	6	6	6	6	6
6	4	2	2	2	2	4	2	4
5½	6	6	6	6	6	6	6	6
5	2	2	2	2	2	2	2	2
4½	--	--	--	--	5	5	--	5
4	1	1	1	1	1	1	1	1
3½	--	--	--	--	--	--	--	--
3	1	1	1	--	--	--	--	1

Work fully fashioned decreases each side every 20 rows __ times. If no number is given, do not work these rows.

	XS	S	M	L	1X	2X	3X	4X
7	--	--	--	--	2	--	--	2
6½	--	--	--	--	--	--	--	--
6	3	--	--	--	--	3	--	3
5½	--	--	--	--	--	--	--	--
5	4	4	4	--	4	4	--	4
4½	--	--	--	--	--	--	--	--
4	4	4	--	4	4	4	4	4
3½	--	--	--	--	--	--	--	--
3	--	--	--	--	--	--	--	--

Work fully fashioned decreases each side every 22 rows 3 times, if indicated below.
If no number is given, do not work these rows.

	XS	S	M	L	1X	2X	3X	4X
7	--	--	--	--	--	--	--	--
6½	--	--	--	--	--	--	--	--
6	--	--	--	--	--	--	--	--
5½	--	--	--	--	--	--	--	--
5	--	--	--	--	--	--	--	--
4½	--	--	--	--	--	--	--	--
4	--	--	--	--	--	--	--	--
3½	--	--	--	--	--	--	--	--
3	--	--	--	3	3	3	3	--

You will now have __ stitches.

	XS	S	M	L	1X	2X	3X	4X
7	80	84	90	96	106	114	124	136
6½	76	78	82	90	98	106	116	126
6	70	72	76	82	90	98	106	116
5½	64	66	70	76	82	90	98	106
5	58	60	64	68	76	82	88	96
4½	52	54	58	62	68	74	80	88
4	46	48	50	56	60	66	72	78
3½	40	42	46	48	52	58	62	68
3	34	36	38	42	46	50	54	58

Continue even until the piece measures approximately 18½"/47cm from the beginning, or the desired length to the armhole, ending after a wrong-side row.

Shape the Cap

Work same as for the set-in classic long sleeve (page 129).

You will have __ stitches remaining.

	XS	S	M	L	1X	2X	3X	4X
7	18	18	18	18	18	18	18	18
6½	16	16	16	16	16	16	16	16
6	16	16	16	16	16	16	16	16
5½	14	14	14	14	14	14	14	14
5	12	12	12	12	12	12	12	12
4½	12	12	12	12	12	12	12	12
4	10	10	10	10	10	10	10	10
3½	8	8	8	8	8	8	8	8
3	8	8	8	8	8	8	8	8

Bind off all stitches.

Set-In—Bell Half Sleeve

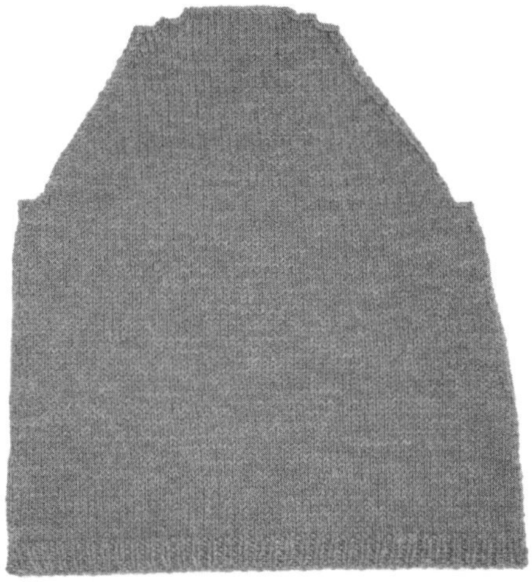

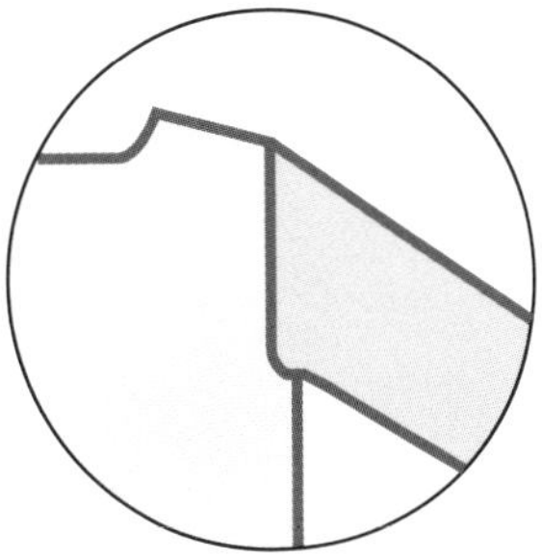
Set-In Shoulder

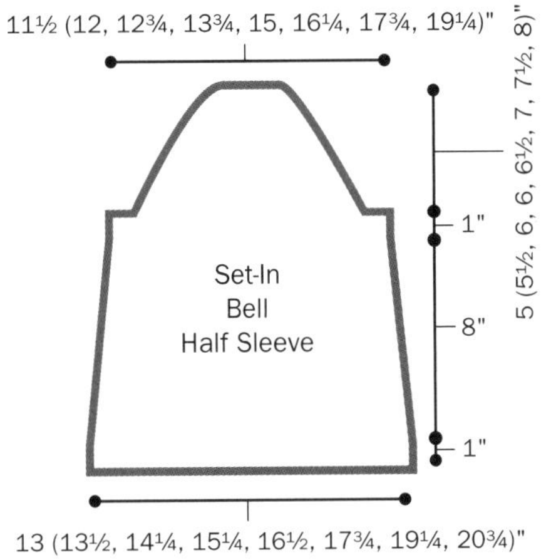
11½ (12, 12¾, 13¾, 15, 16¼, 17¾, 19¼)"
5 (5½, 6, 6, 6½, 7, 7½, 8)"
1"
8"
1"
Set-In
Bell
Half Sleeve
13 (13½, 14¼, 15¼, 16½, 17¾, 19¼, 20¾)"

Finished Measurements

	XS	S	M	L	1X	2X	3X	4X
Length from Underarm	10"/25.5cm	10"/25.5cm	10"/25.5cm	10"/25.5cm	10"/25.5cm	10"/25.5cm	10"/25.5cm	10"/25.5cm
Width at Lower Edge	13"/33cm	13½"/ 34.5cm	14¼"/36cm	15¼"/ 38.5cm	16½"/ 42cm	17¾"/45cm	19¼"/ 49cm	20¾"/ 53cm
Width at Upper Arm	11½"/29cm	12"/30.5cm	12¾"/ 32.5cm	13¾"/35cm	15"/38cm	16¼"/ 41.5cm	17¾"/ 45cm	19¼"/ 49cm

Notes

- This pattern is written for K1P1 ribbed edges. Refer to pages 213–223 for information on how to customize the edge treatment.
- For fully fashioned decreases: On right-side rows, k1, ssk, knit to the last 3 stitches, k2tog, k1; on wrong-side rows, p1, p2tog, purl to the last 3 stitches, ssp (page 255), p1.

Sleeve

Cast on __ stitches.

	XS	S	M	L	1X	2X	3X	4X
7	92	94	100	108	116	124	134	146
6½	84	88	92	100	108	116	126	134
6	78	80	86	92	100	106	116	124
5½	72	74	78	84	90	98	106	114
5	66	68	72	76	82	88	96	104
4½	58	60	64	68	74	80	86	94
4	52	54	58	62	66	72	78	84
3½	46	48	50	54	58	62	68	72
3	38	40	42	46	50	54	58	62

Begin K1P1 rib (page 215), and work even until the piece measures approximately 1"/2.5cm.

Begin stockinette stitch, and work fully fashioned decreases (see Notes) each side every 12 rows __ time(s). If no number is given, do not work these rows.

	XS	S	M	L	1X	2X	3X	4X
7	6	--	--	6	--	--	--	--
6½	--	1	1	1	1	1	1	--
6	--	--	3	3	3	--	3	--
5½	--	--	--	--	--	--	--	--
5	--	--	--	--	--	--	--	--
4½	--	--	--	--	--	--	--	--
4	--	--	4	--	--	--	--	--
3½	1	1	--	1	1	--	1	--
3	--	--	--	--	--	--	--	--

Work fully fashioned decreases each side every 14 rows __ times. If no number is given, do not work these rows.

	XS	S	M	L	1X	2X	3X	4X
7	--	4	4	--	4	4	4	4
6½	--	4	4	4	4	4	4	--
6	--	--	2	2	2	--	2	--
5½	2	2	2	2	2	2	2	2
5	4	4	4	4	--	--	4	4
4½	--	--	--	--	--	--	--	--
4	--	--	--	--	--	--	--	--
3½	2	2	--	2	2	--	2	--
3	--	--	--	--	--	--	--	--

Work fully fashioned decreases each side every 16 rows __ time(s).
If no number is given, do not work these rows.

	XS	S	M	L	1X	2X	3X	4X
7	--	1	1	--	1	1	1	1
6½	2	--	--	--	--	--	--	2
6	4	4	--	--	--	4	--	4
5½	2	2	2	2	2	2	2	2
5	--	--	--	--	--	--	--	--
4½	1	1	1	1	1	1	1	1
4	3	3	--	3	3	3	3	3
3½	--	--	--	--	--	--	--	--
3	2	2	2	2	2	2	2	2

Work fully fashioned decreases each side every 18 rows twice, if indicated below.
If no number is given, do not work these rows.

	XS	S	M	L	1X	2X	3X	4X
7	--	--	--	--	--	--	--	--
6½	2	--	--	--	--	--	--	2
6	--	--	--	--	--	--	--	--
5½	--	--	--	--	--	--	--	--
5	--	--	--	--	2	2	--	--
4½	2	2	2	2	2	2	2	2
4	--	--	--	--	--	--	--	--
3½	--	--	--	--	--	--	--	--
3	--	--	--	--	--	--	--	--

Work fully fashioned decreases each side every 20 rows __ time(s).
If no number is given, do not work these rows.

	XS	S	M	L	1X	2X	3X	4X
7	--	--	--	--	--	--	--	--
6½	--	--	--	--	--	--	--	--
6	--	--	--	--	--	--	--	--
5½	--	--	--	--	--	--	--	--
5	--	--	--	--	1	1	--	--
4½	--	--	--	--	--	--	--	--
4	--	--	--	--	--	--	--	--
3½	--	--	2	--	--	2	--	2
3	--	--	--	--	--	--	--	--

You will now have __ stitches.

	XS	S	M	L	1X	2X	3X	4X
7	80	84	90	96	106	114	124	136
6½	76	78	82	90	98	106	116	126
6	70	72	76	82	90	98	106	116
5½	64	66	70	76	82	90	98	106
5	58	60	64	68	76	82	88	96
4½	52	54	58	62	68	74	80	88
4	46	48	50	56	60	66	72	78
3½	40	42	46	48	52	58	62	68
3	34	36	38	42	46	50	54	58

Continue even until the piece measures approximately 10"/25.5cm from the beginning, or the desired length to the armhole, ending after a wrong-side row.

Shape the Cap
Work same as for the set-in classic long sleeve (page 129).

You will have __ stitches remaining.

	XS	S	M	L	1X	2X	3X	4X
7	18	18	18	18	18	18	18	18
6½	16	16	16	16	16	16	16	16
6	16	16	16	16	16	16	16	16
5½	14	14	14	14	14	14	14	14
5	12	12	12	12	12	12	12	12
4½	12	12	12	12	12	12	12	12
4	10	10	10	10	10	10	10	10
3½	8	8	8	8	8	8	8	8
3	8	8	8	8	8	8	8	8

Bind off all stitches.

Raglan Construction

Raglan—Classic Long Sleeve

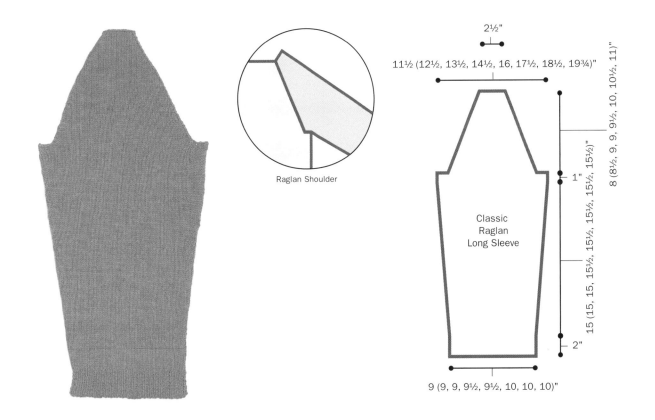

Raglan Shoulder

2½"

11½ (12½, 13½, 14½, 16, 17½, 18½, 19¾)"

8 (8½, 9, 9, 9½, 10, 10½, 11)"

1"

Classic Raglan Long Sleeve

15 (15, 15, 15½, 15½, 15½, 15½, 15½)"

2"

9 (9, 9, 9½, 9½, 10, 10, 10)"

Finished Measurements

	XS	S	M	L	1X	2X	3X	4X
Length to Underarm	18"/45.5cm	18"/45.5cm	18"/45.5cm	18½"/47cm	18½"/47cm	18½"/47cm	18½"/47cm	18½"/47cm
Width at Lower Edge	9"/23cm	9"/23cm	9"/23cm	9½"/24cm	9½"/24cm	10"/25.5cm	10"/25.5cm	10"/25.5cm
Width at Upper Arm	11½"/29cm	12½"/32cm	13½"/34.5cm	14½"/37cm	16"/40.5cm	17½"/44.5cm	18½"/47cm	19¾"/50cm

Notes

- This pattern is written for K1P1 ribbed edges. Refer to pages 213–223 for information on how to customize the edge treatment.
- For fully fashioned increases: On right-side rows, k1, M1R (page 253), knit to the last stitch, M1L (page 253), k1.
- For fully fashioned decreases: On right-side rows, k1, ssk, knit to the last 3 stitches, k2tog, k1; on wrong-side rows, p1, p2tog, purl to the last 3 stitches, ssp (page 255), p1.

Sleeve

Cast on __ stitches.

	XS	S	M	L	1X	2X	3X	4X
7	64	64	64	66	66	70	70	70
6½	58	58	58	62	62	66	66	66
6	54	54	54	58	58	60	60	60
5½	50	50	50	52	52	56	56	56
5	46	46	46	48	48	50	50	50
4½	40	40	40	42	42	46	46	46
4	36	36	36	38	38	40	40	40
3½	32	32	32	34	34	36	36	36
3	26	26	26	28	28	30	30	30

Begin K1P1 rib (page 215), and work even until the piece measures approximately 2"/5cm.

Begin stockinette stitch, and work fully fashioned increases (see Notes) each side every 4 rows __ times.
If no number is given, do not work these rows.

	XS	S	M	L	1X	2X	3X	4X
7	--	--	--	--	--	8	20	32
6½	--	--	--	--	--	6	15	27
6	--	--	--	--	--	7	16	25
5½	--	--	--	--	--	2	11	20
5	--	--	--	--	--	3	9	18
4½	--	--	--	--	--	--	7	13
4	--	--	--	--	--	--	5	14
3½	--	--	--	--	--	--	3	12
3	--	--	--	--	--	2	8	14

Work fully fashioned increases each side every 6 rows __ time(s). If no number is given, do not work these rows.

	XS	S	M	L	1X	2X	3X	4X
7	--	--	--	2	22	18	10	2
6½	--	--	--	--	18	18	12	4
6	--	--	--	--	14	16	10	4
5½	--	--	--	--	14	18	12	6
5	--	--	--	--	10	16	12	6
4½	--	--	--	--	10	14	12	8
4	--	--	--	--	6	14	12	6
3½	--	--	--	--	5	13	11	5
3	--	--	--	1	9	9	5	1

Work fully fashioned increases each side every 8 rows __ time(s). If no number is given, do not work these rows.

	XS	S	M	L	1X	2X	3X	4X
7	--	--	8	16	1	--	--	--
6½	--	--	11	14	3	--	--	--
6	--	--	10	13	5	--	--	--
5½	--	--	4	12	4	--	--	--
5	--	--	3	6	6	--	--	--
4½	--	--	1	10	5	2	--	--
4	--	--	--	4	7	1	--	--
3½	--	--	3	1	6	--	--	--
3	--	--	5	7	1	--	--	--

Work fully fashioned increases each side every 10 rows __ times. If no number is given, do not work these rows.

	XS	S	M	L	1X	2X	3X	4X
7	--	5	7	--	--	--	--	--
6½	--	8	4	2	--	--	--	--
6	--	6	4	2	--	--	--	--
5½	--	--	8	2	--	--	--	--
5	--	--	8	6	--	--	--	--
4½	--	--	9	2	--	--	--	--
4	--	--	9	6	--	--	--	--
3½	--	--	5	7	--	--	--	--
3	--	6	2	--	--	--	--	--

Work fully fashioned increases each side every 12 rows __ times. If no number is given, do not work these rows.

	XS	S	M	L	1X	2X	3X	4X
7	--	7	--	--	--	--	--	--
6½	--	4	--	--	--	--	--	--
6	--	5	--	--	--	--	--	--
5½	--	7	--	--	--	--	--	--
5	--	4	--	--	--	--	--	--
4½	--	7	--	--	--	--	--	--
4	--	4	--	--	--	--	--	--
3½	--	5	--	--	--	--	--	--
3	--	--	--	--	--	--	--	--

Work fully fashioned increases each side every 14 rows __ time(s). If no number is given, do not work these rows.

	XS	S	M	L	1X	2X	3X	4X
7	--	--	--	--	--	--	--	--
6½	--	--	--	--	--	--	--	--
6	4	--	--	--	--	--	--	--
5½	--	2	--	--	--	--	--	--
5	--	4	--	--	--	--	--	--
4½	--	1	--	--	--	--	--	--
4	--	3	--	--	--	--	--	--
3½	--	1	--	--	--	--	--	--
3	2	--	--	--	--	--	--	--

Work fully fashioned increases each side every 16 rows __ times. If no number is given, do not work these rows.

	XS	S	M	L	1X	2X	3X	4X
7	5	--	--	--	--	--	--	--
6½	8	--	--	--	--	--	--	--
6	4	--	--	--	--	--	--	--
5½	7	--	--	--	--	--	--	--
5	2	--	--	--	--	--	--	--
4½	5	--	--	--	--	--	--	--
4	--	--	--	--	--	--	--	--
3½	--	--	--	--	--	--	--	--
3	2	--	--	--	--	--	--	--

Work fully fashioned increases each side every 18 rows __ time(s). If no number is given, do not work these rows.

	XS	S	M	L	1X	2X	3X	4X
7	3	--	--	--	--	--	--	--
6½	--	--	--	--	--	--	--	--
6	--	--	--	--	--	--	--	--
5½	--	--	--	--	--	--	--	--
5	4	--	--	--	--	--	--	--
4½	1	--	--	--	--	--	--	--
4	5	--	--	--	--	--	--	--
3½	3	--	--	--	--	--	--	--
3	--	--	--	--	--	--	--	--

Work fully fashioned increases each side every 20 rows once, if indicated below.
If no number is given, do not work these rows.

	XS	S	M	L	1X	2X	3X	4X
7	--	--	--	--	--	--	--	--
6½	--	--	--	--	--	--	--	--
6	--	--	--	--	--	--	--	--
5½	--	--	--	--	--	--	--	--
5	--	--	--	--	--	--	--	--
4½	--	--	--	--	--	--	--	--
4	--	--	--	--	--	--	--	--
3½	1	--	--	--	--	--	--	--
3	--	--	--	--	--	--	--	--

You will now have __ stitches.

	XS	S	M	L	1X	2X	3X	4X
7	80	88	94	102	112	122	130	138
6½	74	82	88	94	104	114	120	128
6	70	76	82	88	96	106	112	118
5½	64	68	74	80	88	96	102	108
5	58	62	68	72	80	88	92	98
4½	52	56	60	66	72	78	84	88
4	46	50	54	58	64	70	74	80
3½	40	44	48	50	56	62	64	70
3	34	38	40	44	48	52	56	60

Continue even until the piece measures approximately 18 (18, 18, 18½, 18½, 18½, 18½, 18½)"/45.5 (45.5, 45.5, 47, 47, 47, 47, 47)cm from the beginning, or desired length to the armhole, ending after a wrong-side row.

Shape the Cap

Bind off __ stitches at the beginning of the next 2 rows.

	XS	S	M	L	1X	2X	3X	4X
7	7	7	7	7	11	11	11	11
6½	7	7	7	7	10	10	10	10
6	6	6	6	6	9	9	9	9
5½	6	6	6	6	8	8	8	8
5	5	5	5	5	8	8	8	8
4½	5	5	5	5	7	7	7	7
4	4	4	4	4	6	6	6	6
3½	4	4	4	4	6	6	6	6
3	3	3	3	3	5	5	5	5

Work fully fashioned decreases (see Notes) each side every 4 rows __ time(s).
If no number is given, do not work these rows.

	XS	S	M	L	1X	2X	3X	4X
7	11	9	8	4	6	3	1	--
6½	11	9	8	5	5	2	1	--
6	10	9	8	5	6	3	2	1
5½	10	10	9	6	5	3	2	1
5	9	9	7	5	6	4	4	2
4½	10	9	9	6	7	5	4	4
4	9	8	8	6	6	5	4	3
3½	7	6	5	4	5	3	3	1
3	5	4	4	2	3	2	1	--

Work fully fashioned decreases each side every other row __ times.

	XS	S	M	L	1X	2X	3X	4X
7	13	19	23	31	30	38	44	49
6½	11	17	21	27	29	37	41	46
6	11	15	19	25	25	33	37	41
5½	9	11	15	21	24	30	34	38
5	9	11	16	20	20	26	28	33
4½	5	8	10	16	16	21	25	27
4	5	8	10	14	15	19	22	26
3½	5	8	11	13	13	18	19	24
3	5	8	9	13	12	15	18	21

Work 1 row even, if indicated below. If no number is given, do not work this row.

	XS	S	M	L	1X	2X	3X	4X
7	--	1	1	1	--	--	1	--
6½	--	--	1	--	1	1	1	--
6	--	--	--	--	--	--	--	--
5½	--	--	--	--	1	1	1	1
5	--	--	1	1	1	--	--	1
4½	--	1	1	1	--	1	--	--
4	--	1	--	--	1	--	1	--
3½	--	1	1	1	--	--	1	1
3	--	--	--	--	--	--	--	--

You will have __ stitches remaining.

	XS	S	M	L	1X	2X	3X	4X
7	18	18	18	18	18	18	18	18
6½	16	16	16	16	16	16	16	16
6	16	16	16	16	16	16	16	16
5½	14	14	14	14	14	14	14	14
5	12	12	12	12	12	12	12	12
4½	12	12	12	12	12	12	12	12
4	10	10	10	10	10	10	10	10
3½	8	8	8	8	8	8	8	8
3	8	8	8	8	8	8	8	8

Bind off all stitches.

Raglan—Classic Three-Quarter Sleeve

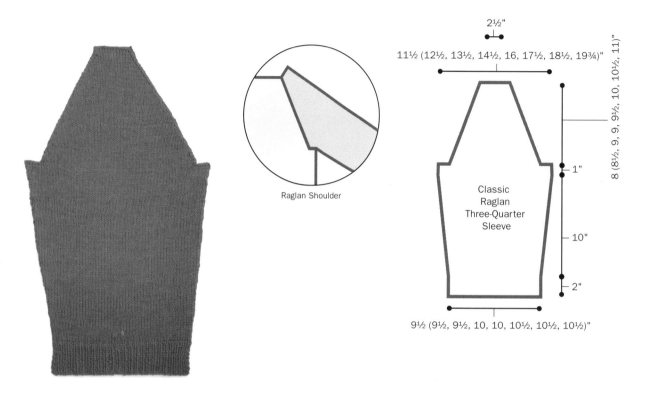

Raglan Shoulder

2½"

11½ (12½, 13½, 14½, 16, 17½, 18½, 19¾)"

8 (8½, 9, 9, 9½, 10, 10½, 11)"

1"

Classic
Raglan
Three-Quarter
Sleeve

10"

2"

9½ (9½, 9½, 10, 10, 10½, 10½, 10½)"

Finished Measurements

	XS	S	M	L	1X	2X	3X	4X
Length from Underarm	13"/33cm	13"/33cm	13"/33cm	13"/33cm	13"/33cm	13"/33cm	13"/33cm	13"/33cm
Width at Lower Edge	9½"/24cm	9½"/24cm	9½"/24cm	10"/25.5cm	10"/25.5cm	10½"/26.5cm	10½"/26.5cm	10½"/26.5cm
Width at Upper Arm	11½"/29cm	12½"/32cm	13½"/34.5cm	14½"/37cm	16"/40.5cm	17½"/44.5cm	18½"/47cm	19¾"/50cm

Notes

- This pattern is written for K1P1 ribbed edges. Refer to pages 213–223 for information on how to customize the edge treatment.
- For fully fashioned increases: On right-side rows, k1, M1R (page 253), knit to the last stitch, M1L (page 253), k1.
- For fully fashioned decreases: On right-side rows, k1, ssk, knit to the last 3 stitches, k2tog, k1; on wrong-side rows, p1, p2tog, purl to the last 3 stitches, ssp (page 255), p1.

Sleeve

Cast on __ stitches.

	XS	S	M	L	1X	2X	3X	4X
7	66	66	66	70	70	74	74	74
6½	62	62	62	66	66	68	68	68
6	58	58	58	60	60	64	64	64
5½	52	52	52	56	56	58	58	58
5	48	48	48	50	50	52	52	52
4½	42	42	42	46	46	48	48	48
4	38	38	38	40	40	42	42	42
3½	34	34	34	36	36	38	38	38
3	28	28	28	30	30	32	32	32

Begin K1P1 rib (page 215), and work even until the piece measures approximately 2"/5cm.

Begin stockinette stitch, and work fully fashioned increases (see Notes) each side every other row __ time(s).
If no number is given, do not work these rows.

	XS	S	M	L	1X	2X	3X	4X
7	--	--	--	--	--	3	11	19
6½	--	--	--	--	--	4	10	18
6	--	--	--	--	--	2	8	14
5½	--	--	--	--	--	1	7	13
5	--	--	--	--	--	1	5	11
4½	--	--	--	--	--	--	4	8
4	--	--	--	--	--	--	2	8
3½	--	--	--	--	--	--	1	7
3	--	--	--	--	--	--	4	8

Work fully fashioned increases each side every 4 rows __ time(s). If no number is given, do not work these rows.

	XS	S	M	L	1X	2X	3X	4X
7	--	--	--	3	18	21	17	13
6½	--	--	--	--	15	19	16	12
6	--	--	--	2	14	19	16	13
5½	--	--	--	--	11	18	15	12
5	--	--	--	--	10	17	15	12
4½	--	--	--	--	7	13	14	12
4	--	--	--	--	6	12	14	11
3½	--	--	--	--	5	11	12	9
3	--	--	--	1	7	10	8	6

Work fully fashioned increases each side every 6 rows __ time(s). If no number is given, do not work these rows.

	XS	S	M	L	1X	2X	3X	4X
7	--	--	11	13	3	--	--	--
6½	--	--	10	14	4	--	--	--
6	--	--	8	12	4	--	--	--
5½	--	--	7	11	5	--	--	--
5	--	--	5	9	5	--	--	--
4½	--	--	4	8	6	2	--	--
4	--	--	2	6	6	2	--	--
3½	--	--	3	3	5	1	--	--
3	--	--	4	6	2	--	--	--

Work fully fashioned increases each side every 8 rows __ time(s). If no number is given, do not work these rows.

	XS	S	M	L	1X	2X	3X	4X
7	--	10	3	--	--	--	--	--
6½	--	8	3	--	--	--	--	--
6	--	5	4	--	--	--	--	--
5½	--	3	4	1	--	--	--	--
5	--	--	5	2	--	--	--	--
4½	--	3	5	2	--	--	--	--
4	--	--	6	3	--	--	--	--
3½	--	--	4	4	--	--	--	--
3	--	5	2	--	--	--	--	--

Work fully fashioned increases each side every 10 rows __ time(s). If no number is given, do not work these rows.

	XS	S	M	L	1X	2X	3X	4X
7	--	1	--	--	--	--	--	--
6½	--	2	--	--	--	--	--	--
6	--	4	--	--	--	--	--	--
5½	--	5	--	--	--	--	--	--
5	--	7	--	--	--	--	--	--
4½	--	4	--	--	--	--	--	--
4	--	6	--	--	--	--	--	--
3½	--	5	--	--	--	--	--	--
3	--	--	--	--	--	--	--	--

Work fully fashioned increases each side every 12 rows __ time(s). If no number is given, do not work these rows.

	XS	S	M	L	1X	2X	3X	4X
7	4	--	--	--	--	--	--	--
6½	--	--	--	--	--	--	--	--
6	2	--	--	--	--	--	--	--
5½	5	--	--	--	--	--	--	--
5	--	--	--	--	--	--	--	--
4½	3	--	--	--	--	--	--	--
4	--	--	--	--	--	--	--	--
3½	--	--	--	--	--	--	--	--
3	1	--	--	--	--	--	--	--

Work fully fashioned increases each side every 14 rows __ time(s). If no number is given, do not work these rows.

	XS	S	M	L	1X	2X	3X	4X
7	3	--	--	--	--	--	--	--
6½	6	--	--	--	--	--	--	--
6	4	--	--	--	--	--	--	--
5½	1	--	--	--	--	--	--	--
5	5	--	--	--	--	--	--	--
4½	2	--	--	--	--	--	--	--
4	2	--	--	--	--	--	--	--
3½	--	--	--	--	--	--	--	--
3	2	--	--	--	--	--	--	--

Work fully fashioned increases each side every 16 rows twice, if indicated below.
If no number is given, do not work these rows.

	XS	S	M	L	1X	2X	3X	4X
7	--	--	--	--	--	--	--	--
6½	--	--	--	--	--	--	--	--
6	--	--	--	--	--	--	--	--
5½	--	--	--	--	--	--	--	--
5	--	--	--	--	--	--	--	--
4½	--	--	--	--	--	--	--	--
4	2	--	--	--	--	--	--	--
3½	2	--	--	--	--	--	--	--
3	--	--	--	--	--	--	--	--

Work fully fashioned increases each side every 18 rows once, if indicated below.
If no number is given, do not work these rows.

	XS	S	M	L	1X	2X	3X	4X
7	--	--	--	--	--	--	--	--
6½	--	--	--	--	--	--	--	--
6	--	--	--	--	--	--	--	--
5½	--	--	--	--	--	--	--	--
5	--	--	--	--	--	--	--	--
4½	--	--	--	--	--	--	--	--
4	--	--	--	--	--	--	--	--
3½	1	--	--	--	--	--	--	--
3	--	--	--	--	--	--	--	--

You will now have __ stitches.

	XS	S	M	L	1X	2X	3X	4X
7	80	88	94	102	112	122	130	138
6½	74	82	88	94	104	114	120	128
6	70	76	82	88	96	106	112	118
5½	64	68	74	80	88	96	102	108
5	58	62	68	72	80	88	92	98
4½	52	56	60	66	72	78	84	88
4	46	50	54	58	64	70	74	80
3½	40	44	48	50	56	62	64	70
3	34	38	40	44	48	52	56	60

Continue even until the piece measures approximately 13"/33cm from the beginning, or desired length to the armhole, ending after a wrong-side row.

Shape the Cap

Work same as for the raglan classic long sleeve (page 159).

You will have __ stitches remaining.

	XS	S	M	L	1X	2X	3X	4X
7	18	18	18	18	18	18	18	18
6½	16	16	16	16	16	16	16	16
6	16	16	16	16	16	16	16	16
5½	14	14	14	14	14	14	14	14
5	12	12	12	12	12	12	12	12
4½	12	12	12	12	12	12	12	12
4	10	10	10	10	10	10	10	10
3½	8	8	8	8	8	8	8	8
3	8	8	8	8	8	8	8	8

Bind off all stitches.

Raglan—Bell Long Sleeve

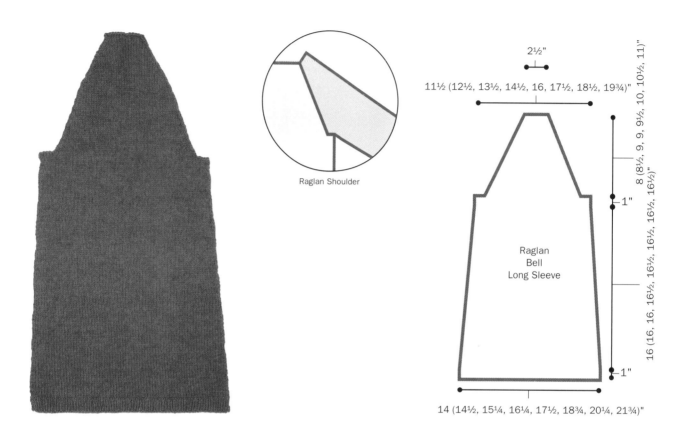

Raglan Shoulder

2½"

11½ (12½, 13½, 14½, 16, 17½, 18½, 19¾)"

8 (8½, 9, 9, 9½, 10, 10½, 11)"

1"

Raglan
Bell
Long Sleeve

16 (16, 16, 16½, 16½, 16½, 16½, 16½)"

1"

14 (14½, 15¼, 16¼, 17½, 18¾, 20¼, 21¾)"

Finished Measurements

	XS	S	M	L	1X	2X	3X	4X
Length to Underarm	18"/45.5cm	18"/45.5cm	18"/45.5cm	18½"/47cm	18½"/47cm	18½"/47cm	18½"/47cm	18½"/47cm
Width at Lower Edge	14"/35.5cm	14½"/37cm	15¼/38.5cm	16¼"/41.5cm	17½"/44.5cm	18¾"/47.5cm	20¼"/51.5cm	21¾"/55cm
Width at Upper Arm	11½"/29cm	12½"/32cm	13½"/34.5cm	14½"/37cm	16"/40.5cm	17½"/44.5cm	18½"/47cm	19¾"/50cm

Notes
- This pattern is written for K1P1 ribbed edges. Refer to pages 213–223 for information on how to customize the edge treatment.
- For fully fashioned decreases: On right-side rows, k1, ssk, knit to the last 3 stitches, k2tog, k1; on wrong-side rows, p1, p2tog, purl to the last 3 stitches, ssp (page 255), p1.

Sleeve

Cast on __ stitches.

	XS	S	M	L	1X	2X	3X	4X
7	98	102	108	114	122	132	142	152
6½	92	94	100	106	114	122	132	142
6	84	88	92	98	106	112	122	130
5½	78	80	84	90	96	104	112	120
5	70	72	76	82	88	94	102	108
4½	64	66	70	74	78	84	92	98
4	56	58	62	66	70	76	82	88
3½	48	50	54	56	62	66	70	76
3	42	44	46	48	52	56	60	66

Begin K1P1 rib (page 215), and work even until the piece measures approximately 1"/2.5cm.

Begin stockinette stitch, and work fully fashioned decreases (see Notes) each side every 14 rows 4 times, if indicated below. If no number is given, do not work these rows.

	XS	S	M	L	1X	2X	3X	4X
7	--	--	--	--	--	--	--	--
6½	4	--	--	--	--	--	--	--
6	--	--	--	--	--	--	--	--
5½	--	--	--	--	--	--	--	--
5	--	--	--	--	--	--	--	--
4½	--	--	--	--	--	--	--	--
4	--	--	--	--	--	--	--	--
3½	--	--	--	--	--	--	--	--
3	--	--	--	--	--	--	--	--

Work fully fashioned decreases each side every 16 rows __ times. If no number is given, do not work these rows.

	XS	S	M	L	1X	2X	3X	4X
7	9	--	--	--	--	--	--	--
6½	5	--	--	--	--	--	--	--
6	--	--	--	--	--	--	--	--
5½	3	--	--	--	--	--	--	--
5	--	--	--	--	--	--	--	--
4½	2	--	--	--	--	--	--	--
4	--	--	--	--	--	--	--	--
3½	--	--	--	--	--	--	--	--
3	4	--	--	--	--	--	--	--

Work fully fashioned decreases each side every 18 rows __ times. If no number is given, do not work these rows.

	XS	S	M	L	1X	2X	3X	4X
7	--	--	--	--	--	--	--	--
6½	--	--	--	--	--	--	--	--
6	6	--	--	--	--	--	--	--
5½	4	--	--	--	--	--	--	--
5	4	--	--	--	--	--	--	--
4½	4	--	--	--	--	--	--	--
4	2	--	--	--	--	--	--	--
3½	--	--	--	--	--	--	--	--
3	--	--	--	--	--	--	--	--

Work fully fashioned decreases each side every 20 rows __ time(s).
If no number is given, do not work these rows.

	XS	S	M	L	1X	2X	3X	4X
7	--	5	5	--	--	--	--	3
6½	--	--	--	--	--	--	--	7
6	1	2	--	--	--	--	--	--
5½	--	6	--	--	--	--	--	4
5	2	--	--	--	--	--	--	--
4½	--	3	3	--	--	--	--	1
4	3	--	--	--	--	--	--	--
3½	4	--	--	--	--	--	--	--
3	--	1	1	--	--	--	--	--

Work fully fashioned decreases each side every 22 rows __ times. If no number is given, do not work these rows.

	XS	S	M	L	1X	2X	3X	4X
7	--	2	2	--	--	--	--	4
6½	--	4	4	2	--	--	2	--
6	--	4	--	--	--	--	--	6
5½	--	--	--	--	--	--	--	2
5	--	4	--	2	--	--	2	2
4½	--	2	2	--	--	--	--	4
4	--	--	--	--	--	--	--	--
3½	--	--	--	--	--	--	--	--
3	--	2	2	--	--	--	--	3

Work fully fashioned decreases each side every 24 rows __ time(s).
If no number is given, do not work these rows.

	XS	S	M	L	1X	2X	3X	4X
7	--	--	--	5	--	--	5	--
6½	--	2	2	4	--	--	4	--
6	--	--	1	--	--	--	--	--
5½	--	--	5	3	--	--	3	--
5	--	1	--	3	--	--	3	3
4½	--	--	--	--	--	--	--	--
4	--	4	4	3	--	--	3	3
3½	--	--	--	--	--	--	--	--
3	--	--	--	--	--	--	--	--

Work fully fashioned decreases each side every 26 rows __ time(s).
If no number is given, do not work these rows.

	XS	S	M	L	1X	2X	3X	4X
7	--	--	--	--	--	--	--	--
6½	--	--	--	--	--	--	--	--
6	--	--	4	4	4	--	4	--
5½	--	--	--	2	--	--	2	--
5	--	--	--	--	--	--	--	--
4½	--	--	--	2	--	--	2	--
4	--	--	--	1	--	--	1	1
3½	--	2	2	1	1	--	1	1
3	--	--	--	--	--	--	--	--

Work fully fashioned decreases each side every 28 rows __ time(s).
If no number is given, do not work these rows.

	XS	S	M	L	1X	2X	3X	4X
7	--	--	--	1	1	1	1	--
6½	--	--	--	--	5	--	--	--
6	--	--	--	1	1	--	1	--
5½	--	--	--	--	--	--	--	--
5	--	--	4	--	2	--	--	--
4½	--	--	--	2	--	--	2	--
4	--	--	--	--	--	--	--	--
3½	--	1	1	2	2	--	2	2
3	--	--	--	--	--	--	--	--

Work fully fashioned decreases each side every 30 rows __ times. If no number is given, do not work these rows.

	XS	S	M	L	1X	2X	3X	4X
7	--	--	--	--	4	4	--	--
6½	--	--	--	--	--	--	--	--
6	--	--	--	--	--	--	--	--
5½	--	--	--	--	2	2	--	--
5	--	--	--	--	2	--	--	--
4½	--	--	--	--	--	--	--	--
4	--	--	--	--	--	--	--	--
3½	--	--	--	--	--	--	--	--
3	--	--	--	--	--	--	--	--

Work fully fashioned decreases each side every 32 rows __ time(s).
If no number is given, do not work these rows.

	XS	S	M	L	1X	2X	3X	4X
7	--	--	--	--	--	--	--	--
6½	--	--	--	--	--	--	--	--
6	--	--	--	--	--	--	--	--
5½	--	--	--	--	2	2	--	--
5	--	--	--	--	--	--	--	--
4½	--	--	--	--	--	--	--	--
4	--	--	--	--	2	2	--	--
3½	--	--	--	--	--	--	--	--
3	--	--	--	1	1	1	1	--

Work fully fashioned decreases each side every 34 rows once; if indicated below.
If no number is given, do not work these rows.

	XS	S	M	L	1X	2X	3X	4X
7	--	--	--	--	--	--	--	--
6½	--	--	--	--	--	2	--	--
6	--	--	--	--	--	--	--	--
5½	--	--	--	--	--	--	--	--
5	--	--	--	--	--	--	--	--
4½	--	--	--	--	--	--	--	--
4	--	--	--	--	1	1	--	--
3½	--	--	--	--	--	--	--	--
3	--	--	--	1	1	1	1	--

Work fully fashioned decreases each side every 36 rows __ times. If no number is given, do not work these rows.

	XS	S	M	L	1X	2X	3X	4X
7	--	--	--	--	--	--	--	--
6½	--	--	--	--	--	2	--	--
6	--	--	--	--	--	--	--	--
5½	--	--	--	--	--	--	--	--
5	--	--	--	--	--	--	--	--
4½	--	--	--	--	3	3	--	--
4	--	--	--	--	--	--	--	--
3½	--	--	--	--	--	--	--	--
3	--	--	--	--	--	--	--	--

Work fully fashioned decreases each side every 38 rows twice, if indicated below.
If no number is given, do not work these rows.

	XS	S	M	L	1X	2X	3X	4X
7	--	--	--	--	--	--	--	--
6½	--	--	--	--	--	--	--	--
6	--	--	--	--	--	--	--	--
5½	--	--	--	--	--	--	--	--
5	--	--	--	--	--	2	--	--
4½	--	--	--	--	--	--	--	--
4	--	--	--	--	--	--	--	--
3½	--	--	--	--	--	--	--	--
3	--	--	--	--	--	--	--	--

Work fully fashioned decreases each side every 40 rows once, if indicated below.
If no number is given, do not work these rows.

	XS	S	M	L	1X	2X	3X	4X
7	--	--	--	--	--	--	--	--
6½	--	--	--	--	--	--	--	--
6	--	--	--	--	--	--	--	--
5½	--	--	--	--	--	--	--	--
5	--	--	--	--	--	1	--	--
4½	--	--	--	--	--	--	--	--
4	--	--	--	--	--	--	--	--
3½	--	--	--	--	--	1	--	--
3	--	--	--	--	--	--	--	--

Work fully fashioned decreases each side every 42 rows once, if indicated below.
If no number is given, do not work these rows.

	XS	S	M	L	1X	2X	3X	4X
7	--	--	--	--	--	--	--	--
6½	--	--	--	--	--	--	--	--
6	--	--	--	--	--	--	--	--
5½	--	--	--	--	--	--	--	--
5	--	--	--	--	--	--	--	--
4½	--	--	--	--	--	--	--	--
4	--	--	--	--	--	--	--	--
3½	--	--	--	--	--	1	--	--
3	--	--	--	--	--	--	--	--

Work fully fashioned decreases each side every 44 rows __ time(s).
If no number is given, do not work these rows.

	XS	S	M	L	1X	2X	3X	4X
7	--	--	--	--	--	--	--	--
6½	--	--	--	--	--	--	--	--
6	--	--	--	--	--	3	--	--
5½	--	--	--	--	--	--	--	--
5	--	--	--	--	--	--	--	--
4½	--	--	--	--	--	--	--	--
4	--	--	--	--	--	--	--	--
3½	--	--	--	--	--	--	--	--
3	--	--	--	--	--	--	--	--

You will now have __ stitches.

	XS	S	M	L	1X	2X	3X	4X
7	80	88	94	102	112	122	130	138
6½	74	82	88	94	104	114	120	128
6	70	76	82	88	96	106	112	118
5½	64	68	74	80	88	96	102	108
5	58	62	68	72	80	88	92	98
4½	52	56	60	66	72	78	84	88
4	46	50	54	58	64	70	74	80
3½	40	44	48	50	56	62	64	70
3	34	38	40	44	48	52	56	60

Continue even until the piece measures approximately 18 (18, 18, 18½, 18½, 18½, 18½, 18½)"/45.5 (45.5, 45.5, 47, 47, 47, 47, 47)cm from the beginning, or desired length to the armhole, ending after a wrong-side row.

Shape the Cap

Work same as for the raglan classic long sleeve (page 159).

You will have __ stitches remaining.

	XS	S	M	L	1X	2X	3X	4X
7	18	18	18	18	18	18	18	18
6½	16	16	16	16	16	16	16	16
6	16	16	16	16	16	16	16	16
5½	14	14	14	14	14	14	14	14
5	12	12	12	12	12	12	12	12
4½	12	12	12	12	12	12	12	12
4	10	10	10	10	10	10	10	10
3½	8	8	8	8	8	8	8	8
3	8	8	8	8	8	8	8	8

Bind off all stitches.

Raglan—Bell Half Sleeve

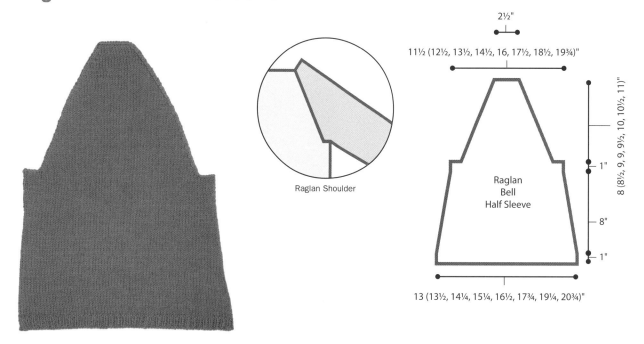

Raglan Shoulder

2½"

11½ (12½, 13½, 14½, 16, 17½, 18½, 19¾)"

Raglan
Bell
Half Sleeve

8 (8½, 9, 9, 9½, 10, 10½, 11)"

1"

8"

1"

13 (13½, 14¼, 15¼, 16½, 17¾, 19¼, 20¾)"

Finished Measurements

	XS	S	M	L	1X	2X	3X	4X
Length from Underarm	10"/25.5cm	10"/25.5cm	10"/25.5cm	10"/25.5cm	10"/25.5cm	10"/25.5cm	10"/25.5cm	10"/25.5cm
Width at Lower Edge	13"/33cm	13½"/34.5cm	14¼"/36cm	15¼"/38.5cm	16½"/42cm	17¾"/45cm	19¼"/49cm	20¾"/53cm
Width at Upper Arm	11½"/29cm	12½"/31.5cm	13½"/32cm	14½"/37cm	16"/40.5cm	17½"/44.5cm	18½"/47cm	19¾"/50cm

Notes

- This pattern is written for K1P1 ribbed edges. Refer to pages 213–23 for information on how to customize the edge treatment.
- For fully fashioned decreases: On right-side rows, k1, ssk, knit to the last 3 stitches, k2tog, k1; on wrong-side rows, p1, p2tog, purl to the last 3 stitches, ssp (page 255), p1.

Sleeve

Cast on __ stitches.

	XS	S	M	L	1X	2X	3X	4X
7	92	94	100	108	116	124	134	146
6½	84	88	92	100	106	116	126	134
6	78	80	86	92	100	106	116	124
5½	72	74	78	84	90	98	106	114
5	66	68	72	76	82	88	96	104
4½	58	60	64	68	74	80	86	94
4	52	54	58	62	66	72	78	84
3½	46	48	50	54	58	62	68	72
3	38	40	42	46	50	54	58	62

Begin K1P1 rib (page 215), and work even until the piece measures approximately 1"/2.5cm.

Begin stockinette stitch, and work fully fashioned decreases (see Notes) each side every 12 rows __ time(s).
If no number is given, do not work these rows.

	XS	S	M	L	1X	2X	3X	4X
7	6	--	--	--	--	--	--	--
6½	1	--	--	--	--	--	--	--
6	--	--	--	--	--	--	--	--
5½	--	--	--	--	--	--	--	--
5	--	--	--	--	--	--	--	--
4½	--	--	--	--	--	--	--	--
4	--	--	--	--	--	--	--	--
3½	1	--	--	--	--	--	--	--
3	--	--	--	--	--	--	--	--

Work fully fashioned decreases each side every 14 rows __ times. If no number is given, do not work these rows.

	XS	S	M	L	1X	2X	3X	4X
7	--	--	--	--	--	--	--	--
6½	4	--	--	--	--	--	--	--
6	--	--	--	--	--	--	--	--
5½	--	--	--	--	--	--	--	--
5	4	--	--	--	--	--	--	--
4½	--	--	--	--	--	--	--	--
4	--	--	--	--	--	--	--	--
3½	2	--	--	--	--	--	--	--
3	--	--	--	--	--	--	--	--

Work fully fashioned decreases each side every 16 rows __ time(s).
If no number is given, do not work these rows.

	XS	S	M	L	1X	2X	3X	4X
7	--	--	--	--	--	--	--	--
6½	--	--	--	--	--	--	--	--
6	4	--	--	--	--	--	--	--
5½	4	--	--	--	--	--	--	--
5	--	--	--	--	--	--	--	--
4½	1	--	--	--	--	--	--	1
4	3	--	--	--	--	--	--	--
3½	--	--	--	--	--	--	--	--
3	2	--	--	--	--	--	--	--

Work fully fashioned decreases each side every 18 rows __ times. If no number is given, do not work these rows.

	XS	S	M	L	1X	2X	3X	4X
7	--	--	--	--	--	--	--	4
6½	--	--	--	--	--	--	--	--
6	--	--	--	--	--	--	--	--
5½	--	--	--	--	--	--	--	--
5	--	2	--	--	--	--	--	2
4½	2	--	--	--	--	--	--	2
4	--	--	--	--	--	--	--	--
3½	--	--	--	--	--	--	--	--
3	--	--	--	--	--	--	--	--

Work fully fashioned decreases each side every 20 rows __ time(s).
If no number is given, do not work these rows.

	XS	S	M	L	1X	2X	3X	4X
7	--	--	--	--	--	--	--	--
6½	--	--	--	--	--	--	--	--
6	--	--	--	--	--	--	--	1
5½	--	3	--	--	--	--	--	3
5	--	1	--	--	--	--	--	1
4½	--	--	--	--	--	--	--	--
4	--	--	--	--	--	--	--	--
3½	--	2	--	2	--	--	2	--
3	--	--	--	--	--	--	--	--

Work fully fashioned decreases each side every 22 rows twice, if indicated below.
If no number is given, do not work these rows.

	XS	S	M	L	1X	2X	3X	4X
7	--	--	--	--	--	--	--	--
6½	--	2	--	2	--	--	2	2
6	--	--	--	--	--	--	--	2
5½	--	--	--	--	--	--	--	--
5	--	--	--	--	--	--	--	--
4½	--	--	--	--	--	--	--	--
4	--	--	--	--	--	--	--	--
3½	--	--	--	--	--	--	--	--
3	--	--	--	--	--	--	--	--

Work fully fashioned decreases each side every 24 rows __ time(s).
If no number is given, do not work these rows.

	XS	S	M	L	1X	2X	3X	4X
7	--	3	3	3	--	--	--	--
6½	--	1	--	1	--	--	1	1
6	--	--	--	--	--	--	--	--
5½	--	--	--	--	--	--	--	--
5	--	--	--	--	--	--	--	--
4½	--	--	--	--	--	--	--	--
4	--	2	2	2	--	--	2	2
3½	--	--	--	--	--	--	--	--
3	--	--	--	--	--	--	--	--

Work fully fashioned decreases each side every 26 rows twice, if indicated below.
If no number is given, do not work these rows.

	XS	S	M	L	1X	2X	3X	4X
7	--	--	--	--	--	--	--	--
6½	--	--	--	--	--	--	--	--
6	--	--	--	--	--	--	--	--
5½	--	--	--	--	--	--	--	--
5	--	--	--	--	--	--	--	--
4½	--	2	2	--	--	--	--	--
4	--	--	--	--	--	--	--	--
3½	--	--	--	--	--	--	--	--
3	--	--	--	--	--	--	--	--

Work fully fashioned decreases each side every 28 rows twice, if indicated below.
If no number is given, do not work these rows.

	XS	S	M	L	1X	2X	3X	4X
7	--	--	--	--	--	--	--	--
6½	--	--	--	--	--	--	--	--
6	--	--	--	--	--	--	--	--
5½	--	--	--	--	--	--	--	--
5	--	--	2	2	--	--	2	--
4½	--	--	--	--	--	--	--	--
4	--	--	--	--	--	--	--	--
3½	--	--	--	--	--	--	--	--
3	--	--	--	--	--	--	--	--

Work fully fashioned decreases each side every 30 rows twice, if indicated below.
If no number is given, do not work these rows.

	XS	S	M	L	1X	2X	3X	4X
7	--	--	--	--	--	--	--	--
6½	--	--	--	--	--	--	--	--
6	--	--	--	--	--	--	--	--
5½	--	--	2	2	--	--	2	--
5	--	--	--	--	--	--	--	--
4½	--	--	--	--	--	--	--	--
4	--	--	--	--	--	--	--	--
3½	--	--	--	--	--	--	--	--
3	--	--	--	--	--	--	--	--

Work fully fashioned decreases each side every 32 rows __ time(s).
If no number is given, do not work these rows.

	XS	S	M	L	1X	2X	3X	4X
7	--	--	--	--	--	--	--	--
6½	--	--	--	--	--	--	--	--
6	--	2	2	2	2	--	2	--
5½	--	--	--	--	--	--	--	--
5	--	--	--	--	--	--	--	--
4½	--	--	--	--	--	--	--	--
4	--	--	--	--	--	--	--	--
3½	--	--	--	--	--	--	--	--
3	--	1	1	1	1	1	1	1

Work fully fashioned decreases each side every 34 rows twice, if indicated below.
If no number is given, do not work these rows.

	XS	S	M	L	1X	2X	3X	4X
7	--	--	--	--	--	--	--	--
6½	--	--	2	--	--	--	--	--
6	--	--	--	--	--	--	--	--
5½	--	--	--	--	--	--	--	--
5	--	--	--	--	--	--	--	--
4½	--	--	--	--	--	--	--	--
4	--	--	--	--	--	--	--	--
3½	--	--	--	--	--	--	--	--
3	--	--	--	--	--	--	--	--

Work fully fashioned decreases each side every 36 rows twice, if indicated below.
If no number is given, do not work these rows.

	XS	S	M	L	1X	2X	3X	4X
7	--	--	--	--	2	--	2	--
6½	--	--	--	--	--	--	--	--
6	--	--	--	--	--	--	--	--
5½	--	--	--	--	--	--	--	--
5	--	--	--	--	--	--	--	--
4½	--	--	--	--	--	--	--	--
4	--	--	--	--	--	--	--	--
3½	--	--	--	--	--	--	--	--
3	--	--	--	--	--	--	--	--

Work fully fashioned decreases each side every 40 rows once, if indicated below.
If no number is given, do not work these rows.

	XS	S	M	L	1X	2X	3X	4X
7	--	--	--	--	--	--	--	--
6½	--	--	--	--	--	--	--	--
6	--	--	--	--	--	--	--	--
5½	--	--	--	--	--	--	--	--
5	--	--	--	--	--	--	--	--
4½	--	--	--	--	--	--	--	--
4	--	--	--	--	--	--	--	--
3½	--	--	1	--	1	--	--	1
3	--	--	--	--	--	--	--	--

Work fully fashioned decreases each side every 48 rows once, if indicated below.
If no number is given, do not work these rows.

	XS	S	M	L	1X	2X	3X	4X
7								
6½								
6								
5½								
5								
4½								
4					1	1		
3½								
3								

Work fully fashioned decreases each side every 52 rows once, if indicated below.
If no number is given, do not work these rows.

	XS	S	M	L	1X	2X	3X	4X
7								
6½								
6								
5½								
5								
4½				1	1	1	1	
4								
3½								
3								

Work fully fashioned decreases each side every 56 rows once, if indicated below.
If no number is given, do not work these rows.

	XS	S	M	L	1X	2X	3X	4X
7								
6½								
6								
5½								
5					1			
4½								
4								
3½								
3								

Work fully fashioned decreases each side every 60 rows once, if indicated below.
If no number is given, do not work these rows.

	XS	S	M	L	1X	2X	3X	4X
7								
6½								
6								
5½					1	1		
5								
4½								
4								
3½								
3								

Work fully fashioned decreases each side every 68 rows once, if indicated below.
If no number is given, do not work these rows.

	XS	S	M	L	1X	2X	3X	4X
7								
6½				1		1		
6								
5½								
5								
4½								
4								
3½								
3								

Work fully fashioned decreases each side every 72 rows once, if indicated below.
If no number is given, do not work these rows.

	XS	S	M	L	1X	2X	3X	4X
7						1		
6½								
6								
5½								
5								
4½								
4								
3½								
3								

You will now have __ stitches.

	XS	S	M	L	1X	2X	3X	4X
7	80	88	94	102	112	122	130	138
6½	74	82	88	94	104	114	120	128
6	70	76	82	88	96	106	112	118
5½	64	68	74	80	88	96	102	108
5	58	62	68	72	80	88	92	98
4½	52	56	60	66	72	78	84	88
4	46	50	54	58	64	70	74	80
3½	40	44	48	50	56	62	64	70
3	34	38	40	44	48	52	56	60

Continue even until the piece measures approximately 10"/25.5cm from the beginning, or the desired length to the underarm, ending after a wrong-side row.

Shape the Cap

Work same as for the raglan classic long sleeve (page 159).

You will have __ stitches remaining.

	XS	S	M	L	1X	2X	3X	4X
7	18	18	18	18	18	18	18	18
6½	16	16	16	16	16	16	16	16
6	16	16	16	16	16	16	16	16
5½	14	14	14	14	14	14	14	14
5	12	12	12	12	12	12	12	12
4½	12	12	12	12	12	12	12	12
4	10	10	10	10	10	10	10	10
3½	8	8	8	8	8	8	8	8
3	8	8	8	8	8	8	8	8

Bind off all stitches.

Saddle Shoulder Construction

Saddle Shoulder—Classic Long Sleeve

Saddle Shoulder

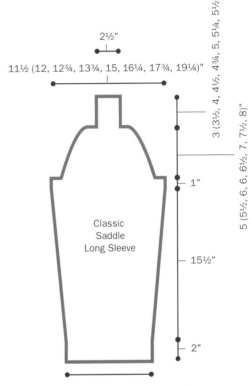

2½"

11½ (12, 12¾, 13¾, 15, 16¼, 17¾, 19¼)"

3 (3½, 4, 4½, 4¾, 5, 5¼, 5½)"

1"

Classic
Saddle
Long Sleeve

5 (5½, 6, 6, 6½, 7, 7½, 8)"

15½"

2"

9½ (9½, 9½, 9½, 9½, 10, 10, 10)"

Finished Measurements

	XS	S	M	L	1X	2X	3X	4X
Length from Underarm	18½"/47cm	18½"/47cm	18½"/47cm	18½"/47cm	18½"/47cm	18½"/47cm	18½"/47cm	18½"/47cm
Width at Cuff	9½"/24cm	9½"/24cm	9½"/24cm	9½"/24cm	9½"/24cm	10"/25.5cm	10"/25.5cm	10"/25.5cm
Width at Upper Arm	11½"/29cm	12"/30.5cm	12¾"/32.5cm	13¾"/35cm	15"/38cm	16¼"/41.5cm	17¾"/45cm	19¼"/49cm

Notes

- This pattern is written for K1P1 ribbed edges. Refer to pages 213–223 for information on how to customize the edge treatment.
- For fully fashioned decreases: On right-side rows, k1, ssk, knit to the last 3 stitches, k2tog, k1; on wrong-side rows, p1, p2tog, purl to the last 3 stitches, ssp (page 255), p1.
- For fully fashioned increases: On right-side rows, k1, M1R (page 253), knit to the last stitch, M1L (page 253), k1.

Sleeve

Cast on __ stitches.

	XS	S	M	L	1X	2X	3X	4X
7	64	64	64	66	66	70	70	70
6½	58	58	58	62	62	66	66	66
6	54	54	54	58	58	60	60	60
5½	50	50	50	52	52	56	56	56
5	44	44	44	48	48	50	50	50
4½	40	40	40	42	42	46	46	46
4	36	36	36	38	38	40	40	40
3½	32	32	32	34	34	36	36	36
3	28	28	28	28	28	30	30	30

Work same as for the set-in classic long sleeve (page 129) until the piece measures approximately 18½"/47cm from the beginning, or desired length to the armhole, ending after a wrong-side row.

You will now have __ stitches.

	XS	S	M	L	1X	2X	3X	4X
7	80	84	90	96	106	114	124	136
6½	76	78	82	90	98	106	116	126
6	70	72	76	82	90	98	106	116
5½	64	66	70	76	82	90	98	106
5	58	60	64	68	76	82	88	96
4½	52	54	58	62	68	74	80	88
4	46	48	50	56	60	66	72	78
3½	40	42	46	48	52	58	62	68
3	34	36	38	42	46	50	54	58

Shape the Cap

Work same as for the set-in classic long sleeve (page 129).

You will have __ stitches remaining.

	XS	S	M	L	1X	2X	3X	4X
7	18	18	18	18	18	18	18	18
6½	16	16	16	16	16	16	16	16
6	16	16	16	16	16	16	16	16
5½	14	14	14	14	14	14	14	14
5	12	12	12	12	12	12	12	12
4½	12	12	12	12	12	12	12	12
4	10	10	10	10	10	10	10	10
3½	8	8	8	8	8	8	8	8
3	8	8	8	8	8	8	8	8

Saddle

Continue even on these remaining saddle stitches for 3 (3½, 4, 4½, 4¾, 5, 5¼, 5½)"/7.5 (9, 10, 11.5, 12, 12.5, 13.5, 14)cm.

Bind off all stitches.

Saddle Shoulder Classic Three-Quarter Sleeve

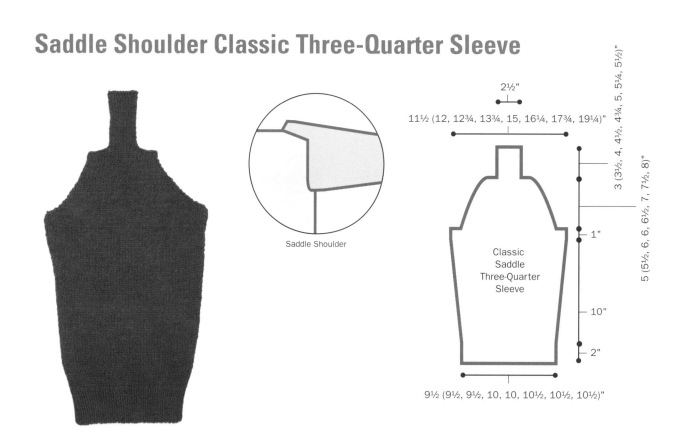

Saddle Shoulder

2½"

11½ (12, 12¾, 13¾, 15, 16¼, 17¾, 19¼)"

3 (3½, 4, 4½, 4¾, 5, 5¼, 5½)"

5 (5½, 6, 6, 6½, 7, 7½, 8)"

1"

Classic
Saddle
Three-Quarter
Sleeve

10"

2"

9½ (9½, 9½, 10, 10, 10½, 10½, 10½)"

Finished Measurements

	XS	S	M	L	1X	2X	3X	4X
Length to Underarm	13"/33cm	13"/33cm	13"/33cm	13"/33cm	13"/33cm	13"/33cm	13"/33cm	13"/33cm
Width at Lower Edge	9½"/24cm	9½"/24cm	9½"/24cm	10"/25.5cm	10"/25.5cm	10½"/26.5cm	10½"/26.5cm	10½"/26.5cm
Width at Upper Arm	11½"/29cm	12"/30.5cm	12¾"/32.5cm	13¾"/35cm	15"/38cm	16¼"/41.5cm	17¾"/45cm	19¼"/49cm

Notes

- This pattern is written for K1P1 ribbed edges. Refer to pages 213–223 for information on how to customize the edge treatment.
- For fully fashioned decreases: On right-side rows, k1, ssk, knit to the last 3 stitches, k2tog, k1; on wrong-side rows, p1, p2tog, purl to the last 3 stitches, ssp (page 255), p1.
- For fully fashioned increases: On right-side rows, k1, M1R (page 253), knit to the last stitch, M1L (page 253), k1.

Sleeve

Cast on __ stitches.

	XS	S	M	L	1X	2X	3X	4X
7	66	66	66	70	70	74	74	74
6½	62	62	62	66	66	68	68	68
6	58	58	58	60	60	64	64	64
5½	52	52	52	56	56	58	58	58
5	48	48	48	50	50	52	52	52
4½	42	42	42	46	46	48	48	48
4	38	38	38	40	40	42	42	42
3½	34	34	34	36	36	38	38	38
3	28	28	28	30	30	32	32	32

Work same as for the set-in classic three-quarter sleeve (page 137) until the piece measures approximately 13"/33cm from the beginning, or desired length, ending after a wrong-side row.

You will now have __ stitches.

	XS	S	M	L	1X	2X	3X	4X
7	80	84	90	96	106	114	124	136
6½	76	78	82	90	98	106	116	126
6	70	72	76	82	90	98	106	116
5½	64	66	70	76	82	90	98	106
5	58	60	64	68	76	82	88	96
4½	52	54	58	62	68	74	80	88
4	46	48	50	56	60	66	72	78
3½	40	42	46	48	52	58	62	68
3	34	36	38	42	46	50	54	58

Shape the Cap

Work same as for the set-in classic long sleeve (page 129).

You will have __ stitches remaining.

	XS	S	M	L	1X	2X	3X	4X
7	18	18	18	18	18	18	18	18
6½	16	16	16	16	16	16	16	16
6	16	16	16	16	16	16	16	16
5½	14	14	14	14	14	14	14	14
5	12	12	12	12	12	12	12	12
4½	12	12	12	12	12	12	12	12
4	10	10	10	10	10	10	10	10
3½	8	8	8	8	8	8	8	8
3	8	8	8	8	8	8	8	8

Saddle

Work same as for the saddle shoulder classic long sleeve (page 189).

Bind off all stitches.

NECKLINE TREATMENTS

Refer to this section for finishing details for the neckline of your choice. Just be certain your neckline opening and neckline treatment icons always match.

HOW MANY STITCHES DO I PICK UP?

Use this table to help determine how many stitches per row you should pick up along the vertical and curved edges in necklines.

Stitch Gauge	Stitch-to-Row Ratio
7	7 stitches for every 9 rows
6½	7 stitches for every 9 rows
6	6 stitches for every 8 rows
5½	6 stitches for every 8 rows
5	5 stitches for every 7 rows
4½	5 stitches for every 7 rows
4	4 stitches for every 6 rows
3½	4 stitches for every 5 rows
3	3 stitches for every 4 rows

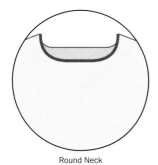

Round Neck

Round Necklines

Crewneck

Use mattress stitch (page 257) to sew the shoulder seams.

With the right side facing and a 16"/40cm circular needle, begin at the left front neck edge. Pick up and knit stitches along the neckline as follows: Pick up one stitch for each bound-off stitch along the horizontal sections, and refer to the table above for the stitch-to-row ratio for vertical and curved sections, adjusting the total number, if necessary, to match the stitch multiple of the stitch pattern of your desired edge treatment. The instructions that follow refer to a K1P1 ribbed neckband worked over an even number of stitches.

Join for circular knitting, placing a marker for the beginning of the round.

K1P1 Rib
(worked in the round)
Pattern Round (RS): *K1, p1; repeat from the * around.

Repeat the pattern round until the neckband measures approximately 1"/2.5cm from the beginning.

Bind off *loosely* in the pattern.

Round Neck

Mock Turtleneck

Work same as for a crewneck, except work even in the pattern until the neckband measures approximately 4"/10cm from the beginning.

Bind off *loosely* in the pattern.

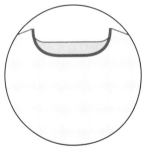

Round Neck

Turtleneck

Work same as for a crewneck, except work even in the pattern until the neckband measures approximately 9"/23cm from the beginning, changing to a needle one size larger at 4½"/11.5cm and another size larger at 7"/18cm.

Bind off *loosely* in the pattern.

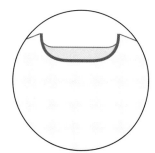

Round Neck

Johnny Collar

Use mattress stitch (page 257) to sew the shoulder seams.

With the right side facing and a 16"/40cm circular needle, begin at the center front neck edge. Pick up and knit stitches along the neckline, ending at the center front, as follows: Pick up one stitch for each bound-off stitch along the horizontal sections, and refer to the table on page 196 for the stitch-to-row ratio for vertical and curved sections, adjusting the total number, if necessary, to match the stitch multiple of the stitch pattern of your desired edge treatment. The instructions that follow refer to a K1P1 ribbed neckband worked over an even number of stitches.

Join for circular knitting, placing a marker for the beginning of the round.

K1P1 Rib
(worked in the round)
Pattern Round (RS): *K1, p1; repeat from the * around.

Repeat the pattern round until the neckband measures approximately ½"/1cm from the beginning, ending at the center front, and use the M1 technique (page 235) to add one stitch at the beginning of the row to balance the stitch pattern.

Place a marker after the first stitch and before the last stitch.

Begin working back and forth in rows, reversing the right side and wrong side of the stitch pattern, if necessary. Use the M1 technique to increase one stitch inside each marker every other row, working new stitches into the pattern as they accumulate, until the collar measures 6"/15cm or until the desired length, *and at the same time*, change to successively larger needles (one size up) every 2"/5cm.

Bind off *loosely* in the pattern.

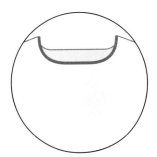

Round Neck

Split Ribbed Collar

Use mattress stitch (page 257) to sew the shoulder seams.

With the right side facing and a 16"/40cm circular needle, begin approximately two-thirds of the way across the neck shaping on the front. Pick up and knit stitches along the neckline as follows, adjusting the number of stitches, if necessary, to have an even number of stitches: Pick up one stitch for each bound-off stitch along the horizontal sections, and refer to the table on page 196 for the stitch-to-row ratio for vertical and curved sections. Then multiply your stitch gauge by 2. Cast on this number of stitches, adjusting it to be an odd number if necessary, for the overlapping section of the neckband. You will have an odd number of stitches in total.

Do not join for circular knitting; this neckband is worked back and forth in rows.

K1P1 Rib

(worked flat, over an odd number of sts)
Row 1 (WS): *P1, k1; repeat from the * to the last st, p1.
Row 2 (RS): *K1, p1; repeat from the * to the last st, k1.

Place a marker after the first stitch and before the last stitch.

Repeat Rows 1 and 2, and use the M1 technique (page 253) to increase one stitch inside each marker every other row until the collar measures 6"/15cm, or the desired length, working new stitches into the pattern as they accumulate, **and at the same time**, change to successively larger needles (one size up) every 2"/5cm.

Bind off *loosely* in the pattern.

Using the photo as a guide, sew the cast-on edge of the collar along the neckline, allowing the collar ends to overlap.

Optional: Sew buttons along one side of the collar for decoration.

Round Neck

Hood

Use mattress stitch (page 257) to sew the shoulder seams.

With the right side facing and a 16"/40cm circular needle, begin at the center front neck. Pick up and knit stitches along the neckline as follows: Pick up one stitch for each bound-off stitch along the horizontal sections, and refer to the table on page 196 for the stitch-to-row ratio for vertical and curved sections, adjusting the total number, if necessary, to have an even number of stitches.

K1P1 Rib
(worked flat, over an even number of sts)
Row 1 (WS): [P1, k1] 3 times, purl to the last 6 stitches, [k1, p1] 3 times.
Row 2 (RS): [K1, p1] 3 times, knit to the last 6 stitches, [p1, k1] 3 times.

Repeat Rows 1 and 2 until the hood measures approximately 1"/2.5cm from the beginning, ending after a wrong-side row. Place markers on either side of the two stitches at the center back of the hood.

Next Row (Increase Row): Work in the pattern as established to first marker, M1 (page 253), slip marker, k2, slip marker, M1, work in the pattern as established to end of row.

Work in the pattern as established, repeating this Increase Row every 1¼"/3cm, until the hood measures approximately 8½"/21.5cm from the beginning.

Continue even until the hood measures approximately 12½"/32cm from the beginning, ending after a wrong-side row.

Divide the stitches evenly onto two double-pointed needles.

Holding the work with wrong sides facing each other, work a three-needle bind-off (page 252).

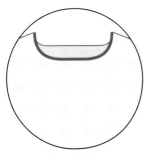

Round Neck

Lace Collar

Use mattress stitch (page 257) to sew the shoulder seams.

With the right side facing and a 16"/40cm circular needle, begin at the center front neck. Pick up and knit stitches along the neckline as follows: Pick up one stitch for each bound-off stitch along the horizontal sections, and refer to the table on page 196 for the stitch-to-row ratio for vertical and curved sections, adjusting the total number, if necessary, to have a multiple of 6 stitches plus 1 stitch.

Lace Edge Pattern
(multiple of 6 sts plus 1)
Row 1 (RS): *K1, yarn over, k1, s2kp2 (page 254), k1, yarn over; repeat from the * to the last st, k1.
Row 2 (WS): Knit.

Repeat Rows 1 and 2 until the collar measures approximately 2"/5cm from the beginning, ending after a wrong-side row.

Change to one size larger needles, and continue in the pattern until the collar measures approximately 4"/10cm from the beginning, ending after a wrong-side row.

Change to one size larger needles, and continue in the pattern until the collar measures approximately 5"/12.5cm from the beginning, or desired length, ending after a wrong-side row.

Bind off *loosely* in the pattern, working the yarn overs and decreases as before.

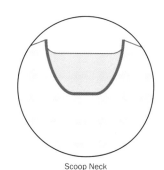

Scoop Neck

Scoop Necklines

Scoop Neck with Garter Stitch Trim

Use mattress stitch (page 257) to sew the shoulder seams.

With the right side facing and a 16"/40cm circular needle, begin at the left front neck edge. Pick up and knit stitches along the neckline as follows: Pick up one stitch for each bound-off stitch along the horizontal sections, and refer to the table on page 196 for the stitch-to-row ratio for vertical and curved sections, adjusting the stitch count, if necessary, to match the stitch multiple of your desired stitch pattern. The instructions that follow refer to garter stitch and can use any multiple of stitches.

Join for circular knitting, placing a marker for the beginning of the round.

Garter Stitch
(worked in the round)
Round 1 (RS): Purl.
Round 2 (RS): Knit.

Repeat Rounds 1 and 2 until the neckband measures approximately ¾"/2cm from the beginning, ending after Round 1.

Next Round: Knit, and use the k2tog technique to decrease 15% of the stitches.

Continue even in the pattern as established until the neckband measures approximately 1"/2.5cm from the beginning, ending after Round 2.

Bind off *loosely* in the pattern.

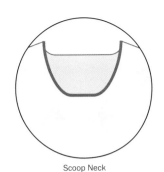

Scoop Neck

Cowl Neck

Use mattress stitch (page 257) to sew the shoulder seams.

With the wrong side facing and a 16"/40cm circular needle, begin at the left front shoulder. Pick up and knit stitches along the neckline as follows: Pick up one stitch for each bound-off stitch along the horizontal sections, and refer to the table on page 196 for the stitch-to-row ratio for vertical and curved sections, adjusting the stitch count, if necessary, to have an even number of stitches in total.

Join for circular knitting, placing a marker for the beginning of the round.

Round 1: Purl.
Repeat Round 1 until the cowl measures approximately ¾"/2cm from the beginning.
Next Round (Increase Round): *P1, M1 purlwise (page 253); repeat from the * around, doubling the number of stitches.

Continue working even, purling all stitches every round, until the cowl measures approximately 5"/12.5cm from the beginning.

Change to one size larger needles and continue working even, purling all stitches every round, until the cowl measures approximately 10½"/26.5cm from the beginning, or approximately ½"/1.5cm less than the desired finished length of the cowl.

Next Round: *K1, p1; repeat from the * around.
Repeat the last round for ½"/1.5cm more.

Bind off *loosely* in the pattern.

V Neck

V Necklines

V-Neck with Mitered Rib Trim

Use mattress stitch (page 257) to sew the shoulder seams.

With the right side facing and a 16"/40cm circular needle, begin at the center front, and pick up and knit an odd number of stitches along the left front neck edge, an odd number of stitches along the back of the neck, and an odd number of stitches along the right front neck edge, as follows: Pick up one stitch for each bound-off stitch along the horizontal sections, and refer to the table on page 196 for the stitch-to-row ratio for vertical and curved sections. You will have an odd number of stitches in total.

Join for circular knitting, placing a marker for the beginning of the round.

Round 1 (RS): *K1, p1; repeat from the * to the last st, k1. (Note that both stitches at the center front are knit stitches.)
Round 2 (Decrease Round): Ssk, continue in rib pattern as established until 2 sts before the end of the round, k2tog.
Repeat Rounds 1 and 2 until the neckband measures approximately 1"/2.5cm from the beginning, ending after an even-numbered round.
Next Round: Work the decrease round as you *loosely* bind off.

V-Neck with Crossover Rib Trim

Use mattress stitch (page 257) to sew the shoulder seams.

With the right side facing and a 16"/40cm circular needle, begin at center left front and end at the center right front. Pick up and knit stitches along the neckline as follows: Pick up one stitch for each bound-off stitch along the horizontal sections, and refer to the table on page 196 for the stitch-to-row ratio for vertical and curved sections, adjusting the stitch count, if necessary, to have an odd number of stitches in total.

Do not join for circular knitting; this neckband is worked back and forth in rows.

K1P1 Rib
(worked flat, over an odd number of sts)
Row 1 (WS): *P1, k1; repeat from the * to the last st, p1.
Row 2 (RS): *K1, p1; repeat from the * to the last st, k1.

Repeat Rows 1 and 2 until the neckband measures approximately 1"/2.5cm from the beginning.

Bind off *loosely* in the pattern.
Overlap the ends at the front V, sewing to secure.

V Neck

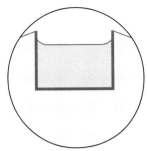

Square Neck

Square Necklines

Square Neck with Mitered K1P1 Rib Trim

Use mattress stitch (page 257) to sew the shoulder seams.

With the right side facing and a 16"/40cm circular needle, begin at the right back neck edge. Pick up and knit stitches along the neckline as follows: Pick up one stitch for each bound-off stitch along the horizontal sections, and refer to the table on page 196 for the stitch-to-row ratio for vertical and curved sections, ensuring that you have an odd number of stitches along each edge of the neckline plus one stitch in each of the 2 front inner corners.

Place a removable marker in each of the 2 front corner stitches. Move this marker up as needed.

Join for circular knitting, placing a marker for the beginning of the round.

Round 1 (RS): *P1, k1; repeat from the * across until 1 stitch before the corner stitch, s2kp2 (page 254), **k1, p1; repeat from the ** until 1 stitch before the second corner stitch, s2kp2; ***k1, p1; repeat from the *** around.
Round 2 (RS): Work in the rib pattern as established until 1 stitch before the corner stitch, s2kp2; repeat from the * around.

Repeat Round 2 until the neckband measures approximately 1"/2.5cm from the beginning.

Bind off in the pattern.

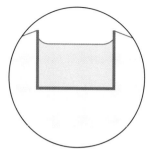

Square Neck

Square Neck with Mitered Garter Stitch Trim

Use mattress stitch (page 257) to sew the left shoulder seam.

With the right side facing and a 16"/40cm circular needle, begin at the right back neck edge. Pick up and knit stitches along the neckline as follows: Pick up one stitch for each bound-off stitch along the horizontal sections, and refer to the table on page 196 for the stitch-to-row ratio for vertical and curved sections, plus 1 stitch in each of the 2 front inner corners.

Place markers on either side of each of the 2 front corner stitches.

Do not join for circular knitting; this neckband is worked back and forth in rows.

Row 1 (WS): *Knit across to marker, slip marker, p1, slip marker; repeat from the * once more, ending with knit stitches along the right back neck edge to the right shoulder.

Row 2 (RS): *Knit across to 2 sts before marker, ssk, slip marker, knit the corner stitch, slip marker, k2tog tbl; repeat from the * once more, ending with knit stitches along the right front neck edge to the right shoulder.

Repeat Rows 1 and 2 until the neckband measures approximately 1"/2.5cm from the beginning.

Bind off knitwise.

Use mattress stitch to sew the right shoulder seam, including the side of the neckband.

Square Neck

Shawl Collar

Use mattress stitch (page 257) to sew the shoulder seams.

With the right side facing and a 16"/40cm circular needle, begin at the lower right front neck edge. Pick up and knit stitches along the neckline from the lower left neck edge to the lower left front neck edge as follows: Pick up one stitch for each bound-off stitch along the horizontal sections, and refer to the table on page 196 for the stitch-to-row ratio for vertical and curved sections, adjusting, if necessary, to match the stitch multiple of the stitch pattern. The instructions that follow refer to a K1P1 ribbed neckband worked over an odd number of stitches.

Do not join for circular knitting; this neckband is worked back and forth in rows.

K1P1 Rib
(worked flat, over an odd number of sts)
Row 1 (WS): *P1, k1; repeat from the * to the last st, p1.
Row 2 (RS): *K1, p1; repeat from the * to the last st, k1.

Repeat Rows 1 and 2 until the neckband measures approximately 7"/18cm from the beginning.

Bind off *loosely* in the pattern.

Sew the sides of the ribbed band to the lower edge of the neck opening, overlapping the left front edge over the right front edge.

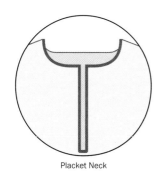

Placket Neck

Placket Necklines

Buttoned Placket Henley

Use mattress stitch (page 257) to sew the shoulder seams.

With the right side facing and a 16"/40cm circular needle, begin at the left front neck edge. Pick up and knit stitches along the neckline as follows: Pick up one stitch for each bound-off stitch along the horizontal sections, and refer to the table on page 196 for the stitch-to-row ratio for vertical and curved sections, adjusting, if necessary, to match the stitch multiple of the stitch pattern. The instructions that follow refer to a K1P1 ribbed neckband worked over an odd number of stitches.

Do not join for circular knitting; this neckband is worked back and forth in rows.

K1P1 Rib
(worked flat, over an odd number of sts)
Row 1 (WS): *P1, k1; repeat from the * to the last st, p1.
Row 2 (RS): *K1, p1; repeat from the * to the last st, k1.

Repeat Rows 1 and 2 until the neckband measures approximately 1"/2.5cm from the beginning, ending after a wrong-side row.

Bind off *loosely* in the pattern.

Button Placket
With the right side facing and a 16"/40cm circular needle, begin at the top of the placket opening on the left front (as worn; on the right-hand side as the piece is facing you). Refer to the table on page 196 for the stitch-to-row ratio. Pick up and knit stitches along the side of the ribbed neckband, continuing down the placket opening, adjusting the number of stitches if necessary to get an odd number.

Repeat Rows 1 and 2 as above until the button placket measures approximately 1"/2.5cm from the beginning.

Bind off *loosely* in the pattern.

Place markers for the desired number of evenly spaced buttons, making the first and last ones approximately ½"/1.5cm from the upper and lower edges of the placket.

Buttonhole Placket

Work same as for the button placket, picking up stitches from bottom to top, until the placket measures approximately ½"/1.5cm from the beginning.

Next Row: Continue in the pattern as established, and make buttonholes opposite the markers by binding off the appropriate number of stitches to match your buttons. Refer to the chart below for more information.

On the subsequent row, cast on the appropriate number of stitches above the bound-off stitches on the previous row.

Complete same as for the button placket.

Overlap the buttonhole placket over the button placket, and sew them together at their lower edges. Sew on the buttons.

Placket Neck

Placket Henley Without Buttons

Work same as for Buttoned Placket Henley, omitting the buttonholes and buttons from the two plackets.

Buttonholes at Different Gauges

	½"/12.75mm	¾"/19mm	1"/24.5mm	1½"/38mm	2"/51mm
7	3 stitches	5 stitches	6 stitches	10 stitches	14 stitches
6½	3 stitches	5 stitches	6 stitches	10 stitches	13 stitches
6	3 stitches	4 stitches	5 stitches	8 stitches	12 stitches
5½	2 stitches	4 stitches	5 stitches	8 stitches	11 stitches
5	2 stitches	3 stitches	4 stitches	7 stitches	10 stitches
4½	2 stitches	3 stitches	4 stitches	6 stitches	9 stitches
4	2 stitches	3 stitches	4 stitches	5 stitches	8 stitches
3½	2 stitches	2 stitches	3 stitches	5 stitches	7 stitches
3	1 stitch	2 stitches	3 stitches	4 stitches	6 stitches

Placket Neck

Buttoned Ribbed High Neck

Use mattress stitch (page 257) to sew the shoulder seams.

With the right side facing and a 16"/40cm circular needle, begin at the left front neck edge. Pick up and knit stitches along the neckline as follows: Pick up one stitch for each bound-off stitch along the horizontal sections, and refer to the table on page 196 for the stitch-to-row ratio for vertical and curved sections, adjusting, if necessary, to match the stitch multiple of the stitch pattern. The instructions that follow refer to a K1P1 ribbed neckband worked over an odd number of stitches.

Do not join for circular knitting; this neckband is worked back and forth in rows.

K1P1 Rib
(worked flat, over an odd number of sts)
Row 1 (WS): *P1, k1; repeat from the * to the last st, p1.
Row 2 (RS): *K1, p1; repeat from the * to the last st, k1.

Repeat Rows 1 and 2 until the neckband measures approximately 3"/7.5cm from the beginning.

Bind off *loosely* in the pattern.

Button Placket
Same as for the Buttoned Placket Henley on page 208.

Buttonhole Placket
Same as for the Buttoned Placket Henley on page 208.

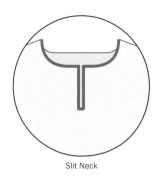

Slit Neck

Slit Necklines

Slit Neck with Johnny Collar

Use mattress stitch (page 257) to sew the shoulder seams.

With the right side facing and a 16"/40cm circular needle, begin at the center front neck edge. Pick up and knit stitches along the neckline, ending at the center front, as follows: Pick up one stitch for each bound-off stitch along the horizontal sections, and refer to the table on page 196 for the stitch-to-row ratio for vertical and curved sections, adjusting the total number, if necessary, to match the stitch multiple of the stitch pattern of your desired edge treatment. The instructions that follow refer to a K1P1 ribbed neckband worked over an even number of stitches.

Do not join for circular knitting; this neckband is worked back and forth in rows.

K1P1 Rib
(worked flat, over an even number of sts)
Row 1 (WS): *P1, k1; repeat from the * to the last st, p1.
Row 2 (RS): *K1, p1; repeat from the * to the last st, k1.

Place a marker after the first stitch and before the last stitch.

Repeat Rows 1 and 2, and use the M1 technique (page 253) to increase one stitch inside each marker every other row until the collar measures 6"/15cm or the desired length, working new stitches into the pattern as they accumulate, ***and at the same time***, change to successively larger needles (one size up) every 2"/5cm.

Bind off *loosely* in the pattern.

Slit and Collar Edging
With the right side facing, begin at the left-hand point of the collar. Referring to the table on page 196 for the stitch-to-row ratio, pick up and knit stitches along the 2 sides of the collar and the neck slit, plus 2 stitches at the slit base.

Next Row (WS): Bind off knitwise.

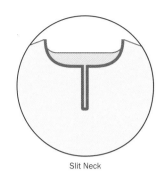

Slit Neck

Zippered High Neck

Note: These instructions refer to a 9"/23cm zipper. If you choose to use a longer (or shorter) zipper, remember to adjust the slit length when knitting your sweater front.

Use mattress stitch (page 257) to sew the shoulder seams.

With the right side facing and a 16"/40cm circular needle, begin at the left front neck edge. Pick up and knit stitches along the neckline as follows: Pick up one stitch for each bound-off stitch along the horizontal sections, and refer to the table on page 196 for the stitch-to-row ratio for vertical and curved sections, adjusting, if necessary, to match the stitch multiple of the stitch pattern. The instructions that follow refer to a K1P1 ribbed neckband worked over an odd number of stitches.

Do not join for circular knitting; this neckband is worked back and forth in rows.

K1P1 Rib
(worked flat, over an odd number of sts)
Row 1 (WS): *P1, k1; repeat from the * to the last st, p1.
Row 2 (RS): *K1, p1; repeat from the * to the last st, k1.

Repeat Rows 1 and 2 until the neckband measures approximately 3"/7.5cm from the beginning.

Bind off *loosely* in the pattern.

Zipper Facing
With the right side facing, begin at the upper edge of the left side of the neckband. Referring to the table on page 196 for the stitch-to-row ratio, pick up and knit stitches along the 2 sides of the neck slit, plus 2 stitches at its base.

Next row (WS): Bind off knitwise.

Sew in zipper (page 258).

EDGE TREATMENTS

Each modular pattern in this book is written to include basic edges.
Knitters, of course, have myriads of possibilities for borders and edges,
from simple garter stitch bands to textured cables and more!
Use this section to find the perfect choice for your project.

Edge treatments are usually worked using knitting needles one or two
sizes smaller than those used to obtain the gauge of the main section
of the garment. Exceptions to this general guideline are noted in the
text. If you'd rather not have the lower edge of your garment draw in,
use just one size of needles for the whole project.

Simple Edges

These simple edge treatments are usually worked using 10–15% fewer stitches than the main fabric.

Garter Stitch

(over any number of sts)

Note: This edge treatment is often worked to a shorter depth than others; the photographed sample has 1"/2.5cm of garter stitch trim.

Row 1 (RS): Knit.
Row 2: Repeat Row 1.
Repeat Rows 1 and 2 for the pattern.

Reverse Stockinette Roll

(over any number of sts)

Row 1 (RS): Purl.
Row 2: Knit.
Rows 3 and 4: Repeat Rows 1 and 2.
Repeat Rows 1–4 for the pattern.

Ribbing

Ribs, the most ubiquitous of all edgings, consist of neat vertical columns of knit and purl stitches. To create a ribbing, knit stitches are worked into knit stitches, and purl stitches are worked into purl stitches. This vertical alignment of stitches tames the lower edge of a garment while remaining elastic. Knitters have countless options for ribbing, with K1P1 and K2P2 being the most common.

K1P1 Rib

(multiple of 2 sts)
Here, knits and purls are arranged in single-stitch columns.
Row 1 (RS): *K1, p1; repeat from the * across.
Row 2: Repeat Row 1.
Repeat Rows 1 and 2 for the pattern.

K2P2 Rib

(multiple of 4 sts plus 2)
In this stretchy rib, knits and purls are arranged in neat two-stitch columns.
Row 1 (RS): *K2, p2; repeat from the * to the last 2 sts, k2.
Row 2: *P2, k2; repeat from the * to the last 2 sts, p2.
Repeat Rows 1 and 2 for the pattern.

Other Knit and Purl Combinations

Knit and purl stitches can be combined in an infinite number of configurations to create a dazzling variety of textures. A balance of knits and purls helps to curtail curling at the edge of a garment. Here are a few patterns to try.

Seed Stitch

(multiple of 2 sts)

In this stitch pattern, knits and purls are alternated throughout the fabric. Typically, this edge treatment is worked with the same size knitting needles as the main fabric.

Row 1 (RS): *K1, p1; repeat from the * across.
Row 2: *P1, k1; repeat from the * across.
Repeat Rows 1 and 2 for the pattern.

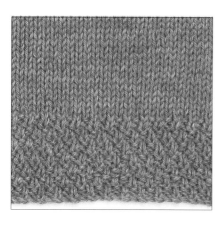

Double Seed Stitch

(multiple of 2 sts)

Here, knits and purls are alternated throughout the fabric, with the pattern shifting every two rows. As with seed stitch, double seed stitch is often worked using the same size knitting needles as the main fabric of a garment.

Row 1 (RS): *K1, p1; repeat from the * across.
Row 2: Repeat Row 1.
Row 3: *P1, k1; repeat from the * across.
Row 4: Repeat Row 3.
Repeat Rows 1–4 for the pattern.

Hurdle Pattern

(multiple of 2 sts plus 1)

In this textured pattern, two rows of K1P1 rib are followed by two rows of garter stitch. The horizontal ridges of the garter stitch counterbalance the vertical ridges of the ribbed rows, creating a sturdy, non-curling edge.

Row 1 (RS): *K1, p1; repeat from the * to the last st, k1.
Row 2: *P1, k1; repeat from the * to the last st, p1.
Rows 3 and 4: Knit.
Repeat Rows 1–4 for the pattern.

Garter Rib Pattern

(multiple of 4 sts plus 2)

This useful pattern has a vertically ribbed appearance without drawing in.

Row 1 (RS): *P2, k2; repeat from the * to the last 2 sts, p2.

Row 2: Purl.

Repeat Rows 1 and 2 for the pattern.

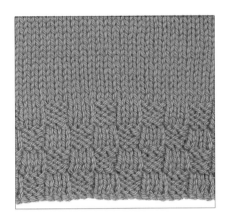

Alternating K3P3 Basketweave Pattern

(multiple of 6 sts)

In this stitch pattern, little "boxes" of knit and purl stitches create a checkerboard effect. It tames the lower edge and is quite easy to knit. It is usually knitted with the same size needles as the main fabric of a project.

Row 1 (RS): *K3, p3; repeat from the * across.

Rows 2–4: Repeat Row 1.

Rows 5–8: *P3, k3; repeat from the * across.

Repeat Rows 1–8 for the pattern.

Cables and Twists

Knitters can use various cables and twisted stitches to add texture to the edges of a garment. Here are some examples to try.

Rope Cables

(multiple of 6 sts plus 2)

Simple two-over-two cables decorate this edge treatment.

Note: This pattern requires a cable needle (cn).

Row 1 (RS): *P2, k4; repeat from the * to the last 2 sts, p2.

Row 2: Knit the knit stitches and purl the purl stitches.

Row 3: *P2, slip the next 2 stitches onto the cn and hold in front, k2 from the left needle, k2 from the cn; repeat from the * to the last 2 sts, p2.

Row 4: Repeat Row 2.

Repeat Rows 1–4 for the pattern, ending after Row 2.

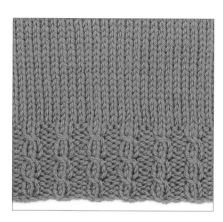

Little Twists

(multiple of 4 sts plus 2)

In this edging, one stitch crosses over another every four rows in miniature mock cables. Bonus: No cable needle is required!

Left Twist (LT): *Skip the first stitch and knit the next stitch through its back loop; knit the skipped stitch, then slip both stitches off the left needle together (see page 255).*

Row 1 (RS): *P2, LT (see above); repeat from the * to the last 2 sts, p2.

Row 2: *K2, p2; repeat from the * to the last 2 sts, k2.

Row 3: *P2, k2; repeat from the * to the last 2 sts, p2.

Row 4: Repeat Row 2.

Repeat Rows 1–4 for the pattern, ending after Row 2.

Zigzags

(multiple of 4 sts plus 2)

Here, alternating left and right twists create interesting texture while taming the edges.

Left Twist (LT): *Skip the first stitch and knit the next stitch through its back loop; knit the skipped stitch, then slip both stitches off the left needle together (see page 255).*

Right Twist (RT): *K2tog, leaving the stitches on the left needle; knit the first stitch the regular way, then slip both stitches off the left needle together (see page 255).*

Row 1 (RS): *P2, LT (see above); repeat from the * to the last 2 sts, p2.

Row 2: *K2, p2; repeat from the * to the last 2 sts, k2.

Row 3: *P2, RT (see above); repeat from the * to the last 2 sts, p2.

Row 4: Repeat Row 2.

Repeat Rows 1–4 for the pattern, ending after a wrong-side row.

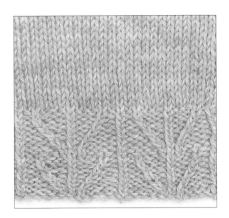

Tree of Life Pattern

(multiple of 12 sts plus 3)

In this pretty edge treatment, stitches are intentionally twisted by working them through their back loops to create an embossed pattern.

Note: This pattern requires a cable needle (cn).

K1-tbl: *Knit the indicated stitch through its back loop, intentionally twisting it (see page 252).*

P1-tbl: *Purl the indicated stitch through its back loop, intentionally twisting it (see page 252).*

Row 1 (RS): *P1, k1-tbl, p4, [k1-tbl] 3 times, p3; repeat from the * to the last 3 sts, p1, k1-tbl, p1.

Row 2: *K1P1-tbl, k4, [p1-tbl] 3 times, k3; repeat from the * to the last 3 sts, K1P1-tbl, k1.

Row 3: *P1, k1-tbl, p3, slip the next st onto cn and hold in back, k1-tbl from the left needle, p1 from the cn, k1-tbl, slip the next st onto cn and hold in front, p1 from the left needle, k1-tbl from the cn, p2; repeat from the * to the last 3 sts, p1, k1-tbl, p1.

Row 4: *K1P1-tbl, k3, [p1-tbl, k1] twice, p1-tbl, k2; repeat from the * to the last 3 sts, K1P1-tbl, k1.

Row 5: *P1, k1-tbl, p2, slip the next st onto cn and hold in back, k1-tbl from the left needle, p1 from the cn, p1, k1-tbl, p1, slip the next st onto cn and hold in front, p1 from the left needle, k1-tbl from the cn, p1; repeat from the * to the last 3 sts, p1, k1-tbl, p1.

Row 6: *K1P1-tbl, k2, p1-tbl, k2, p1-tbl, k2, p1-tbl, k1; repeat from the * to the last 3 sts, K1P1-tbl, k1.

Row 7: *P1, k1-tbl, p1, slip the next st onto cn and hold in back, k1-tbl from the left needle, p1 from the cn, p2, k1-tbl, p2, slip the next st onto cn and hold in front, p1 from the left needle, k1-tbl from the cn; repeat from the * to the last 3 sts, p1, k1-tbl, p1.

Row 8: *[K1P1-tbl] twice, k3, p1-tbl, k3, p1-tbl; repeat from the * to the last 3 sts, K1P1-tbl, k1.

Repeat Rows 1–8 for the pattern, ending after Row 8.

Hemmed Edges

Sometimes a simple and unobtrusive edge treatment is in order. The weight of doubled fabric controls the edge without drawing in.

Crisp Stockinette Hem

(over any number of stitches)

This edge treatment has a purl row on the right side acting as the fold line for the hem. It is simple and elegant.

Note: Be sure to work the hem facing with needles two sizes smaller than those used for the main fabric, to prevent splaying.

Hem Facing

Row 1: Knit.
Row 2: Purl.

Repeat Rows 1 and 2 until the hem facing measures approximately 1"/2.5cm from the beginning, ending after Row 1.

Turning Row (WS): Change to the larger needles, and knit across.
Next Row (RS): Knit.
Next Row: Purl.

Repeat the last two rows until the piece measures approximately 1"/2.5cm from the turning row.

After the entire piece of knitting is finished, fold the hem facing toward the wrong side and *loosely* sew into place, stitch for stitch.

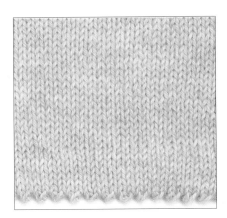

Picot Stockinette Hem

(multiple of 2 sts plus 1)

Yarn over stitches made on the fold line make this edge treatment especially feminine. *Note: Be sure to work the hem facing with needles two sizes smaller than those used for the main fabric, to prevent splaying.*

Hem Facing

Row 1: Knit.
Row 2: Purl.
Repeat Rows 1 and 2 until the hem facing measures approximately 1"/2.5cm from the beginning, ending after Row 1.

Turning Row (WS): Change to the larger needles, and work as follows: K1, *yarn over, k2tog; repeat from the * across.
Next Row (RS): Knit.
Next Row: Purl.
Repeat the last two rows until the piece measures approximately 1"/2.5cm from the turning row.

After the entire piece of knitting is finished, fold the hem facing toward the wrong side and *loosely* sew into place, stitch for stitch.

Lace Edges

These delicate borders are made using yarn over stitches.

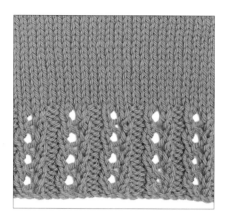

Eyelet Rib

(multiple of 5 sts plus 2)

Here, pretty eyelets decorate a vertical ribbing.

Row 1 (RS): *P2, k1, yarn over, ssk; repeat from the * to the last 2 sts, p2.

Row 2: *K2, p3; repeat from the * to the last 2 sts, k2.

Row 3: *P2, k2tog, yarn over, k1; repeat from the * to the last 2 sts, p2.

Row 4: Repeat Row 2.

Work Rows 1–4 for the pattern.

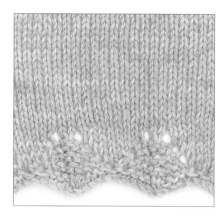

Scalloped Edge

(multiple of 10 sts plus 1)

S2kp2 (centered double decrease): *Slip the next 2 stitches as if to k2tog, k1, pass the 2 slipped stitches over the knitted stitch (see page 254).*

Row 1 (RS): Knit.

Row 2: *K5, p1, k4; repeat from the * to the last st, k1.

Row 3: *K1, yarn over, k3, s2kp2, k3, yarn over; repeat from the * to the last st, k1.

Row 4: *P2, k7; p1; repeat from the * to the last st, p1.

Row 5: *K2, yo, k2, s2kp2, k2, yo, k1; repeat from the * to the last st, k1.

Row 6: *P3, k5, p2; repeat from the * to the last st, p1.

Row 7: *K3, yo, k1, s2kp2, k1, yo, k2; repeat from the * to the last st, k1.

Row 8: *P4, k3, p3; repeat from the * to the last st, p1.

Row 9: *K4, yarn over, s2kp2, yarn over, k3; repeat from the * to the last st, k1.

Row 10: Purl.

Work Rows 1–10 for the pattern.

Multicolor Edges

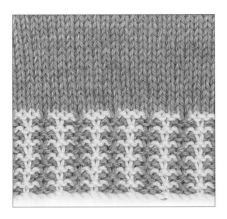

Textured Bird's Eye

(multiple of 4 sts plus 3)

Notes:

1. Two colors are used for this edging. Do not cut the yarns between the stripes. Instead, carry them loosely up the side edge of the fabric.

2. When slipping stitches, always slip them purlwise to prevent twisting them.

Cast on the required number of sts with Color B.

Row 1 (RS): With Color A, *k3, slip the next st with the yarn in back; repeat from the * to the last 3 sts, k3.

Row 2: With Color A, *k3, slip the next st with the yarn in front; repeat from the * to the last 3 sts, k3.

Row 3: With Color B, k1, *slip the next st with the yarn in back, k3; repeat from the * to the last 2 sts, slip the next st with the yarn in back, k1.

Row 4: With Color B, k1, *slip the next st with the yarn in front, k3; repeat from the * to the last 2 sts, slip the next st with the yarn in front, k1.

Repeat Rows 1–4 for the pattern, ending after a wrong-side row.

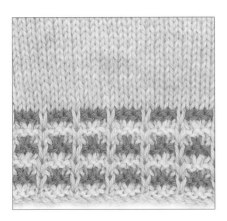

Confetti Slip Stitch

(multiple of 4 sts plus 3)

Notes:

1. Three colors are used for this edging. Do not cut the yarns between the stripes. Instead, carry them loosely up the side edge of the fabric.

2. When slipping stitches, always slip them purlwise to prevent twisting them.

Cast on the required number of sts with Color A.

Row 1 (RS): With Color B, *k3, slip the next st with the yarn in back; repeat from the * to the last 3 sts, k3.

Row 2: With Color B, *k3, slip the next st with the yarn in front; repeat from the * to the last 3 sts, k3.

Row 3: With Color A, k1, *slip the next st with the yarn in back, k3; repeat from the * to the last 2 sts, slip the next st with the yarn in back, k1.

Row 4: With Color A, p1, *slip the next st with the yarn in front, p3; repeat from the * to the last 2 sts, slip the next st with the yarn in front, p1.

Rows 5 and 6: With Color C, repeat Rows 1 and 2.

Rows 7 and 8: With Color A, repeat Rows 3 and 4.

Repeat Rows 1–8 for the pattern, ending after a wrong-side row.

POCKETS

Want to add a convenient and cute pocket to your garment? Find the perfect one here.

Patch Pockets

These pockets are knitted as separate pieces and simply sewn onto the garment. Try on your finished sweater, decide where you'd like to place the pocket, and sew it on!

Simple Patch Pocket

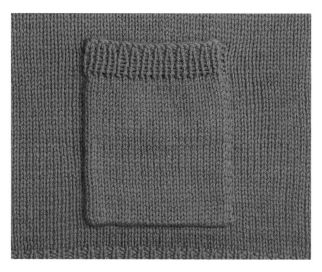

Finished Measurements

	XS	S	M	L	1X	2X	3X	4X
Width	5"/12.5cm	5"/12.5cm	5"/12.5cm	5"/12.5cm	5"/12.5cm	5"/12.5cm	5"/12.5cm	5"/12.5cm
Height (before edging)	5½"/14cm	5½"/14cm	5½"/14cm	5½"/14cm	5½"/14cm	5½"/14cm	5½"/14cm	5½"/14cm

Note

• This pattern is written for K1P1 ribbed edges. Refer to pages 213–223 for information on how to customize the edge treatment.

Pocket

Cast on __ stitches.

	XS	S	M	L	1X	2X	3X	4X
7	36	36	36	36	36	36	36	36
6½	32	32	32	32	32	32	32	32
6	30	30	30	30	30	30	30	30
5½	28	28	28	28	28	28	28	28
5	26	26	26	26	26	26	26	26
4½	22	22	22	22	22	22	22	22
4	20	20	20	20	20	20	20	20
3½	18	18	18	18	18	18	18	18
3	16	16	16	16	16	16	16	16

Begin stockinette stitch, and work even until the piece measures approximately 5½"/14cm from the beginning, ending after a wrong-side row.

Begin K1P1 rib, and work even until the piece measures approximately 6½"/16.5cm from the beginning, ending after a wrong-side row.

Bind off *loosely* in the pattern.

Sew the sides and bottom of the pocket onto the right side of the sweater where desired.

Shaped Patch Pocket

Finished Measurements

	XS	S	M	L	1X	2X	3X	4X
Width at Lower Edge	3"/7.5cm	3"/7.5cm	3"/7.5cm	3"/7.5cm	3"/7.5cm	3"/7.5cm	3"/7.5cm	3"/7.5cm
Width at Upper Edge	5"/12.5cm	5"/12.5cm	5"/12.5cm	5"/12.5cm	5"/12.5cm	5"/12.5cm	5"/12.5cm	5"/12.5cm
Height (before edging)	5½"/14cm	5½"/14cm	5½"/14cm	5½"/14cm	5½"/14cm	5½"/14cm	5½"/14cm	5½"/14cm

Notes
- This pattern is written for K1P1 ribbed edges. Refer to pages 213–223 for information on how to customize the edge treatment.

Pocket
Cast on __ stitches.

	XS	S	M	L	1X	2X	3X	4X
7	22	22	22	22	22	22	22	22
6½	20	20	20	20	20	20	20	20
6	18	18	18	18	18	18	18	18
5½	16	16	16	16	16	16	16	16
5	16	16	16	16	16	16	16	16
4½	14	14	14	14	14	14	14	14
4	12	12	12	12	12	12	12	12
3½	10	10	10	10	10	10	10	10
3	10	10	10	10	10	10	10	10

Begin stockinette stitch, and use the M1 technique (page 253) to increase 1 stitch each side every row __ times.

	XS	S	M	L	1X	2X	3X	4X
7	7	7	7	7	7	7	7	7
6½	6	6	6	6	6	6	6	6
6	6	6	6	6	6	6	6	6
5½	6	6	6	6	6	6	6	6
5	5	5	5	5	5	5	5	5
4½	4	4	4	4	4	4	4	4
4	4	4	4	4	4	4	4	4
3½	4	4	4	4	4	4	4	4
3	3	3	3	3	3	3	3	3

You will now have __ stitches.

	XS	S	M	L	1X	2X	3X	4X
7	36	36	36	36	36	36	36	36
6½	32	32	32	32	32	32	32	32
6	30	30	30	30	30	30	30	30
5½	28	28	28	28	28	28	28	28
5	26	26	26	26	26	26	26	26
4½	22	22	22	22	22	22	22	22
4	20	20	20	20	20	20	20	20
3½	18	18	18	18	18	18	18	18
3	16	16	16	16	16	16	16	16

Continue even until the piece measures approximately 5½"/14cm from the beginning, ending after a wrong-side row.

Begin K1P1 rib, and work even until the piece measures approximately 6½"/16.5cm from the beginning, ending after a wrong-side row.

Bind off *loosely* in the pattern.

Sew the sides and bottom of the pocket onto the right side of the sweater where desired.

Angled Patch Pocket

Finished Measurements

	XS	S	M	L	1X	2X	3X	4X
Width at Lower Edge	13½"/ 34.5cm	13½"/ 34.5cm	13½"/ 34.5cm	13½"/ 34.5cm	13½"/3 4.5cm	13½"/ 34.5cm	13½"/ 34.5cm	13½"/ 34.5cm
Width at Upper Edge	6½"/ 16.5cm	6½"/ 16.5cm	6½"/ 16.5cm	6½"/ 16.5cm	6½"/ 16.5cm	6½"/ 16.5cm	6½"/ 16.5cm	6½"/ 16.5cm
Height	5½"/14cm	5½"/14cm	5½"/14cm	5½"/14cm	5½"/14cm	5½"/14cm	5½"/14cm	5½"/14cm

Notes
- This pattern is written for K1P1 ribbed edges. Refer to pages 213–223 for information on how to customize the edge treatment.
- For fully fashioned decreases: On right-side rows, work 6 stitches in the pattern as established, ssk, knit to the last 8 stitches, k2tog, work in the pattern as established to end of row.

Pocket

Cast on __ stitches.

	XS	S	M	L	1X	2X	3X	4X
7	95	95	95	95	95	95	95	95
6½	88	88	88	88	88	88	88	88
6	82	82	82	82	82	82	82	82
5½	74	74	74	74	74	74	74	74
5	68	68	68	68	68	68	68	68
4½	61	61	61	61	61	61	61	61
4	54	54	54	54	54	54	54	54
3½	48	48	48	48	48	48	48	48
3	41	41	41	41	41	41	41	41

Set Up the Pattern

Row 1 (RS): [K1, p1] 3 times, knit to last 6 sts, [p1, k1] 3 times.
Row 2 (WS): [P1, k1] 3 times, purl to last 6 sts, [k1, p1] 3 times.

Repeat Rows 1 and 2, **and at the same time,** work fully fashioned decreases (see Notes) each side every other row __ times.

	XS	S	M	L	1X	2X	3X	4X
7	23	23	23	23	23	23	23	23
6½	23	23	23	23	23	23	23	23
6	20	20	20	20	20	20	20	20
5½	17	17	17	17	17	17	17	17
5	17	17	17	17	17	17	17	17
4½	14	14	14	14	14	14	14	14
4	11	11	11	11	11	11	11	11
3½	10	10	10	10	10	10	10	10
3	11	11	11	11	11	11	11	11

Work fully fashioned decreases each side every 4 rows __ time(s). If no number is given, do not work these rows.

	XS	S	M	L	1X	2X	3X	4X
7	1	1	1	1	1	1	1	1
6½	--	--	--	--	--	--	--	--
6	1	1	1	1	1	1	1	1
5½	2	2	2	2	2	2	2	2
5	1	1	1	1	1	1	1	1
4½	2	2	2	2	2	2	2	2
4	3	3	3	3	3	3	3	3
3½	2	2	2	2	2	2	2	2
3	--	--	--	--	--	--	--	--

You will have __ stitches remaining.

	XS	S	M	L	1X	2X	3X	4X
7	47	47	47	47	47	47	47	47
6½	42	42	42	42	42	42	42	42
6	40	40	40	40	40	40	40	40
5½	36	36	36	36	36	36	36	36
5	32	32	32	32	32	32	32	32
4½	29	29	29	29	29	29	29	29
4	26	26	26	26	26	26	26	26
3½	24	24	24	24	24	24	24	24
3	19	19	19	19	19	19	19	19

Bind off in the pattern.

Sew the lower and upper edges of the pocket onto the right side of the sweater where desired, leaving the sides open.

Knitted-In Pockets

This sort of pocket is more refined than a patch pocket and is relatively easy to add to a garment.

Horizontal Inset Pocket

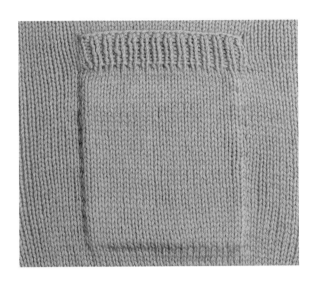

Finished Measurements

	XS	S	M	L	1X	2X	3X	4X
Width at Lower Edge	5"/12.5cm	5"/12.5cm	5"/12.5cm	5"/12.5cm	5"/12.5cm	5"/12.5cm	5"/12.5cm	5"/12.5cm
Width at Upper Edge	5"/12.5cm	5"/12.5cm	5"/12.5cm	5"/12.5cm	5"/12.5cm	5"/12.5cm	5"/12.5cm	5"/12.5cm
Height (before edging)	5½"/14cm	5½"/14cm	5½"/14cm	5½"/14cm	5½"/14cm	5½"/14cm	5½"/14cm	5½"/14cm

Note

- This pattern is written for K1P1 ribbed edges. Refer to pages 213–223 for information on how to customize the edge treatment.

Pocket
Pocket Lining

Cast on __ stitches.

	XS	S	M	L	1X	2X	3X	4X
7	36	36	36	36	36	36	36	36
6½	32	32	32	32	32	32	32	32
6	30	30	30	30	30	30	30	30
5½	28	28	28	28	28	28	28	28
5	26	26	26	26	26	26	26	26
4½	22	22	22	22	22	22	22	22
4	20	20	20	20	20	20	20	20
3½	18	18	18	18	18	18	18	18
3	16	16	16	16	16	16	16	16

Begin stockinette stitch, and work even until the piece measures approximately 5½"/14cm from the beginning, ending after a wrong-side row.

Slip the stitches onto a holder.

Place the Pocket Lining

Work the sweater piece to the height of the desired pocket position (for the top of the pocket), ending after a wrong-side row.

Next Row (RS): Work across to the desired position of the right-hand edge of the pocket. With the right side facing, knit across the stitches of the pocket lining, then slip the same number of stitches from the main fabric as were in the pocket lining onto a holder. Work to end of row.

Pocket Edging

Once the sweater piece is completed, pick up and knit the stitches from the holder. Continue even in K1P1 rib (page 215) for 1"/2.5cm.

Bind off *loosely* in the pattern.

Sew the sides of the pocket edging to the fabric. Sew the pocket lining to the wrong side of the fabric.

Vertical Inset Pocket

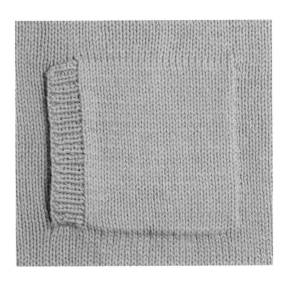

Finished Measurements

	XS	S	M	L	1X	2X	3X	4X
Width at Lower Edge	5"/12.5cm	5"/12.5cm	5"/12.5cm	5"/12.5cm	5"/12.5cm	5"/12.5cm	5"/12.5cm	5"/12.5cm
Width at Upper Edge	5"/12.5cm	5"/12.5cm	5"/12.5cm	5"/12.5cm	5"/12.5cm	5"/12.5cm	5"/12.5cm	5"/12.5cm
Height	6½"/ 16.5cm	6½"/ 16.5cm	6½"/ 16.5cm	6½"/ 16.5cm	6½"/ 16.5cm	6½"/ 16.5cm	6½"/ 16.5cm	6½"/ 16.5cm

Notes
- These instructions are for a pocket on the right-hand side of a garment; for a pocket on the left-hand side, see below.
- This pattern is written for K1P1 ribbed edges. Refer to pages 213–223 for information on how to customize the edge treatment.

Pocket
Pocket Lining
Cast on __ stitches.

	XS	S	M	L	1X	2X	3X	4X
7	36	36	36	36	36	36	36	36
6½	32	32	32	32	32	32	32	32
6	30	30	30	30	30	30	30	30
5½	28	28	28	28	28	28	28	28
5	26	26	26	26	26	26	26	26
4½	22	22	22	22	22	22	22	22
4	20	20	20	20	20	20	20	20
3½	18	18	18	18	18	18	18	18
3	16	16	16	16	16	16	16	16

Begin stockinette stitch, and work even until the piece measures approximately 1"/2.5cm from the beginning, ending after a right-side row.

Slip the stitches onto a spare needle.

Work the sweater piece to the height of the desired pocket position (bottom of pocket opening), ending after a wrong-side row.

Place the Pocket Lining
Next Row (RS): Work across to the desired position of the right-hand edge of the pocket. Slip the stitches knitted on this row up to this point onto a holder, then work to the end of the row.
Next Row: Work across to the pocket edge, then work across the pocket lining stitches.

Continue on these stitches until the desired depth of the pocket, then place these stitches onto a second holder.

Return to the stitches on the first holder, placing them back on a needle. Work to the desired depth of the pocket, making sure to work the same number of rows total as on the other side, ending after a wrong-side row.

Place the stitches from the second holder onto a needle. Place this needle behind the other main needle.

Close Pocket
Next Row (RS): Work across all stitches, working the lining stitches together with the main fabric stitches where they overlap. If your pattern stitch is stockinette stitch, for example, use the k2tog technique.

Pocket Edging
Once the sweater piece is completed, refer to the table on page 196 for stitch-to-row ratio, and pick up and knit an even number of stitches along the vertical edge of the pocket.

Begin K1P1 rib (page 215), and work even for 1"/2.5cm.

Bind off *loosely* in the pattern.

Sew the sides of the pocket edging to the fabric. Sew the pocket lining to the wrong side of the fabric.

For Pocket on Left-Hand Side
Place the Pocket Lining

Work across to the desired position of the left-hand edge of the pocket. Slip the remaining stitches onto a holder.

Next Row: Knit across the pocket lining stitches, then knit across remaining stitches on the needle (left-hand edge of sweater).

Continue working these stitches until the desired depth of the pocket, then place these stitches onto a second holder.

Continue as above.

Slanted Inset Pocket

Finished Measurements

	XS	S	M	L	1X	2X	3X	4X
Width at Lower Edge	5"/12.5cm	5"/12.5cm	5"/12.5cm	5"/12.5cm	5"/12.5cm	5"/12.5cm	5"/12.5cm	5"/12.5cm
Width at Upper Edge	5"/12.5cm	5"/12.5cm	5"/12.5cm	5"/12.5cm	5"/12.5cm	5"/12.5cm	5"/12.5cm	5"/12.5cm
Height	6½"/16.5cm	6½"/16.5cm	6½"/16.5cm	6½"/16.5cm	6½"/16.5cm	6½"/16.5cm	6½"/16.5cm	6½"/16.5cm

Notes

These instructions are for a pocket on the right-hand side of a garment; for a pocket on the left-hand side, see below.

For fully fashioned decreases on the front layer of the fabric: On right-side rows, knit across to the last 3 stitches, k2tog, k1; on wrong-side rows, p1, p2tog, purl across to end the row.

This pattern is written for K1P1 ribbed edges. Refer to pages 213–223 for information on how to customize the edge treatment.

Pocket

Pocket Lining
Cast on __ stitches.

	XS	S	M	L	1X	2X	3X	4X
7	44	44	44	44	44	44	44	44
6½	38	38	38	38	38	38	38	38
6	36	36	36	36	36	36	36	36
5½	34	34	34	34	34	34	34	34
5	32	32	32	32	32	32	32	32
4½	26	26	26	26	26	26	26	26
4	24	24	24	24	24	24	24	24
3½	22	22	22	22	22	22	22	22
3	20	20	20	20	20	20	20	20

Begin stockinette stitch, and work even until the piece measures approximately 1"/2.5cm from the beginning, ending after a right-side row.

Slip the stitches onto a holder.

Work the sweater piece to the desired height of the pocket bottom, ending after a wrong-side row.

Begin Pocket Opening
Next Row (RS): Work across to the desired position of the right-hand edge of the pocket, then slip the remaining stitches of the row onto a second holder without working them.

Working across the front layer, work fully fashioned decreases (see Notes) at the pocket opening every row __ times. If no number is given, do not work these rows.

	XS	S	M	L	1X	2X	3X	4X
7	6	6	6	6	6	6	6	6
6½	6	6	6	6	6	6	6	6
6	4	4	4	4	4	4	4	4
5½	4	4	4	4	4	4	4	4
5	2	2	2	2	2	2	2	2
4½	--	--	--	--	--	--	--	--
4	--	--	--	--	--	--	--	--
3½	--	--	--	--	--	--	--	--
3	2	2	2	2	2	2	2	2

Work fully fashioned decreases at pocket opening every other row __ times.

	XS	S	M	L	1X	2X	3X	4X
7	22	22	22	22	22	22	22	22
6½	20	20	20	20	20	20	20	20
6	20	20	20	20	20	20	20	20
5½	18	18	18	18	18	18	18	18
5	18	18	18	18	18	18	18	18
4½	18	18	18	18	18	18	18	18
4	15	15	15	15	15	15	15	15
3½	14	14	14	14	14	14	14	14
3	20	20	20	20	20	20	20	20

Work fully fashioned decreases at pocket opening every 4 rows once, if indicated below.
If no number is given, do not work these rows.

	XS	S	M	L	1X	2X	3X	4X
7	--	--	--	--	--	--	--	--
6½	--	--	--	--	--	--	--	--
6	--	--	--	--	--	--	--	--
5½	--	--	--	--	--	--	--	--
5	--	--	--	--	--	--	--	--
4½	--	--	--	--	--	--	--	--
4	1	1	1	1	1	1	1	1
3½	--	--	--	--	--	--	--	--
3	--	--	--	--	--	--	--	--

Work one row, if necessary, to end after a wrong-side row.

Slip these stitches onto a third holder.

Place the Pocket Lining
Slip the stitches from the second holder onto a needle, then slip the stitches for the pocket lining from the first holder onto the same needle.

With a second ball of yarn, work to the desired depth of the pocket, making sure to work the same number of rows total as on the front layer, ending after a wrong-side row.

Close Pocket
Place the front layer stitches from the third holder back onto a knitting needle.
Next Row (RS): Work across all stitches, working the lining stitches together with the main fabric stitches where they overlap. If your pattern stitch is stockinette stitch, for example, use the k2tog technique. Make sure your ending stitch count is correct for your size and gauge.

Pocket Edging

Once the sweater piece is completed, refer to the table on page 196 for stitch-to-row ratio, and pick up and knit an even number of stitches along the slanted edge of the pocket.

Begin K1P1 rib (page 215), and work even for 1"/2.5cm.

Bind off *loosely* in the pattern.

Sew the sides of the pocket edging to the fabric. Sew the pocket lining to the wrong side of the fabric.

For Pocket on Left-Hand Side
Place the Pocket Lining

Next Row (RS): Work across to the desired position of the left-hand edge of the pocket, then slip stitches just worked to a holder. Work to end of row.

Work decreases at the pocket opening as described above, replacing k2tog with ssk, and p2tog with ssp (page 255).

When decreases are complete, place the pocket lining and close pocket as described above.

PULLOVER POSSIBILITIES

Three-Quarter-Sleeve Fitted Pullover

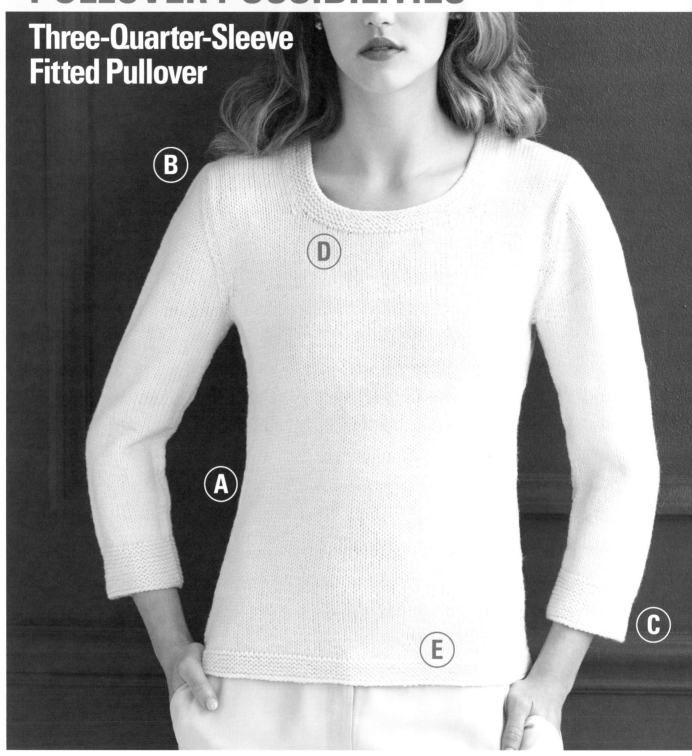

Yarn: Cascade Yarns *Cascade 220* (4)
in color #8010
Gauge: 5 stitches and 7 rows = 1"/2.5cm

A Shaped silhouette
B Set-in construction
C Classic ¾-length set-in sleeves

D Scoop neck
E Garter stitch edge treatment

Striped Saddle Shoulder Pullover

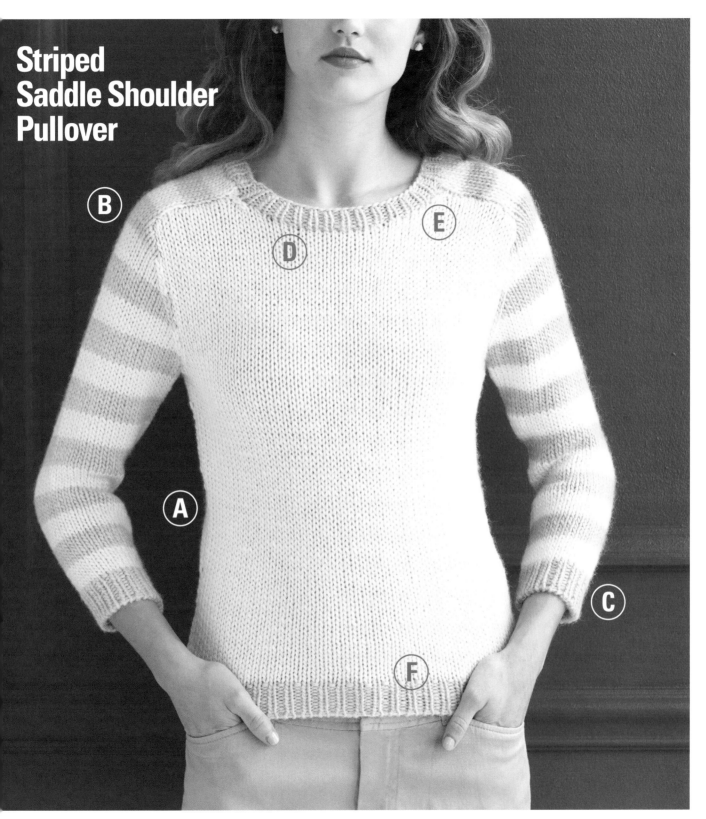

Yarn: Rowan *Cocoon* [5]
in colors #801 and #806
Gauge: 3½ stitches and 5 rows = 1"/2.5cm

A Tapered silhouette
B Saddle shoulder construction
C Three-quarter-length
    saddle sleeves

D Round neck
E Ribbed neckband
F K1P1 rib edge treatment

A-Line Pocket Hoodie

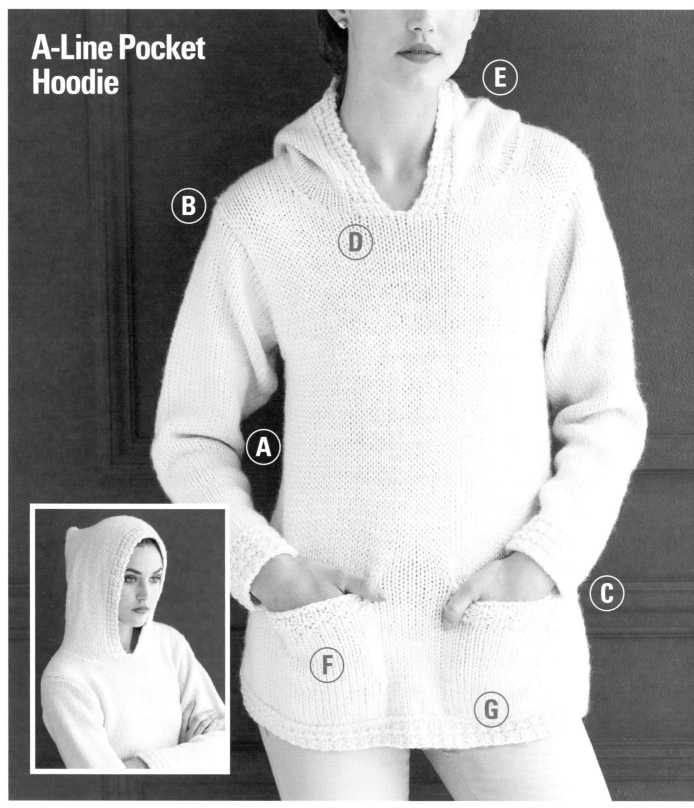

Yarn: Lion Brand *Alpine Wool* (5) in color #099

Gauge: 3½ stitches and 5 rows = 1"/2.5cm

A A-line silhouette
B Square indented construction
C Classic square indented long sleeves
D Round neck
E Hood
F Horizontal inset pockets
G Hurdle rib edge treatment

Empire Waist Top

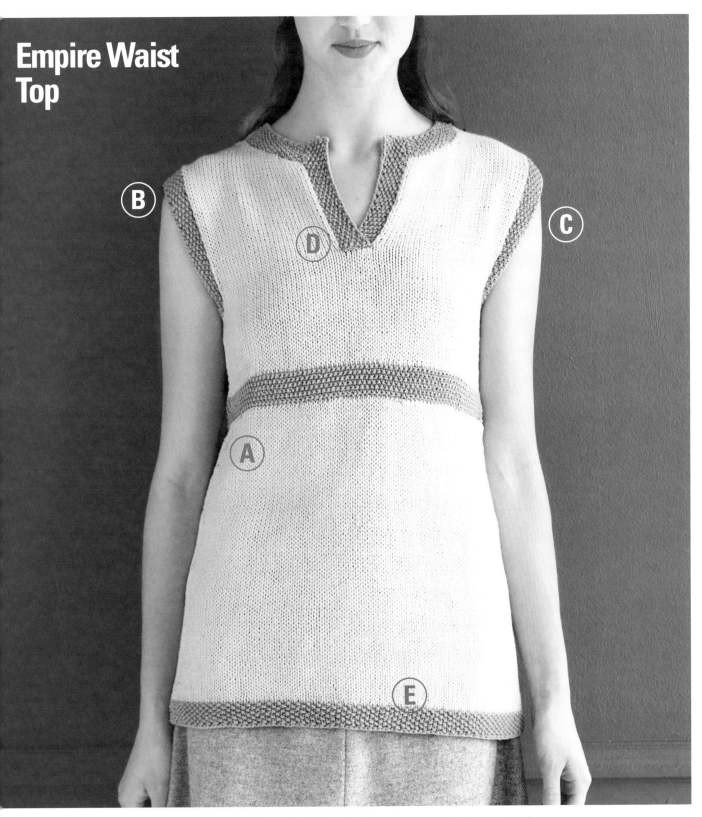

Yarn: Berroco *Modern Cotton* (4)
in colors #1603 and #1611
Gauge: 5 stitches and 6½ rows = 1"/2.5cm

A Empire waist silhouette
B Set-in construction
C Sleeveless

D Placket neck
E Seed stitch edge treatment

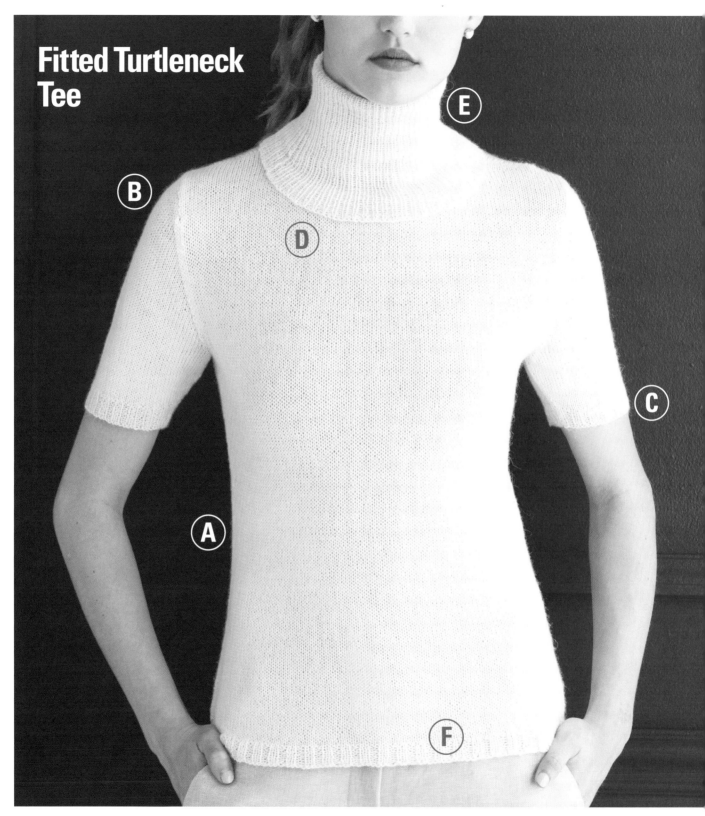

Fitted Turtleneck Tee

Yarn: Classic Elite *Vail* (1) in color #6416

Gauge: 7 stitches and 9 rows = 1"/2.5cm

A Shaped silhouette
B Set-in construction
C Short set-in sleeves

D Round neck
E Turtleneck
F K1P1 rib edge treatment

Fitted V-Neck Pullover

Yarn: Brown Sheep Company *Lamb's Pride Bulky* (5) in color #M-10
Gauge: 3 stitches and 4 rows = 1"/2.5cm

A Shaped silhouette
B Set-in construction
C Classic long set-in sleeves

D V-neck
E K1P1 rib edge treatment

Fill-In-the-Blanks Checklist

Before knitting your custom garment, plan your project using the following handy checklist. It's a great place to make notes and save pertinent page numbers for a project.

Size _____

Body Silhouette Style _____

Armhole Style _____

Sleeve Style _____

Finished Measurements _____

    Circumference at bust _____

    Circumference at waist _____

    Circumference at hip _____

    Total body length _____

    Sleeve length from underarm _____

    Sleeve width at lower edge _____

    Sleeve width at upper arm _____

Materials _____

    Yarn _____

    Needles _____

    Notions _____

Gauge _____

Edge Treatments _____

    Lower edges of back and front _____

    Lower edges of sleeves _____

    Pocket edge treatments, if necessary _____

Neckline Shape _____

Neckline Treatment _____

Pockets, if Applicable _____

Back _____

    Cast-on and lower edge treatment _____

    Shaping from the lower edge to the armholes, if necessary _____

    Armhole shaping _____

    Neck shaping _____

    Shoulder shaping _____

Front _____

    Cast-on and lower edge treatment _____

    Shaping from the lower edge to the armholes, if necessary _____

    Armhole shaping _____

    Neck shaping _____

    Shoulder shaping _____

Sleeve _____

    Cast-on and lower edge treatment _____

    Shaping from the lower edge to the upper sleeve, if necessary _____

    Sleeve cap shaping, if necessary _____

    Saddle shaping, if necessary _____

Finishing _____

    Block to desired finished measurements _____

    Assembly _____

    Add neckline treatment _____

    Sew on buttons, if necessary _____

INSPIRATION & INFORMATION

Refer to this section for information on knitting and finishing techniques (listed alphabetically), common abbreviations, and more.

Abbreviations

Here is a list of abbreviations used in the patterns of this book. For more technical information, see the Knitting Techniques section (on the next page).

cm	centimeter(s)
cn	cable needle
k	knit
k1-tbl	knit the next stitch through its back loop (page 252)
k2tog	knit the next 2 stitches together; a right-slanting decrease (page 254)
k2tog-tbl	knit the next 2 stitches together through their back loops (page 254)
LT	left twist (page 255)
M1	make 1 (increase) (page 253)
M1L	make 1 left (increase) (page 253)
M1-purlwise	make 1 purlwise (increase) (page 253)
M1R	make 1 right (increase) (page 253)
mm	millimeter(s)
p	purl
p1-tbl	purl the next stitch through its back loop (page 252)
p2tog	purl the next 2 stitches together; a right-slanting decrease (page 254)
RS	right side (of work)
RT	right twist (page 255)

s2kp2	slip the next 2 stitches at once knitwise, knit the next stitch, pass the 2 slipped stitches over the knitted stitch; a centered double decrease (page 254)
ssk	slip the next 2 stitches knitwise one at a time from the left-hand needle to the right-hand one, insert the left-hand needle tip into the fronts of both slipped stitches to knit them together from this position; a left-slanting decrease (page 255)
ssp	slip the next 2 stitches knitwise one at a time from the left-hand needle to the right-hand one, return both stitches to the left-hand needle and insert the right-hand needle into them from left to right and from back to front, to purl them together through their back loops; a left-slanting decrease (page 255)
st(s)	stitch(es)
WS	wrong side (of work)
* or ** or ***	repeat instructions after asterisk(s) across the row or for as many times as instructed

Knitting Techniques

Cable Cast-On

Each modular piece in this book begins with a cast-on edge. Here's my favorite cast-on technique, a type of knitted-on cast-on. It's easy and quick and looks lovely.

Start by making a slip knot on your needle, and place the needle in your left hand.

Insert the tip of the right needle knitwise into the loop on the left needle and knit up a stitch *but don't remove the original stitch from the left needle.*

Transfer the new stitch from the right needle back to the left one. One new stitch has been cast on. For each successive stitch to be added, insert the tip of the right needle *between* the first 2 stitches on the left needle to knit up a stitch. As before, don't remove the original stitch, but slip the new one back onto the left needle instead; repeat until you have cast on the required number of stitches.

Binding Off

Binding off is the technique used to end a piece of fabric, to link all the live stitches together so they don't unravel when they are removed from the knitting needles.

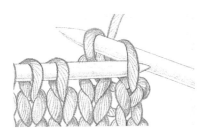

Start by working two stitches in the pattern as established. Then insert the tip of the left needle into the first knitted stitch.

Pull the first knitted stitch over the second one.

Remove this bound-off stitch from the right needle. Repeat for each successive stitch to be bound off, knitting or purling another stitch (working in pattern to maintain elasticity and desired width), and pulling the second stitch on the right needle over the first one.

Three-Needle Bind-Off

This technique allows the knitter to bind off two pieces of fabric and seam them together at the same time. It is used to finish the hood on page 200.

Hold the two pieces of fabric together, still on their needles, with their right sides together, in your left hand. Insert a third knitting needle knitwise into the first stitch on each needle, and knit them together as if they're one stitch.

Slip the new stitch off onto the right needle. Insert the third needle knitwise into the next two stitches on the two left needles and knit them together.

Slip the new stitch off onto the right needle. Pass the first stitch on the right needle over the second stitch to bind it off. Continue across the row, knitting together one stitch from each needle and binding off as you go.

Knit a Stitch Through Its Back Loop (k1-tbl)

Knitters use this decorative technique to intentionally twist a stitch.

Insert the right needle into the stitch from *right to left* and from *front to back*. Complete the stitch by wrapping the working yarn around the needle the regular way to form a knit stitch.

Purl a Stitch Through Its Back Loop (p1-tbl)

Similar to knitting a stitch through the back loop, this technique intentionally twists a stitch.

Insert the right needle into the stitch from from *right to left* and from *back to front*, and complete the stitch by wrapping the working yarn around the needle the regular way to purl the stitch.

Make 1 Increase (M1)

This increase technique uses the horizontal strand of yarn that hangs between the knitting needles. The knitter works into the strand, carefully twisting it to prevent a hole.

These raised increases can slant to the right or to the left to create a beautiful, decorative effect. If no direction is specified, use the M1L increase.

M1 increases: left slanting (M1L)

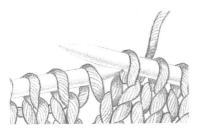

Use the left needle to scoop up the horizontal strand that's hanging between the needles from *front to back*.

Knit into the lifted strand, inserting the right needle *through its back loop*, twisting it to prevent a hole in your fabric. One stitch has been increased.

The increase is worked the same way on the purl side of the fabric, inserting the needle purlwise through the back loop.

M1 increases: right slanting (M1R)

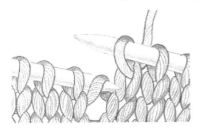

Use the left needle to scoop up the horizontal strand that's hanging between the needles from back to front.

Knit into the lifted strand, inserting the right needle *through its front loop*, twisting it to prevent a hole in your fabric. One stitch has been increased.

The increase is worked the same way on the purl side of the fabric, inserting the needle purlwise through the front loop.

Yarn Over Increase

This decorative method of increasing creates delicate eyelets in the fabric. It is used to make the picot hemmed edge on page 221.

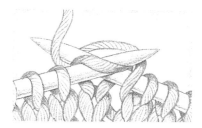

Start by bringing the working yarn to the front, between the tips of the two knitting needles. As you knit the next stitch, the yarn will go over the right needle to create the extra stitch.

Knit Two Together Decrease (k2tog)

This technique decreases two stitches down to a single stitch; it leans to the right.

With the working yarn toward the back, insert the right needle from *front to back*, knitwise, into the first two stitches on the left needle as if they were a single stitch. Wrap the yarn around the right needle as for a knit stitch. Pull the yarn through both stitches, and slip them off the left needle at once.

Knit Two Together Through Their Back Loops (k2tog-tbl)

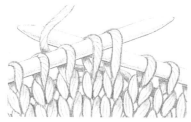

This technique decreases two stitches down to a single stitch while twisting them. Work as for k1-tbl, but inserting the right needle into the first two stitches on the left needle through their back loops as if they were a single stitch and knitting them together as you would for a k2tog decrease.

Purl Two Together Decrease (p2tog)

This decrease method combines two purl stitches. Work as for k2tog, but with the working yarn to the front, insert the tip of your right needle into the first two stitches on the left needle from right to left, purlwise. Then wrap the yarn around the right needle as for a purl stitch, pull the yarn through both stitches, and slip them off the left needle at once.

Slip 2, Knit 1, Pass the 2 Slipped Stitches Over (s2kp2)

Here's a centered double decrease that takes three stitches down to one stitch. It is often used to miter the corners on square neckbands.

Start by slipping two stitches at once *knitwise*.

Knit the next stitch. Pass the two slipped stitches over the stitch you just slipped.

Slip, Slip, Knit Decrease (ssk)

This knit decrease creates a mirror image of the k2tog decrease described at left.

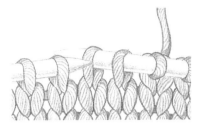

With the working yarn toward the back, insert the right needle from *left to right*, knitwise, into the first and then the second stitches on the left needle, *one at a time*, and slip them onto the right needle.

Insert the tip of the left needle into the fronts of both slipped stitches and knit them together from this position, through their back loops.

Slip, Slip, Purl Decrease (ssp)

This purl decrease technique is often used on wrong-side rows to mimic the left-slanting look of the ssk decrease on the knit side of the fabric. It is the mirror image of a p2tog decrease. With the working yarn toward the front, slip the first two stitches knitwise, one at a time, from the left needle to the right needle. Then slip these two stitches back to the left needle in their twisted position. Finally, insert the tip of the right needle *into the back loops* of these two stitches (going into the second stitch first, and then the first stitch), and purl them together through their back loops as if they were a single stitch.

Left Twist (LT)

This technique is a miniature cable that is worked over two stitches without the use of a cable needle. It is quick and easy to do.

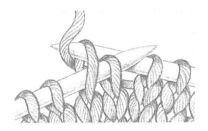

First, skip the first stitch on the left needle, and with the right needle behind the left one, knit the next stitch in its back loop.

Then, knit the first stitch in its front loop the regular way, and then slip both stitches off the left needle together.

Right Twist (RT)

Like the left twist, the right twist is a miniature cable that is worked over two stitches without the use of a cable needle.

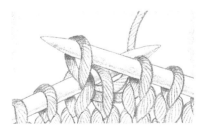

Knit two stitches together the regular way, but do not remove them from the left needle.

Insert the tip of your right needle between the two stitches, and knit the first stitch again *through its front loop*. Slip both stitches off the left needle together.

Finishing Techniques

Blocking

Blocking is the finishing process that helps "set" your project pieces to the desired size prior to seaming and magically evens out the fabric, hiding any badly knit, loose, or tight stitches.

We have several blocking methods to choose from, but here are the most common ones:

- Wet-blocking: First, wash the knitted pieces, following the manufacturer's instructions on the yarn label. Lay them flat on a towel, patting them gently to the measurements shown in the schematic illustrations. Finally, use rustless pins (trust me) to pin the damp fabric down and allow it to dry completely.
- Steam-blocking: Place a damp cloth over each piece, and carefully run a steam iron just above the fabric, allowing the steam to set the stitches in the fabric. Be sure to not let the iron touch the fabric.

Seaming

Knitters use different seaming methods, depending on the location of the seam and whether stitches are being sewn to stitches or to rows. Refer to page 260 for an illustration of how sweater pieces fit together for each type of armhole construction.

Vertical-to-Vertical Mattress Stitch

With the right side of the fabric facing you, lay the fabric pieces flat, side by side. Take care to match stripes, if applicable. Thread a blunt-end yarn needle with the sewing yarn, and bring the needle up from back to front through the left-hand piece of fabric, going one stitch in from the side edge, leaving a 6"/15cm tail.

Take the needle down from *front to back* through the corresponding spot on the right-hand piece, securing the lower edges together.

Insert the needle down from *front to back, into the same spot on the left-hand piece where the needle emerged before,* and bring it up through the corresponding spot in the next row of fabric, grabbing the horizontal bar between the stitches.

Insert the needle down from *front to back, into the same spot on the right-hand piece where the needle emerged befor*e, and bring it up through the corresponding spot in the next row of fabric, grabbing the horizontal bar between the stitches.

Repeat the last two steps several times, always grabbing the horizontal bars between the stitches, until you've sewn a couple of inches. Then pull firmly on the sewing yarn, bringing the pieces of knitting together. The edge stitch of each piece of fabric will roll to the wrong side. Continue this way until the seam is complete.

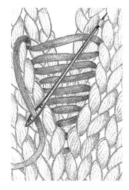

Knitters use this invisible seam for side seams of garments.

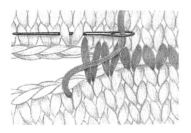

Knitters use this method to join two bound-off edges together, as in shoulder seams.

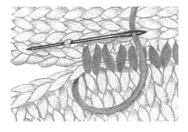

Knitters use this method most often to set sleeves into armholes.

Horizontal-to-Horizontal Mattress Stitch

With the right side of the fabric facing you, lay the pieces flat, one piece above the other, with their bound-off edges together. Using a blunt-end yarn needle with the seaming yarn, bring the needle up from back to front, one-half stitch in on the right-hand edge of the upper piece of fabric just above the bound-off edge, leaving a 6"/15cm tail.

Bring the needle down from *front to back* into the center of the corresponding stitch in the lower piece of fabric, just below the bound-off edge.

Bring the needle up from *back to front* through the center of the next stitch on the lower piece of fabric.

Return to the upper piece of fabric, insert the needle down *into the same spot it emerged before*, and bring it up to the left of the next stitch to the left.

Return to the lower piece of fabric, insert the needle down *into the same spot it emerged before*, and bring it up through the center of the next stitch to the left.

Repeat these steps, pulling tightly every few inches, until the seam is completed.

Horizontal-to-Vertical Mattress Stitch

To start, lay the two pieces of fabric right side up, one on top of the other. The bottom piece should have its cast-on row at the bottom and its bind-off edge at the top; the upper piece should be oriented perpendicular to the bottom piece.

Leaving a 6"/15cm tail and using a blunt-end yarn needle, bring the working yarn up from *back to front* through the center of the first stitch on the bottom piece of fabric.

On the upper piece of fabric, insert the needle from *right to left*, catching the running thread (or bar) that is between the first two stitches at the right-hand edge of the fabric.

Go back to the bottom piece, and insert the needle down *into the same spot it emerged before*, then take it up through the center of the next stitch to the left.

Return to the upper piece, and insert the sewing needle down *into the same spot it emerged before*, bringing it up from *right to left* to catch the next running strand (or bar) between the first and second stitches.

Continue in this fashion until the seam is completed, drawing the yarn tightly every few inches.

Backstitch Seams

This sturdy seam is the perfect choice when you'd like to ease in a little width of your fabric.

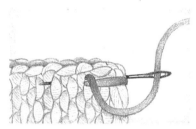 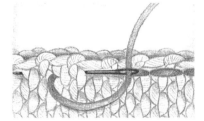

Begin by placing the two pieces of fabric together with right sides facing each other; the wrong side will be facing you. Attach the sewing yarn by inserting the sewing needle two times around the edge of the fabric, about ¼"/.5cm from the edge.

Then, all in one step, insert the tip of the needle back down into the same spot where the yarn emerged from the previous stitch and then back up again approximately ¼"/.5cm to the left. Repeat this last step to complete the seam.

Whipstitch Seams

This type of seam is best when you need to include every bit of your fabric in your sweater, since it does not use a selvedge. It can be worked with the right side or wrong side facing you.

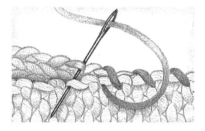

With either the right sides facing each other or the wrong sides facing each other, insert the seaming needle from the back to front through the flat strands of yarn comprising stitches along the sides of the fabric, skipping the knots. Repeat this step to complete the seam.

Sewing In a Zipper

Don't be afraid to add a zipper to a sweater! You'll be surprised how easy it is to do.

Begin with the zipper closed and the right side of the garment piece(s) facing you, and pin the zipper into place, keeping in mind that with hairier fabrics, it's best to allow more of the teeth to show to prevent the fibers from getting caught in the zipper's operation. Use contrasting sewing thread to baste the zipper into place.

Remove the pins, and with matching sewing thread, whipstitch (above) the tape to the wrong side of the fabric.

Next, with the right side of the garment facing you, use backstitch (above) to neatly sew it firmly into place. Fold any excess zipper tape to the wrong side, and tack it down.

Hiding Yarn Tails

Use this technique to secure yarn tails left when beginning and ending a skein of yarn.

Start by using a pointed-end yarn needle to make short running stitches on the wrong side of the fabric in a diagonal line for about 1"/2.5cm or so, actually piercing the yarn strands that comprise the stitches. Be sure that these darning stitches don't show on the public side of the fabric.

Next, stitch back to where you began, going alongside the previous stitches.

Finally, to secure the tail before snipping it off, work another stitch or two, this time actually piercing the stitches you just created.

Snip the yarn close to the fabric.

Picking Up Stitches

Most neckline treatments require that stitches be picked up along the neck opening. Here's how.

Picking Up Stitches Along a Horizontal Edge

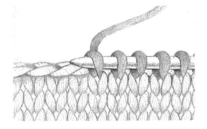

With the right side of the fabric facing you, insert a knitting needle *into the middle* of the first stitch just below the bind-off. Be sure to go into the center of the "V," not into the links of the chain running along the top of the fabric. Next, wrap the yarn around the needle knitwise, and use the tip of the needle to pull up a loop, creating a new stitch. Continue picking up one stitch in each stitch across.

Picking Up Stitches Along a Vertical Edge

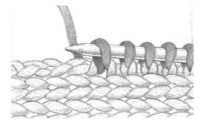

With the right side facing you, insert a knitting needle *between the first and second stitches* in the first row of knitting. Be sure to not insert the needle in the middle of a "V" but rather between two stitches. Next, wrap the yarn around the needle knitwise, and use the tip of the needle to pull up a loop, creating a new stitch. Continue picking up stitches along the edge, referring to the table on page 196 for the correct ratio of stitches to rows.

Picking Up Stitches Along a Curved Edge

When picking up stitches along the curved sections of a neckline, be sure to insert your knitting needle inside the edge in order to hide the unevenness. Note: Try to avoid picking up stitches in obvious holes in your fabric, or else you will make the holes look larger rather than hiding them. (Don't ask me how I know.)

Sweater Assembly

Sweater pieces interlock like a jigsaw puzzle, with the type of armhole construction determining how the front, back, and sleeves fit together.

Refer to the illustrations below when assembling sweaters.

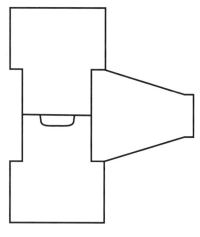

Square Indented
Construction

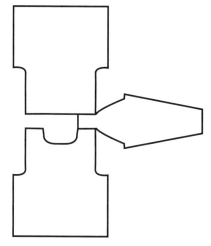

Saddle Shoulder
Construction

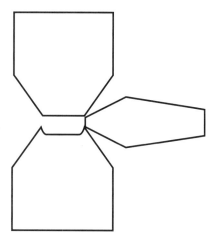

Raglan
Construction

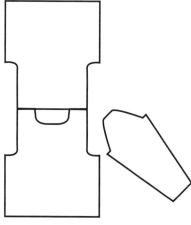

Set-In
Construction

The Knitting Community

To meet other knitters and to learn more about the craft, check out the following nonprofit organization. I currently sit on their Advisory Board and can attest to the educational value—and the pure, knitterly fun—of this great group:

The Knitting Guild Association
www.tkga.com

For an exciting time with thousands of fellow knitters, take workshops with me and other authors at a national knitting event such as Vogue Knitting LIVE. These memorable events are held at various locations around the country. For more information, go to VogueKnittingLive.com.

To meet other knitters online, visit Ravelry at www.ravelry.com.

Be sure to join my fan group on Ravelry to share photos of your projects and see what I'm up to. Go to www.ravelry.com/groups/melissa-leapman-rocks and join in on the fun! You'll be among the first to hear about my quick-to-selll-out knitting cruises!

Check out my online knitting and crochet classes online at Craftsy.com. Use this link to get 50% off all of my classes: www.craftsy.com/ext/MelissaLeapman_postcard

Material Resources

Following is the list of manufacturers and distributors of the beautiful yarns and notions used in this book. Contact them to find a yarn shop local to you!

Berroco, Inc.
1 Tupperware Dr. Suite 4
N. Smithfield, RI 02896-6815
401-769-1212
www.berroco.com

Brown Sheep Company
100662 County Road 16
Mitchell, NE 69357-2136
(308) 635-2198
www.brownsheep.com

Cascade Yarns
PO Box 58168
Tukwila, WA 98138
(800) 548-1048
www.cascadeyarns.com

Classic Elite Yarns
16 Esquire Road, Unit 2
North Billerica, MA 01862-2500
(800) 343-0308
www.classiceliteyarns.com

Coats & Clark
PO Box 12229
Greenville, SC 29612-0229
(800) 648-1479

Lion Brand Yarn
34 West 15th Street
New York, NY 10011
(212) 243-8995
www.lionbrand.com

Rowan
Distributed by Westminster Fibers

Westminster Fibers
165 Ledge St.
Nashua, NH 03060
(603) 886-5041
www.westminsterfibers.com

INDEX

ABOUT THE AUTHOR

With over 1,000 designs in print, Melissa Leapman is one of the most widely published knit and crochet designers at work today. She's worked with leading ready-to-wear design houses, is the author of several bestselling books, including *The Knit Stitch Pattern Handbook*, *Mastering Color Knitting*, and *Knitting the Perfect Fit*, and is a sought-out speaker at national and international knitting events, including Vogue Knitting LIVE and her popular annual knitting cruises. Leapman lives in New York City.

Author Photo by Heather Weston